PAPWA

Copyright © 2023 by Barry John Cohen

The right of Barry John Cohen to be identified as the Author of the Work has been asserted in accordance with the Copyright Act 98 of 1978.

All rights reserved. No portion of this book may be reproduced, stored in a retrieval system, or transmitted in any form or by any means, electronic, mechanical, photocopying, recording, or otherwise without the prior permission of the copyright owner.

First Edition May 2020 in paperback
Second Edition October 2023

Project by New Voices Publishing Services
guiding authors to self-publish
www.newvoices.co.za

Cover designed by Media Mastery

ISBN: 978 0 7961 6724 8
eBook 9780630724263

PAPWA

❦

Barry John Cohen

BY THE SAME AUTHOR

Blazing the Trail: This sport collector's volume chronicles the impact black golf had on overcoming discrimination, their history, and how they broke down the apartheid barriers, banning and protests. It is a rare glimpse into the extraordinary lives of Southern Africa's top black golfers, and their determination to win against all odds, and ultimately their induction into the Southern Africa Golf Hall of Fame, as well as local and international black TPA tournament statistics.

Let me Play: This is the story of Papwa Sewgolum who rose from humble beginnings to challenge the might of the golfing titans on an equal footing, and after winning three Dutch Opens and two Natal Opens beating Gary Player, he was banned from playing in white tournaments and his passport was withdrawn.

Let The Storm Burst: 1895. A group of trekkers travel by wagon through the bushveld to the goldfields. Romance, adventure, and a plot to overthrow the Boer Republic. Into this explosive atmosphere comes the hero, born to an English mother and Afrikaans father, caught between the Boers and the English.

The Boys from Bulawayo: Two former Rhodesians help a mother on the run with her twins who were being sexually abused by hiding them for four years. Then they are arrested and the Australian Federal Police throw the book at them. A challenging legal drama: a Family Court order or the rights of the children?

Mike West: South Africa's Super Soldier - Co-written with Hannes Wessels: Mike West is heading for a life of crime. Then he manages to be accepted to fight in the Rhodesian war where he learns the art of survival, tracking, and killing, before joining the SANDF where he must fight both the Afrikaner internal prejucie and the terrorists for survival.

The CEDRIC KUSHNER Story: Cedric Kushner broke the mould by following his passion insofar as organising and promoting music and boxing events abroad at the highest level and ignoring the naysayers who look at school reports to gauge potential. We are all good at something. We just have to find our passion. What matters in life and what you achieve and the memories you leave behind. Cedric was such a man.

AN UNEXPECTED LIFE: Fighting apartheid. music, video, sailing America Cup boat, scratch cards, Supersport television gaming, touring with the Springboks, CANSA in transition, the Golf Hall of Fame, finally becoming an author and film possiblities, all go to make up a life interacting with giants on the world stage. From treachery to hope, and life's lessons. Barry John Cohen, my unexpected journey.

CONTENTS

FOREWORD	9
LIST OF ACRONYMS	10
INTRODUCTION	12
CHAPTER 1: BLACK GOLFERS	**15**
Caddies – the first black golfers	15
First black golf club	16
Ramnath 'Bambata' Boodhun	19
CHAPTER 2: BLACK GOLF EXPLODES	**23**
A famous caddy victory	23
Bush Golf	24
Papwa: The early years	25
Playing on a White golf course	46
Simon 'Cox' Hlapo	49
CHAPTER 3: TPA TOUR RIVALRY	**54**
Provincial Non-European Opens	54
South African Non-European Opens	58
Comparison: Papwa, Chowglay, Tshabalala	64
CHAPTER 4: THE 'PAPWA' STORY – A CHALLENGE TO APARTHEID	**70**
Discovered	72
Graham Wulff and Oil of Olay	74

Victory	96
Edward Johnson-Sedibe	115
CHAPTER 5: BREAKTHROUGH	**119**
A loophole	119
Permission	125
Firestorm	135
Apartheid thorn	141
CHAPTER 6: THE SHOWDOWN	**161**
Papwa vs Player	161
CHAPTER 7: REACTION	**182**
What goes up must come down	182
Assassination	188
An illicit affair	191
Banned	195
India: Offer you can't refuse	205
Pushback	219
The leading scores were:	229
Cracks in the wall	231
Light peeping through	238
CHAPTER 8: VIVE LA FRANCE	**241**
Handing over the crown	241
CHAPTER 9: END OF THE ROAD	**253**
Papwa's death	253
In Honour: Sewsunker 'Papwa' Sewgolum	261
Gary Player: Questions	271
Final word	278

SOUTHERN AFRICA PLAYER RANKINGS	280
All-Time Southern Africa BEST Golfers	283
All-Time Greatest BLACK Golfers (pre-1994)	284
All-Time Greatest Golfers	284
CHAPTER 10: RECORDING HISTORY	286
Southern Africa Golf Hall of Fame	286
Southern Africa 'Black' Hall of Fame Inductees	287
CHAPTER 11: STATISTICS	291
Southern Africa circuit wins (5)	291
Papwa: Tournament Records	292
Notable Performances	307
AUTHOR'S NOTES	308
BIBLIOGRAPHY	310
Books	310
Newspapers, Magazines, and Interviews	312
Websites	313

FOREWORD

The greatest glory in living lies not in never falling, but in rising every time we fall – Nelson Mandela

The fabric of black golf is interwoven with attempts by the South African apartheid government to prevent golfers of colour to compete against white sporting South Africans on the international stage.

They said he couldn't do it but he became the symbol of the anti-apartheid sport movement, exerting pressure to have South Africa banned from the Olympics, sport boycotts, and our golfers banned from competing in various countries, such that the world took notice

Papwa Sewgolum, against all odds, won the Dutch Open playing in only his second white-tournament, and a total of three times in four attempts. Then after being allowed to play in the white- Natal Open he demolished a top field, runner-up in the South African Open, and two years later when he was again allowed to play the Natal Open, beat the world number 1, the white-champion, Gary Player, head-to-head, only for the apartheid government, after a failed assassination attempt, to ban him from playing in tournaments in South Africa, and thereafter withhold his passport to prevent him playing abroad, such that he died impoverished.

This book is written in a popular, conversational style. It's easily understood by those who don't know much about golf, yet the book's message is of hope and perseverance. It tells the story so that Papwa Sewgolum and his struggles are not forgotten, and in so doing, creates a black golfing hero to inspire the youth.

LIST OF ACRONYMS

ANC	African National Congress
ANI	Adams National Industries
BPGA	British Professional Golfer Association
DISGA	Durban Indian Sports Ground Association
EP	Eastern Province
EPGU	Eastern Province Golf Union
EP(N-E)GU	Eastern Province (Non-European) Golf Union
GC	Golf Club
GU	Golf Union
IDC	Industrial Development Corporation
N-E	Non-European
NE	North Eastern
NIC	Natal Indian Congress
NUSAS	National Union of South African Students
OFS	Orange Free State
OFSGU	Orange Free State Golf Union
PAC	Pan African Congress
PE	Port Elizabeth
PE(N-E)GU	Port Elizabeth (Non-European) Golf Union
PGA	Professional Golf Association
RAF	Royal Air Force
SA	South Africa/n
SAA	South African Airways
SACOS	South Africa Sports Confederation and Olympic Committee

SAGU	South African Golf Union
SAN-ROC	South African Non-Racial Olympic Committee
SA(N-E)GA	South African (Non-European) Golf Association
SAPGA	South African Professional Golfer Association
SASA	South African Sports Association
T(N-E)GU	Transvaal Non-European Golf Union
TPA	Tournament Players Association
UDI	Unilateral Declaration of Independence
UK	United Kingdom
UN	United Nations
US	United States
WP	Western Province
WPGU	Western Province Golf Union
WP(N-E)GU	Western Province (Non-European) Golf Union
ZPGA	Zimbabwe Professional Golf Association

INTRODUCTION

'Man is born free but everywhere in chains – Rousseau

Sport in apartheid South Africa (SA) was a powerful medium used to achieve the ultimate objective for a non-racial democracy in the politics of liberation.

The story of South Africa cannot be told fully, without the inclusion of the contribution of sport in breaking racial barriers. At the heart of the cultural boycott under apartheid was sport as a tool to bring the might of apartheid to its knees. Who can forget the mantra of the South African Council on Sport (SACOS) coined by its then President, Hassan Howa, that there can be "no normal sport in an abnormal society"?

As Sport was used as a tool to breakdown the apartheid system, it has continued to be utilised as a tool for nation building and social cohesion post the 1994 democratic era.

The fabric of black golf is interwoven with attempts by the South African apartheid government not to allow black golfers to compete against their white counterpart and on the international stage, consistent with the 1956 Apartheid Sports Plan. In many ways the contribution of black golf in highlighting the injustices visited upon black sports men and women cannot be overstated. Against this backdrop, 'Papwa' Sewsunker Sewgolum[1] went on to be the poster boy for successful anti-apartheid black sportsmen.

Through his perseverance, he and others enabled the anti-apartheid sport movement to draw the attention of the world sports fraternity to these injustices. Collectively, they contributed immensely towards breaking down the sporting barriers and helped eliminate apartheid. It is important for the voices of the oppressed and their stories to be heard

---

1   He was known as Sewsunker Sewgolum although his real name is **Sewshanker** Sewgolum

Introduction

of golf, and how Papwa Sewgolum rose from humble beginnings to challenge the might of the golfing titans, and compete on an equal footing must be told.

Papwa Sewgolum became the first symbol and torch-bearer of the anti-apartheid sport movement in 1963 after receiving his trophy in the rain. His treatment by the authorities during the 1960s and 70s continued to receive substantial coverage in the media locally, in India, the UK, and elsewhere.

It is a misnomer that rugby and cricket were the prime sport movers involved with the dismantling of apartheid. In fact, it was black SA golf which first drew international condemnation during the 1960s in the form of Papwa Sewgolum, leading India to have SA thrown out of the Olympics in 1964, and later during the 1970s and 80s having numerous SA golfers banned from playing in Europe, such as in Sweden, Netherlands, Tunisia, Greece, Denmark, with tournaments called off in Scotland and elsewhere, and anti-apartheid demonstrations against SA golfers, especially Gary Player, in Britain, Ireland, Australia, New Zealand, and the USA.

To reduce his flesh-and-blood life into pitch-meeting shorthand, you could say that Papwa Sewgolum was the Charlie Sifford (the first African American to play on the PGA Tour) of South African golf.

It's an inadequate analogy, of course, just as the few words typed here get you barely past the starting line of Papwa's life. What I know for sure is that I have done an inadequate job, over the years, exploring the lives of black and brown golfers – golfers who moved mountains to get to the first tee. This space, both today and tomorrow, will try to address that.

This then is Papwa's story; it's a story that continues to resonate, how he rose above the challenges, only for those in authority to react and try and stop the sweeping winds of change.

CHAPTER 1: BLACK GOLFERS

The belief that people of colour did not play golf during the 20th century is another apartheid myth, with Ramnath 'Bambata' Boodhun being the first South African player of colour to participate in the 1929 British Open.

Caddies – the first black golfers

The first golf club in the colony of SA is purported to be the Cape Golf Club (later the Royal Cape Golf Club) which was established on Waterloo Green at the Wynberg Military Camp in November 1885. The layout of the course is not known but from the photographs it appears to be laid on open veld with minimal trees in a straight line out and in. Playing conditions, at their best, were rough and ready.

However, this was not the first golf club with a membership as there is a report, dated 30 May 1878 in *The Natal Witness*, of a golf club, the first of its kind, having been started at Cronstadt (Kroonstad), 'the materials from Edinburgh having arrived, and members in full swing'. This is confirmed by a letter to the editor of *The Friend of the Free State and Bloemfontein Gazette*, dated 17 June 1880, from an enthusiastic golfer from Cronstadt describing the fledgling Cronstadt Golf Club.

Subsequently in 1890, T.W. Hoseason was reported to have laid out and started the Kroonstad golf course where the Post Office now stands.

One imagines that Hoseason would have known of the founding of the club some 12 years previously and would have mentioned this to R. G. Fall in 1930 when he wrote about the founding of the first club. It can only be assumed that the club started in 1878 did not last long and that by the time Hoseason arrived in Kroonstad in 1889 the first club was long forgotten.

The first reported medal competition was held in August 1886 at Wynberg where General Torrens, acclaimed as the founder of golf in SA, went on to win with a gross 94. This (or Cronstadt) was possibly the start of black golf as no doubt Cape Coloured, Indian, and Malay caddies were trained and employed to caddy the golf bags or simply carry the clubs and balls of the white golfers. Thus caddies were introduced to the game of golf.

As such, golf started for people of colour with caddies using rolled bent wire for clubs and katoki or bluegum seed-pods or the like for golf balls.

Many of the caddies, unlike their white counterparts, played with a reverse grip, which became known as the 'caddy grip'. The reason was because while they were idling their time waiting for a 'bag', they would set up some holes using empty tins placed in the ground in the smallish area allocated to caddies, and challenge each other.

Using their very lightweight bent wire, with the 'clubface' rolled up, the only way they could get the 'ball' into the air quickly was to use the reverse grip, which later became famous as the 'Papwa grip'.

First black golf club

The first club for black golfers was founded in Natal, when the Durban Indian Golf Club was formed in January 1927. This small nine-hole golf course, not far from the Durban Club's course at Greyville between Mansfield Road School and the racecourse, was situated at the Indian Recreation Grounds (Currie's Fountain), later the Mecca of non-racial sport.

Currie's Fountain got its name in 1878 when a terrible drought hit Durban causing a severe shortage of water. This prompted Councilor H.W. Currie to sink an artesian well in search of water in the area below the Durban Botanic Gardens. Eventually he struck water, and the well-named Currie's Fountain, delivered 50,000 gallons of it to the town every day through pipes laid for the purpose.

'Curries' was a name associated with the days of vibrant struggle, particularly in the 1960s and 1970s, influencing the interaction of black people within a socio-political and cultural environment in Durban and SA. The anti-apartheid formations and political activists

Chapter 1: Black Golfers

held many gatherings, meetings and rallies, sometimes under the pretext of organising sport and cultural programmes. Some of the major political events included a strike against Land Tax in 1913, when 6,000 people assembled to listen to Thumbi Naidoo, a political activist and friend of Mahatma Gandhi, the burning of the Dompas Campaign in 1959 led by Inkosi Albert Luthuli, the launch of Cosatu in 1985, and the re-launch of the Women's League in 1986.

Convenors of the Durban Indian Golf Club.

Top Row.—J. Mayhoo Maharaj, C. M. Singh, N. Maharaj, C. B. Singh and R. L. Boodhan (hon. secretary).
Bottom Row.—J. B. Maharaj (hon. treasurer), '. Moosa (captain), T. S. Purbhoo (president), [. Mahomed (vice-president).

In the Durban Indian Club there is one scratch player and five with a handicap of 1, six with 3 and eight with 4. In the club championship, now under way, there are 60 competitors, 20 to qualify for the final stage.

The course was opened in the first week in June by the late Advocate Albert Christopher under the auspices of the Durban Indian Sports Ground Association (DISGA) with a membership of nine; at the opening tournament in July 1927 there were 57, and a year later there were over 100 members. The Durban Indian Golf Club did have some 'Africans' as members although the vast majority were Indians.

As the ground was swampy, a considerable amount of money was spent on French drains to clear the surface water, and portions of the land had to be filled with refuse and top soil dressing to make the fields playable.

The golf course consisted of just nine holes covering a distance of 1,884m. Par for the course was 34. It overlapped with the cricket, football and tennis playing fields, which effectively meant that golf could be played mainly on Sundays when it was free from the other codes not using the area. Membership enrolment fees were two shillings and sixpence (R4.70). Monthly subscription fees were one shilling (R1.80). Mr T.S. Parbhoo had the honour of being the very first Club President.

The players, drawn mostly from the ranks of the caddies, were very keen, playing mainly every Sunday because all the members worked during the week, even though in conservative SA it was frowned upon to play sport on a Sunday instead of setting the day aside for Christian religious observance.

It was obvious that many of the members had played good golf previously. In the first year, there was one member off scratch, five with a handicap of one, six off three, and eight off four, with 60 competitors playing in the first club championship in 1929 won by E. Marrian, from R.L. Boodhun (Ramnath Bambata's brother).

The handicapping may have been a bit lax, and the allocation of par not entirely up to modern European standards. But it must be remembered that the course, as was the case with every other non-European bush course in SA, was bad, very bad, and a hole 225m in length might be well worth a bogey of four.

On 31 March 1954, the Club changed its name to the Durban Golf Club. The Club was never in a position to reject an application for membership in regard to race or colour, such that in April 1980 it was to accept and welcome a 'white' member.

Ramnath 'Bambata' Boodhun[2]

Boodhun was born in Durban, his parents came from Bihar and arrived as indentured labourers to work in the sugarcane fields. He lived in Madras Road, Berea, at the end of the Durban Country Club course (later Royal Durban) situated within the Greyville racetrack.

Bambata was named after Chief Bambatha kaMancinza who was involved in the 1906 'poll tax' rebellion which saw 3,000 – 4,000 Zulus, including the Chief, killed, and is regarded in some quarters as the start of the 'anti-apartheid' struggle.

Born not far from the Royal Durban Golf Club, it was natural that he should become a caddy, as was the custom for all young Indian boys of that quarter. His exceptional smartness, no less than his aptitude for the game, was shown at a very early age. He attracted the attention of George Fotheringham (SA Open champion 1908, '10, '11, '12, '14), newly out of Carnoustie and the first professional engaged by the Durban club.

Fotheringham took him into the shop, where as an apprenticeship he learnt to make and repair clubs, and he became an excellent club-maker and 'carried' for Fotheringham in all his matches. Boodhun copied the style of Fotheringham such that he became a pocket-size version in this position for the next 20 years, later as an assistant first to Bill Horne, and then to the new professional of the club, Jock Brews

---

2   Note: The correct spelling is Boodhun, not Boodhan.

(SA Open champion 1921, '23, '26, '28) who went on to play in The Open Championship in 1926.

He considered Fotheringham to be the finest player that was ever in SA. His game developed under somewhat difficult circumstances considering the rigid 'colour' bar in colonial SA, his shot-making was absolutely uncanny, and on those occasions his mashie-work and putting had to be seen to be believed.

His weight was just over 45kg, yet his driving was as long as anyone else, professional or amateur in the country, with the possible exception of Jock Brews and Bert Elkin of Pretoria at their very longest.

Even as a boy of 15, it was a common amusement among those who knew, to back Bambata against up-country visitors who prided themselves as to their ability. 'The little Indian never lost!'

Source: Sujatha Boodhun

Because of his popularity among golfers in SA, the club eventually gave him the privilege on the Durban Links to play and coach before 9am, and he also coached at Beachwood Golf Club.

He was considered by many the most exceptional player in SA; and were it not for the 'colour' bar (because of the Colonial policies he was not allowed to participate in 'white-Open' tournaments), there is little doubt that South Africa's golf history would have been materially different.

Chapter 1: Black Golfers

At the same time, he was a pioneer of black golf and founder member of the first black club in SA, the Durban Indian Club, together with his brother, R.L. Boodhun, who was the secretary, as well as being a committee member of the Indian Golf Association.

In 1929 in return for his services, a subscription was raised for him to go overseas to compete in international tournaments.

By then the Indian Golf Association was well established, and Ramnath 'Bambata' Boodhun, the champion Indian golfer from Natal, was the first black golfer of quality to join Sid Brews (future runner-up to Henry Cotton in 1934) and play in the May 1929 British Open in Scotland, with Walter Hagen the defending champion.

When he arrived in England, Bambata had only five clubs, with no more than a mashie, and with no mashie-niblick. He found the English courses hard and the greens fast, with the closed texture of their fairways compared to the soft ground of Durban, while the bunkers demanded a deeper-faced club. By the time he competed in the British Open he had nine clubs including a niblick (a normal set consists of 14 clubs).

The weather was bitterly cold with rain pouring down continuously. Bambata said that his hands and feet were completely numbed with the cold, and his putting touch left him. He looked and felt cold. Added to these difficulties was the shadow which had covered his game. The ball slipped tantalisingly past the hole as Bambata lost his confidence on the greens and had to fight to keep his game from crumbling. All things considered, his score of 87 was a credible performance. The leading score at Muirfield was 74.

The following day, he played the second round at Gullane, scoring 82. Again the weather was partly responsible for his poor score. He found it painful to swing a club, and the bitter cold and wet caused the skin of his hands to crack. His score of 169 was far too high to qualify.

The transition from being the star on the tropical courses of Natal to the links courses of Scotland Europe with their yawning pot bunkers waiting to gobble up an errant golf ball was clearly a difficult one. He also played in the 1929 German Open, but had not managed to win an overseas tournament by the time he died in 1934.

His participation in these tournaments and his intention to qualify

Papwa

as an assistant professional created a new awareness of the existence of black golf prowess in South Africa. Despite Boodhun's lack of success on the European circuit, his endeavours inspired others and played a role in the formation of a number of golf clubs in Natal, Transvaal, Cape Province and Orange Free State.

In 1939, the Durban Indian Sports Ground Association presented a cup to the Durban Golf Club, the 'Bambata cup', to perpetuate the memory of Bambata. This is played for annually by the Royal Durban caddies on their championship day, and in 1968, Papwa Sewgolum, the greatest Indian golfer, won the R.L. Bambata Boodhun Trophy over 36 holes for the first time.

As R.G. Fall wrote (1953) concerning Boodhun: A most brilliant player. He was certainly the greatest little (7st – 100 lbs) golfer Southern Africa has ever produced, and had he enjoyed the privileges which go with a white skin, there is scarcely room for doubt about his becoming an Open champion.

CHAPTER 2: BLACK GOLF EXPLODES

A famous caddy victory

After Alf Padgham[3] won the 1936 British Open he toured SA where he managed to win the 1936 SA and Western Province Opens in-between playing regular exhibition matches.

When Padgham and compatriot, Allan Dailey (a Ryder Cup golfer) were challenged to a match at Durban Country Club against two Indian caddies a year after Padgham's arrival in South Africa, they had reason to assume that they would win.

 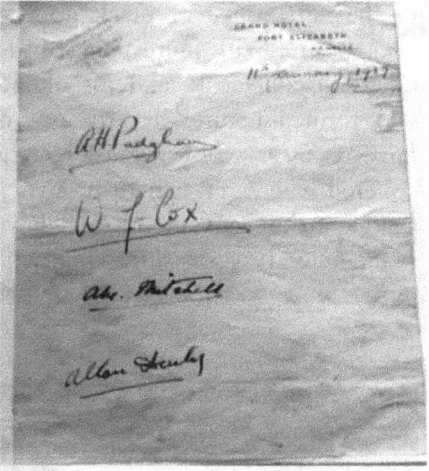

Source: Barry Cohen

Instead they were astonishingly defeated, when two Indian caddies, Jack Nathan and A. Sewpersadh (also a newspaper vendor), played sterling golf to win 2/1 at Beachwood Golf Club, a victory that is now part of SA caddie folklore.

---

3 Padgham also came 2nd, 3rd, 4th and beat Bobby Locke in an exhibition match.

Papwa

When you consider that these caddies were able to beat a Major winner and Ryder Cup stars, it says a lot for the untapped talent waiting for an opportunity – an opportunity which sadly never happened due to the colonial and governing policies of the time. Were they good enough to compete overseas with the best? We will never know.

In the 1930s, there was increasing interest among the many caddies working at the various clubs to take up golf as well as activity on the golfing front among the black communities generally.

Clearly the threat that Padgham or anyone else these Indian golfers ever met at Sunningdale Park would be beaten was no idle boast. If the British Open champion and a partner could be beaten over a championship course, what would have happened to them over the rough-and-ready affair at Currie's Fountain is anyone's guess.

Bush Golf

In the early days of black golf, ramshackle 'courses' popped up everywhere. With more than a little ingenuity, members carved out nine-hole courses. Brickfields, ditches, drainage trenches and a marshy vlei formed natural hazards not normally found on the splendid fairways reserved for whites.. Greens were roughly smoothed patches covered with sand, called 'browns', because oil was mixed with the sand to make them smooth, and they were tiny, averaging three metres in diameter. It was easier to putt with a mashie than with an orthodox putter.

'There is a spice of adventure about golf as the natives play it. They never know from one day to another whether they are going

to find their course in the condition in which they left it. Someone may have dug some pot clay out of one of the greens. That is just too bad and they make another. Or a sewerage trench may have been dug across the course. That is equally bad luck. Their concern is that their courses may disappear altogether to make way for development. They play the game seriously and it would be a pity if they were deprived of their courses'. (RG Fall)

Carved out of the bush with no fences golf courses were full of hazards including dangerous animals.

Such was the sport's growing popularity that clubs continued to spring up and grow, many consisting of small groups of enthusiasts playing on these rough and ready courses laid out on bare veld. 'That putting is difficult goes without saying. A small space was cleared and top-dressed with sand, but in spite of everything the ball weaved a very wobbly way towards the hole with most putts.'

Papwa: The early years
Papwa Sewgolum's great-grand-parents had come to SA in 1860 along with many other indentured Indians from North India via Calcutta to work in the sugarcane plantations on the Natal North Coast. They hoped to make a new life in the land of milk and honey, and prosper, and to get away from their grinding poverty and punishing colonial taxes (which would eventually lead to Gandhi's march to the sea against the salt tax) much like Bambata's grandparents.

Papwa

His father had already told Papwa stories about the great Mahatma Gandhi, one of two black lawyers in SA. Papwa, meaning small or darling child, was of Indian descent. But he was designated 'coloured' in the country's prismatic social structure.

He was born in December 1928 to his mother, Parvathy, who was going blind, in a tin shanty in Riverside, in a part of the world with a history of oppression. "Papwa lived amongst the poorest of the poor in the Riverside area. They lived very modestly." The family had very little money and it was a constant struggle to make ends meet.

Papwa's parents planted vegetables and spices in a small cultivated area at the rear of the house, but this was insufficient for a growing family, and Parvathy would often send the children into the bushes to look for wild fruit, roots and vegetables.

Their home was about one kilometre from the all-white Beachwood Golf Club, and two years after the opening of the first black golf club, the Durban Indian Golf Club at Currie's Fountain.

Source Thayalan Reddy

Chapter 2: Black Golf Explodes

Although times were hard, Riverside had unparalleled views across a magnificent green belt, stretching from the Umgeni River mouth with its abundant bird life on the Umgeni Estuary, across the Indian Ocean and towards the beachfront. A mere 12 minutes walk to the beach, set one kilometre from the banks of the Umgeni River, yet close to the city centre of Durban.

Despite the family's physical and financial hardships, it is easy enough to imagine the blissful natural surrounds in which the young Papwa grew up.

Pounding surf crashed on the shore not far from the little shack which he called home. The tropical air was humid as Papwa, aged seven, and his father left for their late afternoon fishing along the Umgeni River to supplement his meagre wages as the smell wood and paraffin smoke, and the scent of garlic and ginger wafted over them.

Papwa held the greaseproof paper with their bait, dough made from flour and water, and his father explained that by placing some dough in a milk bottle in the water, it would attract smaller fish to swim into the bottle. These could be used as bait for bigger fish.

Just then they heard a shout of 'fore' as a white ball crashed into the colourful bougainvillea bush close by. His dad retrieved the ball, only to be accosted by an elderly red-faced man holding a stick as he came crashing through the bush wanting to know whether the 'coolie' was stealing his golf ball.

Such was his introduction to the game of golf and it peaked Papwa's interest. When the man was told that the ball had nearly hit his little boy, he offered a half-hearted apology and gave his father a tickey as a reward for finding the ball.

During the peace and quiet of fishing, Papwa's father explained the game of golf, and how the great Ramnath 'Bambata' Boodhun, a Hindu man like them, who started out as a caddy-boy, had gone to play in the white man's British Open at Muirfield, the greatest tournament in the world.

Papwa immediately told his father that he would be as great as Bambata, perhaps even greater and that he too would go and play in The Open. His father looked down at his little 'laaitjie' boy, and smiled, proud to have his son tagging along for company. 'Little boys

Finding a palm nut, his father demonstrated how to hit the 'ball', and how to putt. Papwa was intrigued. Later, they made their way back home and his father pointed out the Durban golf course, and the strange white men as they hit the white ball into the bush, retrieved it, and then hit it back into another bush.

To Papwa it seemed funny, and excitedly he described the scene to his mother. The strange men with canvas bags, and strange sticks which looked like thin bamboo shoots, some with knobs on them, hitting this little white ball trying to roll it into a small hole with a flag, on what appeared to be a freshly-mown lawn, clapping each other on the back, while Indian coolie boys carrying bags had to keep very quiet because this would make the white man very angry as they watched and exchanged money amongst them at the end of the hole. Papwa also learnt many words of these white man's language, such as *Damn, Hardlines, Putter, Bunker, Good shot,* and so on.

It may have been a world away for a poor Indian boy, but Papwa was fascinated, and the seed was planted. He too would one day stride those fairways followed by hordes of supporters with the sole aim of getting the white ball into the hole. His mother smiled at his babbling, and then prepared their small spiced fish supper and it was time for bed.

While his father played football for the local Indian team, Papwa would sneak away, squirming his way through the Beachwood Golf Club's fence and watch these strange white men at play, waiting for

Chapter 2: Black Golf Explodes

the opportunity to 'find' a golf ball. He had his father whittle him a syringa[4] stick putter, and after placing tin cups in the sandy ground at home, he challenged his father and little brother to a 'game of golf.'

Every night he putted over his 'green', placing balls around the cup, first from two-feet, and when he had holed these, he would place them once again around the cup, but this time a foot further away, until he had sunk all these putts before extending further back.

Like other Indian boys, he also fashioned golf clubs from palm leaf midriff and rolled iron, and taught himself to swing with what was to become his famed cross-handed grip (hands positioned the opposite way to the traditional grip, an unconventional hold) to get the ball quickly into the air due to the light weight of his 'clubs'.

This grip had become popular with the other caddy boys throughout the country for the same reason, and was called the 'caddy grip'.

Papwa's future provincial rival, Ismail Chowglay would also use this grip with much success in Cape Town, and later Vincent Tshabalala, who was destined to win the French Open, used this grip with his long irons. Many top golfers today use Papwa's cross-handed grip for putting, even chipping, but virtually no one uses it today for all shots. 'I believe a man should swing a club the best way he knows how,' Papwa told Golf Digest in 1964.

As he did not go to school after Grade 4, he sometimes played 'golf' with his friends after a midday swim in the Umgeni River using their mid-ribs of palm leaf clubs and palm nut golf balls. Three sticks were set up around the river bank, indicating where the holes were:

> *But it was their mannerisms – obviously modeled on their pet 'Bwana' – their power drives, the wrist play, the disgust after a bad shot, the putting stances. Everything, and even after all the practice swings, mimicry, etc., they cracked the old palm nut as to the manner born, with perfect timing, as far as any man born of woman could hit a palm nut with a palm-leaf mid-rib, on river-sand, in the same set of circumstances.*

As Papwa's hands were still tiny, they were separated with no

---

4 Tall syringa trees were originally imported to South Africa from India as an ornamental plant with its scented lilac flowers

overlapping or interlocking of fingers to assist the wrist in holding the club. He swung the 'club' back past parallel almost bouncing off his right shoulder, with his hip fully turned, and his left heel raised, then with his trademark dip, he bent his knees to get to it, he swung downwards as hard as possible, often falling back onto his right foot, which later became a part of his style, and whipped his right hip through the swing to generate club head speed.

His putting style was interesting, with his left foot leading his right, and turned slightly inwards helping to counteract the wind and steady him. Given his grip, he would 'pop' the ball, putting down into the stroke.

Before long Papwa had found an old broken wooden-shafted rusted 6-iron club in the bush alongside the fairway, which his father cut down for him as it was far too long and heavy, and with the few balls he found, Papwa began playing whenever he went to watch his dad fishing. (The famous Seve Ballesteros and Lee Trevino would also start out as caddies with one club).

A 6-iron was the perfect club to start with as it could be used for all sorts of shots. By way of explanation, besides using woods, whose club-face angle is around 9-12 degrees, and go the furthest, especially off a tee, but which are the hardest to hit, irons club-face angle range from 1 – 9 plus a wedge (a number 10) with the club-face around 60-65 degrees. The shorter the club the higher the number, and the easier and higher but shorter distance the shot will go.

In the evening after playing Papwa would wash the club in soapy water to clean the dirt off the grooves of the club's face and clean his ball.

From time-to-time he would sneak onto Durban Golf Club where he watched the maestro Bobby Locke win the 1938 SA Open, which happened just before Locke joined the Air Force as a fighter pilot during World War 2. (Locke would go on to win over 80 tournaments, including four British Opens, and nine SA Opens, until he virtually lost the sight of his one eye in a train-crossing accident in 1959). He was regarded as the greatest putter in the world (in 1945 he played 1800 holes of tournament golf and never had a three-putt).

Locke's pre-putt ritual was legendary. First, he would look behind

Chapter 2: Black Golf Explodes

Bobby Locke playing in the 1938 SA Open

the hole, then from side to side, and finally from behind his ball to make certain of all the twists and turns knowing the ball would also move away from any mountain or koppie and towards water.

He would approach the hole, examining the way the grass was leaning; if it was leaning towards the hole, it would be a fast putt, and a slow putt if it was away from the hole. Finally, he looked at the position of the cup in the hole, and if the hole was more upright at the back he could hit the putt just a little firmer.

Then he would crouch down on his haunches behind the ball, twirling his famous wooden-shafted blade putter until he could actually visualise the path along which he needed to putt the ball.

Now standing over the ball with his right foot behind the left, he took the blade back in a curve following the line of his feet, and closing the face, pressing forward he brought it down onto the ball, minimising the bounce as the blade made contact and conveying the spin onto the ball.

He gave the false hope to many an opponent that he would hook the ball offline, but he always hit it in the middle of the putter in the right direction, and magically, it would hook as it made its way into the hole, as despite his later heavy set he danced after it like a ballerina.

Papwa

Nobody ever hooked their putts, yet Locke was the greatest putter the world had seen, and he viewed the putt as having three opportunities to go into the hole, from the left side, the right side, or directly into the hole. As Papwa learnt, his confidence and concentration grew.

Then suddenly his father, his role model, passed away in 1938 when Papwa was about to turn 10. The loss to the family was devastating. Not only was dad a provider, but also a loving husband, a gentle humble father, a teacher and friend to Papwa, with whom he could share his ideas and passion. His humility was to rub off on Papwa.

While his father was alive, family life was straight-forward and happy; the life of traditional Hindus who worshipped their gods at home and in their temples.

His sister helped around the house, but Indian women did not work outside of the family home, so he had no alternative but to go out and try and earn some money together with his older brother Mohan who found work as a municipality labourer, to support his blind mother, sister, and younger brother.

Initially, he found the occasional work as a weekend caddy, and then permanent work as a thread-cutter at 15 shillings per week in Mr Kallidene's garment factory in Prince Edward Street in Durban, but when he plucked up the courage to ask for a raise given his family's circumstances, Mr Kallidene fired him after checking the work roster and noticing Papwa was often absent on Mondays when the caddies had their early morning golf.

But just then, as if preordained, Papwa received an unlikely opportunity to fill in for an absent caddy at Beachwood. As scrawny as he was Papwa leaped at the opportunity – finally he would work on the golf course his father always used to warn him not to be caught on, fearing the consequences of the harsh apartheid laws that would befall his son if they did.

By now Papwa's mother had lost her eyesight completely and was blind, such that she was unable to cope alone. When he was not caddying he would help out in the vegetable garden watering, weeding and harvesting. His mother would instruct him on how to prepare spiced Indian curry dishes.

He was making ends meet caddying at the Beachwood Country

Chapter 2: Black Golf Explodes

Club, earning one shilling and sixpence (1/6d) per round (possibly an extra tip and refreshment) even though the heavy leather bags were almost as tall as him – and caddies were also allowed to play on Monday when the course was 'closed'. (Indians were not allowed to play on the course as a *de facto* form of segregation which had become institutionalised throughout the country). It was here that Papwa learnt the art of golf.

I had no love for the game of golf when first I started. I was 13, and my father had died leaving me to help my mother and younger brother. My stomach was my introduction to golf, and at seven shillings a week I wasn't able to fill it often.

His caddy duties included keeping the golf clubs clean during the round and afterwards advising his player about the pace and undulations of the greens, keeping a watch on his player's ball with each shot they made, and for the not so accomplished golfer (which in all fairness is most recreational golfers), to find their wayward shots in the rough, bushes, and occasional strange places.

After the round of golf a ticket was given to the caddy with a rating as to his performance and effort in carrying out their duties. At the end of the month the best caddy received a financial reward from the Caddy Master of a few shillings. Papwa was popular with the members for his reading of the greens, judging distance, and advice, such that he was a regular winner of the reward.

So Papwa learnt to play, first by knocking palm nuts along the beach shore with his palm leaf mid-ribs, and later by caddying for and watching the rich white folk hack around the golf course, sometimes giving advice but usually remaining quiet when they admonished him for their poor shot-making.

There were times when he brought home as little as 7/6d (R14.50) per week as he did not get a bag to carry every day, and the family often went hungry. But he was now involved with the game of golf and after he was given another old second-hand golf club. He practiced whenever he could.

He would start out every morning with his 6-iron and two old golf balls and hit these balls two kilometres, all the way to the golf club, including over the river. On his return at 4pm, after carrying two bags during the day (if he was lucky), he would once again hit the golf balls on his journey back home honing his technique.

There were sand dunes on both sides of his home, and a stream between them, and later each evening he would hit golf balls from one end to the other.

All caddies were allowed to play at Beachwood on a Monday (likewise at many other clubs) from 5–9am. So in the early morning hours around 04:30 they would catch the bus to steal a round on those hallowed grounds, just as long as they could play 18 holes before the club members started to arrive at 08:30.

If they missed their opportunity, they had to wait another week before they could play. Of course, people of colour were not allowed to be members of these golf clubs.

Allowing caddies to play on Mondays encouraged them to have a chance at the game of golf. It also allowed them to be responsible for filling in divots and familiarize themselves with golf etiquette.

Eventually, Papwa started to enter local tournaments and became more interested in the game when he won a minor Indian competition where the prize was a case of cool-drinks. Soon his golfing prowess was good enough for him to win the highest competitions in the non-white golfing world.

When I played caddy matches there was a bunch of my mates jeering at my grip and once in a fit of temper I broke a club, but never again! That club cost me six months wages. Much has been made about my unorthodox grip, but it works for me and that is all that matters.

It wasn't long before he had shot an unofficial 64, beating the Beachwood par-73 course record of 66 set by Sandy Guthrie, and then later in 1957 he shot a 59, but because it was a 'caddy tournament' and he was not a member of the SAGU, the course record score was not officially recognised. This was only the second recorded sub-60 in South Africa, the other was scored by Louis Crozet at Queenstown GC in 1925.

Club Captain Martindale advised Papwa, now aged 16, to enter the 1945 Natal Indian Open. Martindale financed his entry and provided

Chapter 2: Black Golf Explodes

his son Alan's gear and clubs.

Talented Alan Martindale was later to captain the Western Province's golf team in the 1960s, and he was also the Captain of Metropolitan Golf Club where future two-time major winner, Sally Little had started playing.

At that time, Currie's Fountain golf course consisted of nine indifferent holes repeated from different tee-boxes masquerading as an 18-hole course. Scattered about the course were the wrecks of old cars and trams. During the round, the players' traversed two soccer fields, a car race track, and a tennis court. There were no greens to speak of, and the holes were set into uneven sand that was not regularly rolled.

Papwa won this championship at the Currie's Fountain course, his first big tournament victory. This was a phenomenal achievement, and the next day he recounted this wonderful victory, and that the organisers were reluctant to give him the trophy because of his youth. Martindale wasted no time, and pressure was placed on the organisers until they relented and presented Papwa with his first trophy.

He had won in grand style, stunning spectators with his powerful grip which allowed him on his backswing to get the club up quickly with plenty of time to get his hips through ahead of the club on the downswing, but that year would be remembered for another reason.

Around this time the Indian government requested that the discriminatory treatment of Indians in SA be included on the agenda of the very first session of the General Assembly at the newly formed United Nations (UN). This after the government of General Jan Smuts had enacted the notorious 'Asiatic Land Tenure and Indian Representation Act', the so-called 'Ghetto Act', in the face of an outraged Indian population and the strongest of protests from the Indian Government, in that this legislation sought to limit Indian political representation, and define where they could live, own land, and trade.

Outraged, India immediately imposed trade sanctions and withdrew their High Commissioner, whilst Mahatma Gandhi gave the Durban community his blessing to launch a two-year passive resistance struggle, but to no avail.

The authorities didn't take this lying down and Jan Smuts addressed the UN Assembly arguing the right of the country to defend its policies and that the UN was not the right forum for discussing this matter. Smuts' argument was rejected and the requisite two-thirds majority demanded that the government conform to the basic principles of the newly-formed UN Charter in its treatment of the Indian population. Smuts did not comply.

Worse was to come, as the National Party was to take over from Smuts' liberal United Party in 1948, winning more seats although less votes. At last the Boers, defeated in the 1899 – 1902 Anglo-Boer war, took back control of the country on the basis of *'never again'*, given that the British had 'killed' two-thirds of their women, old men, and especially children in their concentration camps due to starvation and disease. Now they started to impose their own form of 'apartheid' on all people of colour.

For the illiterate Papwa, with no access to information, these political developments meant little.

Their day-to-day diet consisted either of rice or flat wheat bread (chapati). This was usually supplemented with the puree of a legume (called dal), a few vegetables, and when they could afford it, a small bowl of yogurt. Chilies and other spices added zest to this simple fare. Although meat was a rarity, fish, fresh milk, and fruits were also consumed.

In 1951, Papwa married Suminthra in a low-key arranged marriage where they met for the first time at the wedding after their parents first consulted their horoscopes.

For almost all Indians the family is the most important social unit. Almost all marriages were arranged by family elders on the basis of caste, degree of consanguinity, economic status, education (if any), and astrology.

Within families there is a clear order of social precedence and influence based on gender, age, and in the case of a woman, the number of her male children. The senior male of the household – whether father, grandfather, or uncle – is typically the recognised family head, and his wife is the person who regulates the tasks assigned to female family members. Males enjoy higher status than females; boys were often pampered while girls were relatively neglected. This pattern of preference is connected to the institution of dowry since the family's obligation is to provide a suitable dowry to the bride's new family represents a major financial liability.

Traditionally, women were expected to treat their husbands as if they were gods, and obedience of wives to husbands has remained a strong social norm.

Suminthra quickly brought five beautiful children into the world: Romilla, Dinesh, Rajen, Sewnarain, and Deepraj.

Although Papwa was a better golfer than the men for whom he caddied, the South African racial laws prevented him from demonstrating his prowess. He would regularly shoot in the 60s and had already made a hole-in-one on Beachwood's par-4 16th hole. He was soon winning local open tournaments for 'non-Europeans,' often by more than 20 shots, and routinely setting course records.

The segregation of sporting facilities and residential areas meant that Papwa and his family had to live in their shanty home in an area reserved for them, and he was not allowed to enter any white tournament. However, he played in the non-European events staged in Natal from 1954, and where he was almost unbeatable.

Papwa Sewgolum with peers. Picture courtesy of LLA.

Relatively short in stature for a successful golfer at 5 foot 6 inches (165cm), weighing only 145lbs, Papwa's physique was similar to that of Gary Player. In order to achieve distance off the tee, especially given his unorthodox grip, he had to swing his hips aggressively into the shot, something else which had so-called knowledgeable golfers shaking their heads.

By now others were taking notice of the quiet Indian although many purists were bothered by Papwa's unorthodoxy.

Reg Sweet was the sports editor for the *Sunday Tribune* and *Daily News* and wrote a 1957 article entitled 'Back-to-Front Indian Golfer (Plus 1) is a Champion'. Still, Sweet felt everything was wrong, from his awkward swing to his back-to-front grip.

A scratch golfer is someone who should play to par for the golf course, usually around 72. Handicaps are usually higher than par, and you have to be very good to have a plus handicap, which means your score must average under par.

'Papwa really does play to a plus one handicap,' Sweet wrote. In fact he is the only plus Indian golfer in Natal, and in the matter of golf at the top level, he compares with the best of them.

Look at these figures. The official record at Beachwood is a 66 by Sandy Guthrie. The club record stands to Alan Martindale, with a 68 – and this is a par 73 course. Papwa's own best is a 64, or nine under par. And the remarkable thing about this soft-spoken Indian is the way he holds the club. It looks the most awkward grip in the world until he makes his shots', and he went on to urge; 'there are good reasons why golfers as good as this should be given every encouragement'.

Sweet proceeded to describe Papwa's win in a caddie match against Ram, handicap of four, the Beachwood head waiter, who played barefooted. With six-holes to go in the pouring rain, and holding his three-wood down the leather on the shaft to get a better grip, Papwa was four down. Both players were playing with a mixture of clubs. Ram used a two-iron closing its face instead of a putter. Gradually Papwa reeled him in with an immaculate long drive on the 270 yard 15th, a long putt and the hole was his.

Onto the 16th, Ram was the first to wilt as he pulled his drive into the bank. Wiping his wet clubs with a towel, Papwa hit a perfect five-iron straight into the heart of the green with a satisfying whack. Conversation between players and caddies took on a serious turn as they lined up their respective putts. Papwa's ball fell into the front edge, now it was Ram's turn, as his putt slid by, touching the right lip.

All square with the 18th, a par-three to play, and the 20 or so gallery of caddie friends calling out support as though they were playing for the British Open. Ram's tee-shot was short, Papwa's pulled-up three feet from the pin. Now it was Ram's turn, but he froze as he putted well short, and conceded Papwa's putt.

A handshake and the gathering dispersed, not for a hot shower and refreshment but back to the bar and dining room for Ram to serve the club's white patrons, and the caddy enclosure for Papwa. Such were the dictates of the regulations they lived under.

Although an individual sport, golf managed to hammer one of the first nails into the apartheid sport's coffin, as the simple, poor, illiterate Natal-born Indian, 'Papwa' Sewsunker Sewgolum began to make waves on both the local and international fairways.

Self-taught, Papwa would be an immediate success, but this brightness was tarnished by the humiliation heaped on him in his own country.

At this time, Gary Player won his first international tournament in Cairo – in 1955, the Egyptian Open – and went out the same afternoon and practiced until it was dark. Brian Wilkes, a fellow pro who was with the group making the trip was flabbergasted.

'What the hell do you think you're doing Gary?'

'Brian,' replied Player, 'In four years I am going to win the British Open.' It took him four.

These were the early years for Gary when he needed somebody to snap at, and his dad, Harry 'Whisky' Player was there for him – 'Geddy, that's the finest golf shot you ever made,' and, 'Geddy, if you live to be a thousand you will never hit it any better.'

'Whisky Player' got his name as a young man of action at a downtown Johannesburg hotel. He had led a delegation of miners into the hotel to celebrate the impending marriage of one of their number, and when refused anything appropriate with which to celebrate, he clambered up on the table and shouted, 'We want whisky!'

'All of us Players were high-strung,' he said as he stood watching his son practice. 'That's the fantastic thing about Geddy, the way he has mastered himself. I would have flapped. I would have had my chips under all that pressure. Not him. Oh, when it was just the two of us out there, we bloody well had our fights, all right. He'd tell me he couldn't make it, and I'd tell him he was talking rot. I'd tell him he was falling back off his shots, and he'd say, "I don't want to hear it," and I'd say, "well, the hell with you," and then later he'd put his arm around me and kiss me and say, "I'm sorry, Dad, I've just got to explode sometime, and you are the only one who can take it".'

When Player came to Durban to play, Papwa would occasionally caddy for him. These on-course encounters shifted towards the competitive when funded by Oil of Olay founder Graham Wulff, Papwa joined Player to play in the 1959 British Open at Muirfield.

The year 1956 also saw the removal of coloureds from the voting roll; it was the year after the writing up of the Freedom Charter, followed by the Treason Trial. Prime Minister J.G. Strijdom, followed by Hendrik Verwoerd, saw the Nationalist Party enshrine its policy of race absolutism.

1957 brought an amendment to the Group Areas Act prohibiting three forms of statutory occupation by all races insofar as places of public entertainment, of refreshments, and as a member or guest in any club. This enabled the State President to use this provision to issue the proclamation to prohibit non-racial or mixed sport.

By the late 1950s, the National Party government was battling to deal with the complex race issue and there was a groundswell of antagonism from countries around the world, especially those in Africa and Asia, in addition to pressures faced at home.

The sweeping race laws in this deeply divided country were also proving a challenge for sports administrators as there was uncertainty concerning its implementation and substantial penalties for non-compliance. Could people of colour compete, and if so, where? And who could attend, and could each race group mix with the other? Meanwhile activists formed bodies to combat racism in sport.

Papwa was unknown in such activist circles, but through a series of strange coincidences, illiterate non-political 'Papwa' Sewsunker' Sewgolum's name was to become a symbol for those fighting against oppression.

By this stage a number of potential golf champions had emerged such as Simon 'Cox' Hlapo, Edward Johnson-Sedibe, Ismail Chowglay, and shortly thereafter, Richard Mogoerane, Laurence Buthelezi, Vincent Tshabalala, and later Joe Dlamini; all these players could hold themselves against any white opponents, but had yet to make an impact.

What is often lost in the record books is not only the daily discrimination and loss of opportunities forced upon them by the apartheid government, but the fact that these leading players, well into their 30s, which is the prime time of any golf professional, were only now starting to compete on proper 'white' courses.

There is no way one can compare the courses they had to play on to even enable them to play in major non-european events because of the so-called 'parallel but equal' apartheid policy where government and municipality funds were used only to build white courses.

This was even more evident insofar as caddies were allowed to play at the white course where they caddied, but only on a Monday when the course was closed. On the other hand, white professionals practiced daily on manicured top-class golf courses. Many of these professionals played fulltime, unlike their counterparts, who still caddied for a living.

At best, they could rise to caddy-master in their chosen profession. However, they were not allowed to engage in teaching or work in the professional's shop despite the fact that they were more than qualified.

In 1959, those township caddies denied the opportunity to compete on the 'white' SA Tour set their sights on playing in 'The British Open' in the UK.

At this time all that the average white golfer knew about non-European golf was the annual caddy competition at his club. He knew, of course, that some of the caddies played very fine golf; he was made to realise it whenever he watched some of the lads swinging clubs, or apologies for clubs, either on the course or the adjacent caddy enclosure. But it was not until the former Indian caddy, Papwa Sewgolum, and the Transvaal African, Johnson-Sedibe took part in the British Open, and Papwa won the Dutch Open with an excellent score, that the average golfer realised how far blacks had advanced in the world of golf.

In 1960, it was the turn of Lawrence Buthelezi, a former Beachwood Durban caddy, and later the Howick caddy master, to participate in The Open. In 1961 it was William Manie's turn, and 1962 Ismail Chowglay competed, all without success.

What is important, however, was that they could compete and that they aimed beyond the 'veld' courses they had to play on and attempts by the authorities to make them feel inferior.

The SA Non-European Open Championship was first played at Kimberley in 1949 after the formation of the SA Non-European Golf Association. Papwa Sewgolum only appears for the first time in 1960; significantly, he was already 31 years old.

This is perhaps surprising as by then Papwa was well known in Natal where he had won the Natal Non-European Championship numerous times and, more significantly, he was already the 1959 Dutch Open champion. There must be some reason for him not winning the national championship sooner than this. It was not until 1961 that the championship was held in Natal, and before that, except for Milnerton in 1960, it seems that Papwa was not willing to travel, probably due to financial reasons.

Papwa's dominance over his competitors was such that there was Papwa's level, then quite some distance before Chowglay and later Tshabalala, then Hlope and Mogoerane, followed by the rest. He dominated the tournaments, and his positive golfing personality and confidence awed his opponents. An overview of his dominance substantiates this.

The important years for Papwa on the non-European golf scene in SA were the 1960s and into the 1970s. Previously, he had won the Natal Non-European Championship in 1954, '55, '57, '58, and '59, but it was in 1959 that he made his first visit to Europe where he played in The Open Championship and hit the world headlines by winning the Dutch Open.

In 1960, he launched his remarkable career on the golf courses of SA, and it was perhaps his victory in the SA Non-European Championship at Milnerton that year that marked the beginning.

Chapter 2: Black Golf Explodes

In the 11 years from 1960 to 1970, he won the National Non-European title no less than nine times which included one draw (out of ten attempts), and it was during this same period that he played and won provincial tournaments all over the country.

In addition, he made history at East London in 1961 by being the first golfer of colour to play in the 'whites only' South African Open Championship. When his often busy schedule allowed, he did play in what might be considered the more important non-european provincial championships, and his record in these events in the years 1960 to 1970 speaks for itself.

But it was not always one-sided. Walmer Country Club again made their course available for the Eastern Province (EP) Non-European Championships in 1963. This was won by Ismail Chowglay whose score of 309 was one shot better than Papwa who was making his first visit to Port Elizabeth. Papwa made a strong challenge for the title, scoring a record 71 in the last round, but it wasn't quite enough. Chowglay was given a warm welcome by golfers in the Peninsula on his return to Cape Town.

The tables were turned in 1964 when Papwa beat Chowglay by an easy ten shots, but in 1968 Chowglay again turned the tables on him.

Kimberley was an important centre for black golfers in the 1960s, not least because of the support they were given by the Kimberley Golf Club, and Papwa was always ready to play in the Griqualand West Non-European Championship. In fact, he won four times in a row from 1961 to 1964, and then again in 1966 and '67.

His avoidance of the Free State would almost certainly have been because a local, law that prohibited Indians from remaining in the Province overnight. There are only two recorded instances of Papwa playing in the Orange Free State (OFS) Non-European Championship, and these were in Bloemfontein in 1966 where he won, followed by Hlapo and Mogoerane, and in 1968, when he and Ismail Chowglay drove into the Free State for the day, and then left for Kimberley, returning the next day.

The Bloemfontein Golf Club had become the regular venue for the OFS Non-European Championship and once again hosted the 1968 event which was won by Richard Mogoerane (302) from Papwa and

Cox Hlapo (306). Papwa was leading Hlapo and Nkosi by one shot after 36 holes but failed to master the breezy conditions on day two.

The Transvaal was a regular crucible of black golfing activity, and it was inevitable that sooner or later Papwa would make his first appearance there. He entered the 1964 Transvaal Non-European championship at the Benoni Country Club and went on to win it in fine style, stamping his authority on the tournament with an excellent 65 in the third round.

In the final round, Papwa sunk a 15-foot putt on the eighteenth hole for a birdie to complete a brilliant day's performance and win the 72-hole Transvaal Open championship. Sewgolum had a four-round record aggregate of 284, 20 strokes better than his current rival, Eric Boorman, with the defending champion Cox Hlapo slumping to 10th position on 313. Sewgolum was in top form over the last 36 holes. His purse was R100.

Papwa returned the following year and won at Glendower. He won again in 1966 and was runner-up in '67 to Richard Mogoerane, while Chowglay won in 1968, but he won again in 1969 and '70 when he beat Vincent Tshabalala, Solly Sepeng and Ronald Anooplal who all tied for 2nd.

In 1972, Papwa (now 43) was beaten by two shots by Vincent Tshabalala for the title. Later that year in a tournament sponsored by Luyt Lager, Papwa tied with Cox Hlapo (now 46) only to lose the sudden-death playoff.

Papwa was not a regular visitor to the Cape but, when he did make the trip, he usually went home with the title, although Ismail Chowglay provided intermittent opposition.

There were tournaments where Papwa was simply unstoppable. His first appearance in the Western Province Non-European Championship was in 1960 which he won, then in January 1964 at Royal Cape he demolished the competition, running further away from the field with every hole he played.

Opening with an excellent 68, he was followed by Chowglay on 71. That was the last time Chowglay saw Papwa. Thanks to a brilliant 65 in round two, he went on to win by no less than 27 shots. And this was with champion golfer Ismail Chowglay in the field! His total of

Chapter 2: Black Golf Explodes

275 was the second-best score ever shot over 72-holes at Royal Cape, with Gary Player shooting 271 in 1960.

Windy conditions upset most of the players' scorecards. However, a 4-under par first nine if the final round threatened more of round one fireworks, but he produced poor golf by his own standards over the second nine. Wally Johannsen, in second place overnight after two rounds, fell away, and Chowglay and Philip van Dieman came up into joint 2nd place.

He was 2nd to Chowglay in 1968, and on his fourth visit in 1969 the championship was played on the new Athlone course and, true to form, Papwa came out on top, and finally in 1976 (now aged 47) he won 'by the proverbial mile,' yet again.

In his home province of Natal, Papwa reigned supreme for many years. When he won the Natal Non-European Championship in 1960, it was the fourth time in a row and his sixth victory in seven years. But he was not finished there. In 1961 he won at Umbogintwini once again by a mile 'going away', and again at Kloof CC in 1962, then at Circle Country Club in 1963, and Maritzburg in 1964. His winning streak ended in 1965 when he was runner-up by one shot to Raydmuth Rajdaw at Kloof CC, but took off again with a win in 1966.

Also, in 1968, the golfing maestro provided some thrills for the big gallery which followed throughout the final round of the Natal Non-European Open played on a Tuesday. All black tournaments were played on a Monday and Tuesday (36-holes each day), unlike their counterpart white tournaments which were played daily from Thursday to Saturday (36-holes). Papwa clinched the title and prize money with scores of 71 76 69 70. He was followed home by J. Ranjith with 299. A field of 120 golfers from all over SA took part.

He won again in 1969 and '70. In 1971 he lost the title to Vincent Tshabalala, who won the following year again, but he won again in 1974, and then lost to Ismail Chowglay in a three-hole sudden-death play-off in 1976. The last results on file were those for 1977 when he won for the last time.

Along with the provincial 'majors', there were numerous tournaments for small purses held around the country, with the first 'official' SA Non-European Open in 1949 won by Ronnie Ditsebe. In

1950 the winner was Jacob Gumbi, '51 and '52 Eddie Johnson-Sedibe, '53 Bob Nkuna, '54 Les Khatidi, '55 Simon 'Cox' Hlapo from Ismail Chowglay (as he emerged onto the scene), '56 'Polly' November, '57 Simon Hlapo, '58 David Motati, and '59 Simon Hlapo once again.

Playing on a White golf course

Some indication of the difficulties facing the black golfing community is evident from the report on the 1956 SA Non-European Open which was played in Cape Town on a rough and ready course of nine holes laid out on the Cape Flats. The grass greens were described as being as 'unpredictable as an April day in Britain'. The Championship was won by A. (Polly) November with the incredible score of 305. Simon Hlapo came down from the Transvaal and finished in 6th place.

In those early days, there was no question of their being able to use a 'white' golf course, and the championships were played on the courses laid out by the golfers themselves on any areas of open veld with sufficient space to accommodate a course, usually only nine holes. These courses were built near the main towns and cities, were inevitably very rough and ready, but they had to make do. We can therefore assume that when the venue is given as being Kimberley or Bloemfontein, this refers to the 'make-do veld' courses in those towns. This was until 1960 at Milnerton.

The 1960 SA Open was again scheduled in Cape Town, and to this end, a new 18-hole course was laid out in two months at Wettonville close to the Wetton railway station. The coloureds had been driven off the only available course of their own at Thornhill. The press commented at the time that, 'the going will be rough, but it is wonderful what these enthusiastic golfers can achieve with a man like Peter Louw to guide them.'

They were in a real quandary. 'How could they invite their friends from the Transvaal, Natal, Griqualand West, Free State and EP to play over a scratch-about after only two months in the building for the national title of best black golfer?'

Two men came to their rescue: Mr F.L. Cannon, President of the Western Province Golf Union (WPGU), and 26-year-old Anton (Tony) Buirski, Captain of Milnerton GC, an attorney, who agreed to make

Chapter 2: Black Golf Explodes

their course available. This was in the face of fierce opposition from the club's president, Sir de Villiers Graaff, leader of the opposition United Party, who was concerned that the club would be invaded by swarms of blacks (the De Villiers Graaff Trust owned the land) – the first time that such a thing had ever happened in the history of golf in South Africa. Her Worship, the Mayor of Cape Town, Mrs Joyce Newton-Thompson consented to hold a mayoral reception in the Woodstock Town Hall and to present the prizes.

History was made when the SA Non-European Champion-ship was played for the first time on a 'white' course. This set a precedent and, except for 1969 when the Championship was played over the Athlone course, the Championship was only ever played on a 'white' course thereafter.

The tournament attracted a considerable attention. Many leading players, all the local professionals, and many golf administrators were among those who watched. African Consolidated Theatres were also there to take pictures for the cinemas. There were kind messages, including a cable from the New Zealand Golf Union and a beautiful shield from the Australian Golf Union.

One of the players was asked how this course compared with those in his own district. 'Sir,' was the courteous reply, 'that is indeed a difficult question to answer. You see, I have never been allowed to play on a European course previously.'

It was not all smooth sailing for the players. With the south-easter blowing harder than it had done for years – and that south-easterly wind can really 'pump' – Milnerton proved a real challenge to the best golfer – poor 'Bra Cox' Hlapo (winner of the championship three times during the previous six years) suffered more than the others. He was blown clean off his game. While on his artificial sand greens in the Transvaal he putted well, or even on rough grass greens on which he putted with an iron, he was altogether at sea on good grass greens, with a proper putter in his hand.

Hlapo's swing was as smooth as butter! Not one of the others hit the ball quite so far with such an effortless, graceful swing. In November 1959 at Kroonstad, he won the Non-European Free State Championship with two 68s. In winning the SA title in 1958 with 290, he had a second round of 66. He had an incredible feat, but this was a different challenge as he was all at sea, leading to a huge score.

Nevertheless as R.G. Fall (Editor *SA Golf*) stated: 'If you had seen some of those non-European swings in that hurricane at Milnerton: seen some of those No. 2 iron shots straight as a bullet, 'quail high' straight to the mark against the wind, you would, like I did, begin to wonder.'

Papwa did make the trip to Cape Town and ended up winning his first South African title. It was not to be the last.

Over 800 spectators, many of them Europeans followed Papwa round the Milnerton course early in January during his last round when he won the SA Non-European Championship with returns of 80 80 74 74 – a fantastic effort given the ferocious south-easter that threatened to blow every player off his feet. And he only won by two strokes from one of the Western Province players, R.L. Brown, who also had a 74 on the second day, when par could be rated at 78. It could have been rated at 80 during some portions of the first day.

The postscript to the Wettonville project is that the Milnerton Golf Club offered their course to the Association for the Championship, the first time a white club had ever done so. This marked a turning point. Never again was the Non-European Open Championship played on a make-shift course carved out of the open veld. The Wettonville project did not go to waste and later that year played host to the Western Province Open Championship.

The question of European golf clubs lending their courses for significant black tournaments is important. Now blacks were at least competing on an equal playing field although they were not allowed to practice there before the event. Milnerton had set a sporting precedent. Never again would blacks play a major tournament on a 'scratch-about' course that did not provide a fair test.

While Milnerton was the first European club to offer the non-Europeans their course for a big meeting, other European clubs subsequently made similar gestures. Maritzburg Country Club were hosts for the competitors in the Natal Midlands Non-European Open, which Papwa won after a tie with Lawrence Buthelezi, now the Maritzburg Country Club, Howick caddy master, shooting record

Chapter 2: Black Golf Explodes

scores including 72s.

Buthelezi had been leading right up to the 18th hole, where Papwa holed a 20 metre shot to drawn level, and in the play-off he thrashed Buthelezi 142 to 156.

Mention of the 72 by two black golfers at Maritzburg Country Club leads one inevitably to the question: 'Just how good are these players? How would they compare with the best of the Europeans were they to be given a fair chance of getting accustomed to golf on championship courses?'

1963 Transvaal Open, Benoni: Simon 'Cox' Hlapo and Dave Motati with their caddies standing on the first tee.

Source: Bernnadett Hlapo

Simon 'Cox' Hlapo

The record books may be incomplete, but one thing cannot be questioned: before the arrival of Papwa Sewgolum in 1960, there was one name you always found in the top three, usually at number one, Simon 'Cox' Hlapo.

'Cox' proved beyond doubt that he was the most consistent African golfer in the country before the advent of Papwa Sewgolum in

1960, and there were repeated calls for the T(N-E)GU to do something to enable Cox to play in the British Open – 'he'll certainly not disgrace us.'

Barred from playing on white golf courses, still playing on their bush pop-up courses, the challenge for black golfers was how to finance a trip abroad with the British Open, especially following Bobby Locke's successes, their focal point.

'Bra Cox' or 'The Great Cox', as he was affectionately known, matriculated at Marian Hill High school in Kwa-Zulu Natal. His classmates and friends at the time were Archbishop Emeritus Desmond Tutu, the music maestro, Professor Mzilikazi Khumalo, and former Drum magazine editor, Stan Motjuwadi. Can you imagine the combination, Hlapo a sportsman, Tutu a man of the cloth, Khumalo, an artist, and Motjuwadi, a journo par excellence.

The role played by Simon Hlapo is of particular importance, given where black golf was positioned at the time. His was a name that showed up on every leader board. He dominated the game of golf not only with his aggressive style of play but with his uncompromising personality. At that time, blacks were barred from playing alongside their fellow white countrymen, although segregation had not been officially endorsed in the statute books during the 1940s and early 1950s. This was also a time when black golfers were forced by the political laws of the time to have separate tournaments.

Born in Alexandra Township in 1924 Cox lived an ordinary working class life as a Putco bus driver working the morning shifts, so by 11am, he would be hitting golf balls at the Mofolo golf course close to home in Dube, Soweto, on Mehlomakhulu Street (this golf course was later invaded by shack dwellers who made the field their home). One thing in his favour was that his big boss at the Putco depot, Uncle Sam Mnisi, was the president of the SA(N-E)GU, and uncle Mnisi was understanding of Bra Cox's passion for golf. 'On reaching home, I would take my clubs and run to the Mofolo golf course. Even if I hit six balls I was always very happy after such a practice. Every ball I hit meant something to my game.'

He started playing in the 1940s at two patches of open veld; one at Alexandra near Wynberg along the old Pretoria Road and the other

Chapter 2: Black Golf Explodes

in Sophiatown on the outskirts of Tobby Street between Sophiatown and Linden, and it was there where the tall strong and humble Bra Cox enjoyed his game.

In 1949 he joined the Wynberg GC, where he was taught by one of the greats of golf, J. Jass and Uncle Sam, and he dominated the 'black' golfing fraternity between 1955–1959, before being overshadowed by Papwa Sewgolum, when black golfers were permitted to start using proper courses.

After playing the game for little over five years, he won the highest honour in South Africa when he was 30 years old, his first SA Championship played over the New Year weekend, and to make it more memorable, his team won the huge *Drum* Golf Trophy.

Suddenly black golf had their new hero, and adverts featuring 'Bra Cox endorsing Brylcreem appeared in the newspapers.

He was called the Maestro of the sand greens, mainly because of the unique way he hit the ball during his drives and chipping. 'When he had focused his playing form and rhythm, we all knew he was untouchable, we all knew we were in trouble', commented Richard 'Boikie' Mogoerane.

Bra Cox, although cool and icy on the golf course, was a bundle of fun off it, frequently playing practical jokes on his friends and indulging in his favourite past time of 'singing' when he wasn't helping to fix other people's cars for free. He won over 27 tournaments including the SA Non-European Open in 1955, '57, '59, runner-up in 1961, and as late as 1964, '67, and in '68, then aged 44, he was still able to finish in the top five.

Following another generous sponsorship by Alf Magerman of £100 at the Kroonstad Open tournament, Bra Cox won with a record breaking score of 68 68 (136) followed by David Motati (140), Ronnie Ditsebe (141) and D Harrison (141).

He captured the Orange Free State Open in 1953, '60, '61, '62 and '63, 3rd in '68, the Transvaal Open in 1957, '59, '61, '62 and '63, and the Northern OFS Championship and the North Eastern Transvaal Open in 1959, Griqualand West 2nd in 1966, 3rd '64 and '67.

His last major win was the Luyt Lager Tournament in 1972, aged 48, when most of his peers had given up competitive golf, and finally

Papwa

he won the 3M Classic at the Soweto Country Club in 1983 aged 59.

Bra Cox was present in 1963 when Papwa Sewgolum received his prize in the rain after winning the Natal Open at Durban Country Club, where he witnessed that historic occasion, but sadly both were not allowed inside the clubhouse because of the colour of their skin.

In 1971 he played with the champion USA black golfer Lee Elder in an exhibition SAPGA Tournament with Gary Player and Vincent Tshabalala and a host of other black golfers. 'Gary felt the pressured by the threat of isolation when competing at international championships. He was booed and taunted by anti-apartheid protesters at several tournaments. One condition for a non-racial tournament featuring Elder was that all South African black golfers should play, and funds raised should go towards a secondary school. This was how apartheid was killed,' commented newspaper editor, Leslie Sehume.

Bra Cox became a role model to many black golfers. 'Every player wanted to play like him,' said John Mashego. Sadly he was too old when the doors opened for black golfers to compete in major tournaments.

Like so many other wonderfully talented golfers of the time, his

Chapter 2: Black Golf Explodes

career was curtailed due to politics but it didn't prevent him from playing both the game itself and a role in the administration of black golf affairs.

He died in 1986 aged 61, the towering father of black golf, penniless, but his community, friends and family rallied and ensured he received a proper send-off.

In 2011 he was inducted into the Southern Africa Golf Hall of Fame, and in 2018, the then-Minister of Sport, Tokozile Xasa, awarded him the 'Andrew Mlangeni Green Jacket' award.

CHAPTER 3: TPA TOUR RIVALRY

Provincial Non-European Opens

Papwa Sewgolum, Ismail Chowglay, David Motati with two officials.

Source: Peter Sauerman

White golfers played a small part in inspiring their black golfing colleagues. This could be seen in the colourful names attributed to black golfers, such as Atrol 'Sid Brews' Mazibuko and David 'Bobby Locke' Motati, together with other interesting nicknames such as 'Otto' Lee, 'Goli-Goli' Mdeni, 'Baby-face boy' Chowglay, 'Bra Cox' Hlapo, 'Bambata' Boodhun, 'Boikie' Mogoerane, 'Star' Naidoo, 'Polly' November, J. 'Fiver' Mazibuko, 'FM' Paul, 'Doe' Khumou,

Chapter 3: TPA Tour Rivalry

'Ram' Rajdaw, 'Eddia' Johnson-Sidebe, and 'Papwa' Sewgolum.

In 1954, Papwa (25) won his first Natal Non-European Open, and in 1955 Chowglay (22) won the Western Province Non-European Open. Likewise, Gary Player (19) earned his first provincial title in 1955, winning the East Rand Open, and then proceeded to win the SA Open the following year.

His rigorous practice regimen contributed to his success, and he was quoted as saying, 'the harder I practice, the luckier I get'. Papwa and Gary's paths were yet to cross.

Ismail Chowglay and Papwa Sewgolum, born four years apart, both disadvantaged by apartheid were not permitted to play on the 'white' SA Tour until into their thirties. Between them they won at least 52 Non-European Provincial Open titles (probably more, as the records are incomplete), Sewgolum 38 (second 9) and Chowglay 14 (second 8), and 12 SA Non-European Open tiles, with Sewgolum winning 10 (second 1) and Chowglay 2 (second 5).

Chowglay was a left-hander who played with the same reverse grip as Papwa – the caddy grip. He was born in a cottage overlooking the Royal Cape Golf Club and grew up in a modest home with 11 other children.

He started as a caddy, learning to read greens and how to play. The caddy master helped him with his driving, and his talent was nurtured by Phil van Dieman as well as the great coloured golfer, and future South African Non-European Open champion, 'Polly' November.

Chowglay, tall and lean, wearing a straw hat (which made him look even taller), full of fun and an engaging smile with a gold front tooth, joined the bush Royal Heatherton Golf Club at Milnerton and soon won the club championships beating November in a closely fought final round, and again the following year.

As a labourer at the South African Navy field, Chowglay practiced during his lunch hour and caddied every Saturday for extra income. His hard work paid off and by 1955 he was 4th in the Western Province Non-European Open, which he won the following year, whilst he was runner-up to November in the SA Non-European Open.

Even though there are gaps in the results of a number of provincial and national Non-European tournaments, it is interesting to review how the dominant golfers, Sewgolum, Chowglay, and Tshabalala fared when competing against each other. This is not to take away from the fact that many of Papwa's victories were often by the proverbial mile, sometimes by 10, 20, and as high as the 27 shots ahead by which Papwa beat Chowglay and Van Dieman for the WP Non-European Open title in 1964. Every now and then his rivals rose to challenge him until eventually, Vincent Tshabalala took over his mantle.

Although Papwa dominated black provincial golf in Natal, their records in other centres, especially the Cape where Chowglay prevailed (similarly 'Cox' Hlapo dominated early on in the Transvaal as well as the OFS before Richard Mogoerane) should be examined.

Papwa did not play in the WP Championship every year, but when he did make the trip to Cape Town, he was a significant threat. Papwa demolished the field at Royal Cape in January 1964. The 1968 Western Province Non-European Championship was played on the newly-opened Athlone course and was won by the holder, Chowglay with a score of 297. Papwa was runner-up on 305. Chowglay played steady golf throughout while Sewgolum got off to a poor start with 83 in the first round and couldn't recover.

In 1969, it was at the relatively new Athlone course when he came back to Cape Town as the SA Non-European Champion and won the WP Non-European Championship as well. His four round total was 74 74 76 72 (296) with Vincent Tshabalala runner-up on 298. Papwa had to wait for the last round before he obtained the lead, but his brilliant 72 was too good for the opposition.

Ismail Chowglay, the former champion, had a great victory in the 1971 Western Province Championship held at the Athlone GC. With scores of 79 76 72 75 (302) he beat defending champion Abe van Rooyen (306) into 2nd place. His prize money was R200.

The 1973 WP Non-European Championship was again won by Chowglay played on the Athlone course. He was still the leading player in the WP at the time.

1976 it was once again Papwa Sewgolum (now 47) at a canter, winning by six shots against Johnson Chetty. His scores were 78 70 76 77 (301). Papwa and Noel Maart were level after 45 holes, but then Papwa started to forge ahead. This was to be his final victory outside of Natal.

Chapter 3: TPA Tour Rivalry

Apart from setting a new Kimberley Golf Club course record in 1961, Papwa Sewgolum competed on many occasions during the 1960s in Kimberley.

The 1960 Griqualand West title was won by Papwa Sewgolum with scores of 69 72 72 72 – 285. There is debate whether this was played at the "new course" in Kimberley or at some other course. The "old course" at this time was not in use and the other course available was the Versatiles golf course at Green Point. Papwa did not like playing the so-called "bush" courses, so it must be presumed that it was at the new course on the Johannesburg road.

In 1961 the Griqualand West Non-European Championship was definitely played over the "new grass course" of the Kimberley Golf Club and was won by Papwa Sewgolum with scores of 75 68 69 73– 285. He finished 23 shots ahead of runner-up Jacob Gumbi. Papwa was given something of a run in the final round by Dick Phala who was three under after 10 holes but his challenge was short-lived. There was a field of just on 30 players and the local golfers were most impressed by the standard of play. Papwa's record-breaking 68 in the second round was particularly noteworthy.

The Griqualand West Non-European Championship in 1963 was again played at the Kimberley GC and again won by Papwa. He scored 285, eight shots ahead of Chowglay on 293.

History was repeated in the 1964 Griqualand West Championship when Sewgolum won with scores of 77 72 74 72 – 295 from Chowglay with scores of 75 75 73 78 – 301. The two were level with one round to go but Papwa's mastery was never more evident than during the final round when, battling against a strong wind and a dust storm, he shot his second sub-par score of the tournament carding a one-under 72.

Played yet again at the Kimberley GC the Griqualand West Non-European Championship in 1965 was won by Sewgolum for the fifth time in a row with a score of 281. Second was Cox Hlapo or 286 whose first round 75 let him down.

With opening rounds of 78 and 78, Papwa trailed Percy Mazibuko by seven shots and David Motati by five after the first day of the 1967 Griqualand West Non-European Open but made up the deficit on the second day with 75 and 69, and came out the winner on a score of 300.

Papwa

The two earlier challengers fell away and 2nd place was filled by Solly Sepeng 78 78 75 72 – 303 from Simon 'Cox' Hlapo 78 79 74 76 – 307.

South African Non-European Opens

Just like the domination of the SA 'White' Open by Bobby Locke in winning nine Opens in nine attempts, and Gary Player winning it thirteen times, so Papwa completely dominated the SA 'Black' Open through the 1960s once he had broken the ice. In the 11 years up to and including 1970, he won the title nine times including sharing it once (in ten attempts). This was with Vincent Tshabalala at Alexander GC in East London in 1965, and for a final tenth time in 1974.

At the S.A. Non-European Championship, Kimberley: Mrs. F. W. Pitman, P.L. Paul (who shared fourth place with Cox Hlapo); Lawrence Buthelezi; F.W. Pitman, managing director, Gordon's Dry Gin Co.; A. Maqubela, president, S.A. Non-European Golf Association.

Having won again in 1961 (where Mr. Cannon became the first European sponsor for the SA Non-European Association), the following year at Kimberley, Papwa was not at his best – 1962 was not a good year generally for Papwa – and he finished in 8th place behind

Chapter 3: TPA Tour Rivalry

Ismail Chowglay, with Hlapo also only finishing 5th.

The SA Non-European Golf Association were hoping to play their championship over the Bloemfontein Golf Club's course but the permit from the Government for non-Europeans to play over a course occupied by European golfers was not granted due to the Free State statute which forbade any Indian from staying overnight in the Province. Instead, it was played at the Kimberley Golf Club.

The most energetic and able organiser of the tournament was again Peter Louw, vice-President of the SA Non-European Golf Association, to whom much of the credit for the successful event was due.

Unlike the 'supposed parallel' white tour, there was little distinction between amateurs and professionals.

Ismail Chowglay *1962 SA N-E Open*

As ever, many people gathered round to give support to the tournament. There was a civic reception at which the Mayor of Kimberley, Mr G.J. Hugo, presented the winner, Ismail Chowglay, the Western Cape champion, and possibly the finest left-hand golfer in the country (except for New Zealander Bob Charles, winner of The Open, who married Verity, a SA girl, and when not competing abroad spent much of his time living in Johannesburg), with his prize money of R300 after scores of 72 74 74 77 (297), Chowglay had every reason to feel optimistic about the future of his career.

Ismail hit his 3-wood 240m and never bothered with a driver. He also preferred not using a tee, and would merely push up some turf or make a tee from sand. His short game was legendary, even though his bag never contained the full set of 14 clubs. His back-to-front grip enabled him to steer the ball low into the wind to the flag, and he was exceptional straight off the tee landing on the fairway time-after-time.

Suddenly Ismail was now the flavour of the month and was even approached by sponsors, featuring in advertisements for 'Wilson Three-X Mints'.

Following his victory, a resolution was taken by the South African (Non-European) Golf Association (SA(N-E)GA) to send the Cape and SA champion to 'The Open', where the media confused him with representing Egypt because 'there were supposedly no players of colour in South Africa'. A levy was placed on each of the nine affiliates to the association to assist with Chowglay's trip, whilst tour players held card games and other fundraising efforts.

Unfortunately he failed to progress beyond the qualifying round. After opening with a reasonable 75, he then blew up with an 83 and missed the cut.

With the assistance of Cape champion golfers Phil van Dieman and Polly November (who first recognised and furthered Ismail's talent), Chowglay was widely believed by 1962 to be the equal or better than Papwa Sewgolum after annexing the 1962 SA Non-European Open. However, it was only in 1972 that Ismail, the 6' 2" reigning Western Province champion, regained the SA Non-European Open, beating Tshabalala and Mogoerane into 2nd place.

Left-handed Ismail Chowglay playing with the reverse grip together with Papwa Sewgolum (right) looking on.

Chapter 3: TPA Tour Rivalry

Four years apart, what a journey Papwa and Ismail had travelled! Both of Indian descent, both playing with the back-to-front grip, both denied the ability to compete on the white SA tour until they were in their 30s, and both near the end of their careers.

Still there was a little fire left, with Ismail winning at least one further WP Non-European title in 1973, and beating Papwa in their final battle into 2nd place for the 1976 Natal Non-European title, and in 1983 at the senior age of 51 amazingly winning (oldest player to win on the TPA Tour, but alas no senior tour available to him), for probably the last time a provincial title when he won the Transvaal Non-European title (fifteen years after his previous triumph). In all, he won at least 14 provincial titles (despite holding down a full-time job), which was only bettered (substantially) by Papwa.

Ismail would die, like Papwa, poverty-stricken in 1992 at the still youthful age of 59, possibly South Africa's best left-handed golfer.

The SA Non-European Golf Association was non-racial insofar as their clubs and their unions determined that there shall be no differentiation between Coloured, Indian and African golfers.

In 1962, the government gave R3,000 to the SA Non-European Golf Association 'as tangible proof of the government's desire to support the establishment of separate sports facilities for non-whites'. It was suggested that this was the policy the government was holding out as justification for banning the previous week's Transvaal non-white golf tournament at the white-Irene golf course. As such it was described as 'an apartheid grant', and many prominent members of the community were by no means happy with this. Another donor to this fund was Gary Player who gave R60.

The 1963 South African Non-European Open was played at Walmer CC, and anticipation was rife. Would Chowglay once again dethrone the iconic Sewgolum? The tournament committee consisted of Messrs Peter Louw (vice-president), D.R. Phala (secretary/ treasurer), Louis Nelson (assistant secretary and now Papwa's manager), and Samson Mnisi (assistant treasurer).

At the end of round one, Chowglay, the defending champion was one ahead of Papwa equaling the course record, and maintained this lead after round two. But this changed and after round three, as Papwa

Papwa

found himself three shots ahead of Chowglay thanks to his deadly putting. As Chowglay's game fell apart, Papwa simply ran away with the championship.

A 75 in the third round gave him a lead by three strokes over Chowglay, while a 74 in the last round added another nine strokes to his lead as Papwa went on to win by 13 strokes, Chowglay still being the challenger although that is perhaps not the right word.

It is true that the ball was not running well for Chowglay in the last two rounds. Time and again the putts were just slipping past, but there was no doubt who was the better man on the day. Papwa was out in 34 in the last round, but neither he nor Chowglay shone in the last nine holes, played in a continuous heavy drizzle.

Throughout the tournament Papwa's chipping was deadly, and most of the time so was his putting, but it was the approaches that made the putting-count so low. Accordingly, Papwa won back his national title from the previous year's winner Ismail Chowglay with scores of 75 77 75 74 (301).

Papwa received the J.M. Jass Floating Trophy; named after the founder of the SA(N-E)GA in 1947, who died in 1953, and with it a professional purse of R500, donated by Gordon's Dry Gin Co.

What was so remarkable about the play of the two leaders was their grip. Papwa, a right-hander, gripped the club with the left hand under the right on the shaft: Chowglay, a left-hander, gripped with the right hand under the left. Call it what you will – the wrong grip, or the reverse grip – it worked for these two golfers.

Everything possible was done to make the tournament a success: food, refreshments and equipment were on hand when required, and a record attendance was most capably catered for. As ever, the ladies of the golf section did much to add to the success of the meeting, whilst the Mayor of Port Elizabeth, Monty van der Vyver, arranged a civic reception in the Port Elizabeth Feather Market Hall. Several speakers paid tribute to Peter Louw, vice-president of the SA(N-E)GA, for the admirable manner in which he had organised the tournament.

In 1964, Papwa Sewgolum was once again the winner at Glendower GC with scores of 71 72 70 75 (288), where he was followed by a huge gallery. He received the first prize of R200 plus

Chapter 3: TPA Tour Rivalry

1963 Sewsunker Sewgolum is seen teeing off in the final round of the SA Non-European Open at Walmer Country Club, Port Elizabeth. He won by 13 strokes from Ismail Chowglay (holder, on the left). S Dondashe is in the middle. Papwa's left-hand-under-right-hand grip is plainly visible. It is two handed, not overlapping (Photograph by A Doulman, Weimar)

R12.50 for each of the first three rounds for the leading score of the day. Stylish Edward 'Otto' Lee and Johannes Semenya tied for 2nd on 300, with 'baby-face' Chowglay 4th, followed by 'Cox' Hlapo and David 'Bobby Locke' Motati.

Prizes were presented including the J. Jass trophy to Papwa by Mrs I.W. Pitman at a civic reception in the Coronationville Hall at which the Mayor of Johannesburg, M.J.F. Oberholzer, M.P.C. and the Mayoress were present.

Papwa

With a purse of R500, the tournament which was played over three days under the banner of the SA(N-E)GA attracted an entry of 190 players, with the result that there was a pre-qualifying event with 40 golfers going into the championship proper.

He did not play in the 1966 event held in Bloemfontein which was won by David Motati. Clearly, Papwa's victories were having an effect on the explosion of black players at the non-european golf courses as courses were popping up everywhere.

Comparison: Papwa, Chowglay, Tshabalala

When Tshabalala came onto the scene, he, together with Papwa and Chowglay, featured in numerous non-European tournaments. In many of them, either one or two of them simply did not feature, but it is interesting to note their respective records when they, in fact, did play against each other (although, as mentioned, some of Sewgolum's victories were by the proverbial mile).

*Tshabalala was 14 years younger than Sewgolum and 10 years younger than Chowglay.

SOUTH AFRICAN NON-EUROPEAN OPEN

1956		I Chowglay
1957		
1958		
1959		
1960	**S Sewgolum** 80 80 74 74 (308)	
1961	**S Sewgolum** (297)	
1962	I Chowglay 72 74 74 77 (297)	
1963	**S Sewgolum** 75 77 75 74 (301)	I Chowglay 74 77 80 83 (314)
1964	**S Sewgolum** 71 72 70 75 (288)	

Chapter 3: TPA Tour Rivalry

1965	S.Sewgolum/V Tshabalala	
	77 74 69 71 (291) 74 74 73 70 (291)	
1966		V Tshabalala
1967	**S Sewgolum**	I Chowglay (289)
	70 69 72 71 (282)	
1968	**S Sewgolum**	V Tshabalala (293)
	70 70 71 74 (285)	
1969	**S Sewgolum**	
	71 76 73 75 (295)	
1970	**S Sewgolum**	V Tshabalala
	77 67 69 74 (287)	(295)
1971	V Tshabalala	**S Sewgolum** (293)
	(292)	
1972	I Chowglay	V Tshabalala
	74 74 75 74 (297)	
1973		I Chowglay
1974	**S Sewgolum**	V Tshabalala
	77 69 75 70 (291)	70 70 72 80 (292)
1975		
1976		
1977	V Tshabalala	
	73 75 73 70 (291)	
1979		I Chowglay
1983	V Tshabalala	

PROVINCIAL NON-EUROPEAN OPEN

TRANSVAAL NON-EUROPEAN OPEN

1964	**S Sewgolum** (284)	*65 course record
1965	**S Sewgolum**	
	70 70 71 71 (282)	
1966	**S Sewgolum**	
	69,70,70,73 (282)	

1967		S Sewgolum
1968	I Chowglay 73 69 73 73 (287)	
1969	S Sewgolum	I Chowglay
1970	S Sewgolum	V Tshabalala
1971		
1972	V Tshabalala (295)	S Sewgolum (297)
1973-82		
1983	I Chowglay	

O.F.S. NON-EUROPEAN OPEN

1964	I Chowglay	
1965		
1966	S Sewgolum 69 70 70 73 (282)	
1968		S Sewgolum (304)
1969	S Sewgolum	

NATAL NON-EUROPEAN OPEN

1954	S Sewgolum	
1955	S Sewgolum	
1956		S Sewgolum *lost playoff
1957	S Sewgolum	
1958	S Sewgolum	
1959	S Sewgolum	
1960	S Sewgolum 74 72 75 73 (294)	
1961	S Sewgolum 73 73 71 73 (290)	

Chapter 3: TPA Tour Rivalry

1962	S Sewgolum	
1963	S Sewgolum	
1964		S Sewgolum (294)
1965	S Sewgolum	
	72 71 73 75 (291)	
1966	S Sewgolum	
	70 71 73 74 (288)	
1967	S Sewgolum	
1968	S Sewgolum (286) *63 3rd round	
1969	S Sewgolum *by 21 shots	
1970	S Sewgolum	
1971	V Tshabalala	S Sewgolum
1972	V Tshabalala	
	73 69 69 71 (282)	
1973		
1974	S Sewgolum	
1975	S Sewgolum	I Chowglay (303)
	73 73 77 71 (294)	
1976	I Chowglay *play-off	S Sewgolum
1977	S Sewgolum	

WESTERN PROVINCE NON-EUROPEAN OPEN

1956	I Chowglay	
1957		
1958		
1960	S Sewgolum	
1961		I Chowglay
1962		
1963	I Chowglay	
1964	S Sewgolum	I Chowglay (302)

	68 65 72 70 (275)	
1965	I Chowglay	
1966	I Chowglay	
1967	I Chowglay	
1968	I Chowglay (297)	**S Sewgolum** (305)
1969	**S Sewgolum** 74 74 76 72 (296)	V Tshabalala (298)
1970		
1971	I Chowglay 79 76 72 75 (302)	
1973	I Chowglay	
1974		
1975		
1976	**S Sewgolum** 78 70 76 77 (301)	

EASTERN PROVINCE NON-EUROPEAN OPEN

1963	I Chowglay (309)	**S Sewgolum** (310)
1964	**S Sewgolum**	I Chowglay
1965-67		
1968	I Chowglay	**S Sewgolum**

GRIQUALAND WEST NON-EUROPEAN OPEN

1960	**S Sewgolum** 69 72 72 72 (285)	
1961	**S Sewgolum** 75 68 69 73 (285) *68 course record	
1963	**S Sewgolum** (285)	I Chowglay (293)
1964	S Sewgolum 77 72 74 72 (295)	I Chowglay 75 75 73 78 (301)

Chapter 3: TPA Tour Rivalry

1965	**S Sewgolum**
	71 69 70 71 (281)
1966	
1967	**S Sewgolum** (300)
1969	**S Sewgolum**
	78 78 75 69 (300)

CHAPTER 4: THE 'PAPWA' STORY — A CHALLENGE TO APARTHEID

Two roads diverged in a wood, and I – I took the one less travelled by, and that has made the difference' – Robert Frost

Papwa Sewgolum was able to change the individual-focused sport of golf, and prove that blacks can become the face of change.

The profile of a champion is rather like a complex jigsaw puzzle. There are many pieces, and without all of them he is incomplete. Sound technique is only one of the pieces. Another is fitness. There has to be peace of mind, proper diet, patience, courage, an ability to enjoy the adversity of pressure, intelligent playing strategy. Perhaps most important of all, there must be this commitment to excellence – Gary Player

Chapter 4: The Papwa Story - A Challenge to Apartheid

Golf is a game generally associated with the wealthy. One has to pay considerable tuition fees to learn the game, purchase expensive golf clubs, balls, clothing, special shoes – and then pay up to R500 or more to play 18 holes.

While South Africa's black nouveau riche are now found frequenting the golf courses in our democratic dispensation, the majority of black golfers in past years were working-class citizens who learnt the game while caddying for whites. In the whole of Durban, for example, there was just one golf course for blacks, Currie's Fountain.

But ultimately no memorial, no biography, no written account or account of any other nature will be able to reflect the ignominy, hurt and shame that the crippling racial laws inflicted on the emotions of the majority of South Africans. They were restricted from participating in the broadest possible opportunities – such as to play golf where and when they wanted to.

Due to an almost total lack of proper equipment or anything resembling an actual golf facility, and the endemic poverty affecting the black majority in SA when compared to the white population, and despite the obvious talent, the standard of play was lower than that of the affluent white golf scene.

Talented black golfers of the past include names like Ramnath Boodhun, R.T. Singh, Vincent Tshabalala, Jacob Gumbi, Ronnie Ditsebe, Bob Nkuna, Les Khatidi, Reggie Mamashela, Solly Sepeng, Johannes Semenya, Lawrence Buthelezi, Raydmuth Rajdaw, Edward Johnson-Sedibe, David Motati, Richard Mogoerane, Ismail Chowglay, Simon Hlapo, Johnson Chetty, Daddy Naidoo, Ronald Anooplal and many others.

The most celebrated black golfer, however, was 'Papwa' Sewsunker Sewgolum.

Papwa was a SA professional golfer of ethnic Indian origin, who carved a niche for himself in golfing folklore when he became the first golfer of colour to win a provincial 'white' open in SA. He became an international symbol of the sports boycott movement and hated race laws following pictures of him receiving his trophy outside in the rain were published across the world, because he was not allowed to enter the 'whites-only' clubhouse due to petty apartheid.

He is regarded as **'the greatest black golfer produced in this country'**, and one who would certainly have been among the country's best ever golfers of all races were it not for apartheid. His story contrasts the lot of the poor sportsmen of the world to that of the wealthy and, in his case, reveals a life of both triumph and tragedy.

He was famous for both his unorthodox method of holding the club, with a back-handed grip, hands positioned the opposite way to the traditional grip, the left hand lower on the club shaft than the right. as much as he was for his 'short game' – pitching, chipping, putting and bunker shots within 100m of the hole.

Always a drawcard with an enthusiastic gallery, 'Papwa's army' or the 'Indian army', followed him round courses he used to move across quicker than most'. He would walk quickly up to his ball, take a few practice swings, and even if in a bunker, blast out without further ado. He also putted with his unorthodox grip, but as a spectator muttered, 'who cares – he still sinks 'em doesn't he?' His long irons were punched crisply, and around the green his approach shots were deadly.

As a teenager, he began shooting sub-par rounds as well as several unofficial 62s – well below the Beachwood course record of 66.

Analysts said he was able to draw on his deep spirituality as a practicing Hindu to release any physical and psychological tension in his body – on and off the course.

Discovered

When you are just surviving, you cannot dream.

A chance encounter on a Durban golf course in 1957 launched one of the most remarkable stories in the history of local sport as Papwa's break came one afternoon in 1957 when he was caddying in a fourball which included heavyweight businessman Graham Wulff who lived in Howick in the Natal Midlands. Wulff was a member of Beachwood Golf Club and a golf fanatic who played almost every day, and who was playing a round of golf with his two business partners in his chemical factory, Jack Lowe and chemical engineer Edmund Anderson, together with another Beachwood member, David Andrews

Chapter 4: The Papwa Story - A Challenge to Apartheid

who made up their four-ball. On the fifth hole, the volatile Andrews hit a weak drive and asked his caddy who was carrying his clubs for advice on club selection for his second shot.

With 146m remaining and playing into the lightest of breezes, Papwa drew a 6-iron from the bag and handed it to him. The man took his advice but turned on Sewgolum in frustration when he fluffed his shot, taking his frustration out on his bare-foot caddy's selection.

Papwa didn't take kindly to the abuse, and when tempers frayed, he placed the bag on the ground, turned and walked toward the clubhouse. Wulff, who regarded Papwa as quite timid and respectful, was silenced by the reaction, then Wulff whistled and called him back.

'Hey, caddy, where do you think you are going?'

'To the clubhouse, Sir', Papwa replied quietly, 'to fetch a first-class caddy'.

Turning to the barefoot Indian man Wulff looked at him quizzically. 'Is that right boy? So what made you so sure a 6-iron was the club for that shot?'

Papwa hung his head for a few moments eyeing his bare feet, then said: 'I play a bit in my spare time, Sir'. Wulff, dropping a ball in exactly the same spot, asked Papwa whether he would demonstrate using the same iron to reach the green. "Well, why don't you show us what you can do?" said Wulff.

There were stifled smirks, sniggers of derision, using his unorthodox grip, and exchanged glances as Papwa with his awkward grip, the left hand lower on the club shaft than the right. But the four's petty cruelties were short-lived as he addressed the ball and had a practice swing. But the swing was supple, the rock and roll motion, with a snap in the wrist at the top of the swing, and the ball soared high, then dropped, momentarily landing and biting four metres beyond the flag, then spinning backwards to within a mere foot of the pin.

Andrews and the rest of the four-ball were stunned, then grins and generous smiles appeared on their faces, particularly when Freddy Govender, the caddy on Wulff's bag revealed that Papwa was a plus-one golfer who had secured a string of victories in local non-European Championships.

After witnessing his extraordinary skill, Wulff decided to take Papwa under his wing, encouraging him to consider a career in golf.

Papwa was given a permanent job at his cosmetic factory to support his wife and child, and time off to practice the sport, often with Wulff. Actually, he spent more time at the golf course than working.

Wulff had heard all about Sewgolum's exploits on the "non-European" golf circuit and wanted to help where he could. He was also among the most open-minded.

The more they played, the more convinced Wulff became that Papaw was an extraordinary talent, who if given the chance could compete at the highest level.

It helped that he was rich. Wulff had recently patented what would become the "Oil of Olay" brand, the women's cosmetic beauty cream, and was reputed to be one of the wealthier men in Natal. He was also amongst the most open-minded.

Graham Wulff and Oil of Olay

At the time, Wulff was well on his way to becoming a giant of the international cosmetics industry following his successful invention in 1952 of one of the leading skin-care cosmetic, 'Oil of Olay'.

He was born on a 25-acre farm in Highlands North outside Johannesburg, and lost his father when he was only four years old. He and two siblings were raised by his mother. Times were tough, but he managed to put himself through school.

After matric, Wulff began working as a laboratory assistant at Modderfontein dynamite factory. It was there that he developed a love for science and set his sights on obtaining his B.Sc. through UNISA, which he did by correspondence in three years.

After qualifying as an industrial chemist, Wulff was promoted, and then moved to the South African Pulp and Paper Industries. After graduating with a B.Sc degree which enabled him to join the Industrial Development Corporation (IDC) he established plants at various wool washeries, and, began doing research on skin preparations from lanolin, a derivative of wool-grease.

Part of the process in washing wool involved extracting the grease

Chapter 4: The Papwa Story - A Challenge to Apartheid

from the matted fibre. This grease was then used at the heavy steel mills of ISCOR (Iron and Steel Corporation) on the Witwatersrand. Always seizing opportunities, he joined Herman Beier after the war in a company that made lanolin from wool grease used in the production of a number of addition products including various creams and salves.

Tall with a thickset build and a distinctive handlebar moustache Wulff wasn't settled at Beier, so he moonlighted in the cosmetic field, and soon formed a company with advertising executive, Jack Lowe as his partner.

Wulff noticed his wife Dinah's frustration with the thick, waxy beauty creams that came in shoe-polish tins and left her skin looking greasy, so set about inventing a new beauty product for her.

Such a preparation had to penetrate the skin rapidly while remaining stable and compatible – one that could not only moisturise her skin, but also leave her feeling beautiful and feminine.

Wulff knew that it was not only how a beauty preparation affected ones skin that was important to a woman, but also the positive, more imperceptible attributes she associated with the product – hence the pink colour, subtle fragrance and attractive packaging.

What was to become a billion-dollar empire and an internationally recognisable brand, all started in Wulff's garage in Durban, where he set up a small laboratory, and began experimenting with various specialty bases from chemical manufacturers

He chose materials in conjunction with cholesterol around the world, the beneficial and benign ingredient of lanolin, experimenting on his first wife and anyone prepared to try it out.

His experiment with cosmetics was to have an interesting and lucrative spinoff. Cockroaches were a pest in the hot humid tropical Durban climate.

Some skin preparations had been left out overnight on the laboratory table to await results. In the morning he was surprised to see a number of dead cockroaches amongst the preparations, and wondered what could have been the cause.

He realised he had stumbled onto the solution which every household in Durban would pay for. But which preparation and how had it caused their death?

So he devised a plan, and returned at midnight when all was dark. Using a torch he aimed the beam at the laboratory table and observed the scurrying cockroaches' antlers twitching.

The cockroaches seem to be attracted by the face powder that he was preparing. They rubbed their feelers into the powder, cleaned it into their mouths, and died shortly thereafter.

He had inadvertently stumbled upon a powder that was safe and would eradicate the cockroaches. This soon led to *The Natal Mercury's* well-known humorous columnist *'The Idler'*, devoting an article to the chance find in their 01 February 1952 edition.

Meanwhile Wulff called the pink beauty powder PEA-BEU and put it into production in the children's garden log cabin using a wartime home-made flour sifter.

With his formula complete and the first batch mixed by hand, Graham enlisted the help of an advertising agency that he found in the Yellow Pages. Lowe quickly became Graham's lifelong friend and business partner, and the two soon created a company to produce and market Oil of Olay.

Wulff and Jack Lowe, the former copywriter, tested the product on their wives and friends and were confident in its uniqueness and quality.

Wulff and Lowe's next job was how to market the powder. They were nothing if not unconventional.

They noticed that the Durban Corporation ran Durban unlike other municipalities. Their health department was checking restaurants and shops for unhealthy conditions, especially cockroaches. These inspectors were wearing pith helmets and white coats.

So they devised a devious plan. Having registered the name 'PEA-BEU Corporation', they dressed their employees likewise in pitch helmets and white coats, and directed them to go house-to-house and introduce themselves as being from PEA-BEU Corporation, but stress the emphasis on Corporation and pronounce the first part of the name softly.

Home and flat owners thought this was a compulsory immunisation campaign against cockroaches and sales rocketed. Now they had the finances to expand their cosmetic range and launch Oil of Olay. To that end they set up a factory with chemist Edmund Anderson.

Together, Graham and Dinah fine-tuned everything from absorption and texture to the delicate pink shade and instantly recognisable fragrance.

Olay Active Hydrating Beauty Fluid Lotion provided an immediate surge of hydration to soothe dry skin. It penetrated to help skin replenish its own essential moisture and diminish the appearance of fine lines. The light, non-greasy formula was dermatologically tested and non-comedogenic (that is, it didn't clog pores and encourage the formation of blackheads).

At last, the legendary Oil of Olay Beauty Fluid was born. It was unique in the early days because it was a pink fluid rather than a cream, packaged in a heavy glass bottle. He chose the name "Oil of Olay" as a spin on the word "lanolin", a key ingredient.

Olay's marketing was also unique, since it was never described as a moisturiser, or even as a beauty fluid. Nowhere on the packaging did it actually say what the product actually did.

Print advertisements used phrases like "Share the secret of a younger looking you" and talked about the "beauty secret" of Oil of Olay.

At the same time, he realised that there were a lot of cosmetics in the market all claiming to be the aging cream solution, so given their lack of finances he invented a 'beauty consultant' of repute who advised on the use of the product.

Advertisements were written as personal messages to the reader from a fictitious advice columnist named 'Margaret Merril'. The first symbol rhymed and was easy on the tongue, and so the adventure began.

Wulff and Lowe ran the company under the banner of Adams National Industries (ANI), but did not sell the product to the trade. Instead it waited for pharmacies to ask for it based on consumer requests.

They ran adverts in *Readers' Digest* and newspapers which often looked like editorials, and at times 'she' would recommend Oil of Olay written in lower case so that it appeared to be a substance rather than a product. Further, Merril advised the reader to ask their pharmacist to get it for them. Thus the mysterious Oil of Olay was launched and repeat orders came flooding in.

Meanwhile Merril was in hot demand. Everyone from women with conditions, to the media wanted to interview this elusive beauty consultant. Talks were confirmed then cancelled as Wulff came up with various excuses.

Surely the fraud would soon be discovered, but it was many years before the truth surfaced. By this stage even a rose, the 'Margaret Merril Rose' had been named and entered into flower shows, with success in Japan.

Wulff's efforts in his home laboratory soon paid off, and within five years, Olay was enjoying phenomenal success in South Africa because he had struck an important chord with women – 'looking good and feeling good were inseparable'.

In 1959, Wulff felt it was time to introduce Olay to the world[5], as they expanded into England and Ireland as Oil of Ulay, Australia as Oil of Ulan, Oil of Olaz in the Netherlands, Italy, France and Germany (later in 1970 into the USA and Canada). Needless to say, the Olay business flourished[6].

Since 1957 Papwa had been employed in the factory placing caps on the Oil of Olay bottles and receiving £10 a month salary, but in reality he was playing more golf than working.

Wulff, though, was frustrated that Papwa couldn't participate in 'white' tournaments, and to this end, he and Lowe came up with the idea of Papwa playing in Australia, a country in which Lowe had recently spent a year.

They arranged for a film to be made of Papwa demonstrating his reverse grip with Athlone professional, Phil Ritson (the future world-famous USA golf coach, later inducted into the Southern Africa Golf Hall of Fame in 2010).

---

5   Today it accounts for well over $3-billion of Proctor & Gamble's annual revenue

6   ANI sold out to Richardardson-Vicks Inc. in 1970 who later sold it on to Proctor & Gamble

Chapter 4: The Papwa Story - A Challenge to Apartheid

It was sent to the Australian PGA, and shown to the appropriate authorities, but neither would grant him a visa to go there. Clearly, the Australian authorities did not encourage dark skins. 'The Australian darkie colour bar is as effective as ours,' said Wulff with some bitterness. There was a rumour that Pretoria politicians put pressure on the Aussie authorities although this was never proven.

This was 1958 when Papwa, now 29, was no longer a youngster. He had already shown his potential by winning the Natal Non-European Open four times in the last five years (his only loss was in a play-off for the title).

Meanwhile Wulff bought Papwa a decent set of clubs and his family a comfortable single-storey house nearby. However, Suminthra, deeply superstitious, vetoed the idea of relocating and Wulff was forced to sell the property.

'Papwa' Sewsunker Sewgolum

SA Open winners: G Player 1956, 60 D Hutchinson 1959, H Henning 1957

Papwa dominated the non-European tournaments, yet it seemed that he, like his fellow black golfers, would never get the opportunity to measure himself against the likes of Bobby Locke, Harold Henning, and the jewel in South Africa's golfing crown, Gary Player.

These heroes of the public had lifted South Africa's already rich golfing heritage to among the top of the world and were regularly winning major tournaments against the very best in Europe, America and Australia.

To compete, Papwa would need to get accreditation from the PGA. Although SA hosted several so-called 'Open' tournaments, Papwa was barred from entry as these were classified by the government as

Papwa

'white-only' events.

Lowe having successfully introduced Oil of Ulan, as it was known to Australia, it was now Graham's turn to introduce it to England.

Their cosmetic business was thriving and Wulff needed to fly to England to set up the European leg of his operation.

When it came to encouraging Sewgolum to enter the British Open at Muirfield two years later, Wulff wouldn't take no for an answer. It didn't matter that Sewgolum was illiterate, had no passport and wouldn't be allowed to board an SAA flight to Europe because of his skin colour. Wulff had a cunning plan.

Lowe and Anderson then entered Papwa for the lucrative Open Championship, one of four 'Majors' to be played at Muirfield, Scotland.

At that time anyone calling himself a professional (even if he was not affiliated to a club) and amateurs with a 1 or better handicap could enter the qualifying rounds, with the aim of winning the trophy called the 'Claret Jug'.

Papwa had heard of the British Open as his father would tell him stories of the great Bambata who went to play in the Open.

It didn't matter that Papwa was illiterate, had no passport, and wouldn't be allowed to board an SAA flight to Europe because of his skin colour. Wulff had a cunning plan.

So Wulff and his partners raised the money and took Papwa to play in the British and Dutch Opens in 1959. Papwa's promise to his dad was becoming a reality.

Graham Wulff was Papwa's benefactor

Chapter 4: The Papwa Story - A Challenge to Apartheid

Meanwhile, Papwa, being illiterate, encountered obstacles with things as simple as getting a passport and receiving permission to leave the country, and even when he obtained those, he hit another barrier. When Wulff tried to buy tickets for the flight to London, they were told that South African Airways (SAA) didn't carry black passengers.

But that didn't stop either one of them. They both had their reasons and were both determined to reach their goal. A symbiotic relationship emanated from this. Both may have come from different worlds, yet in this respect they were quite similar.

Already the chairperson of the South African Aero Club, vice-president of the Durban Wings Club, and chairperson of the South African Wings Club, flying was Wulff's greatest passion so, undaunted, Wulff bought a light aircraft. He would fly Papwa out of South Africa in his new four-seater Piper Comanche 250 ZS-DRT to have a crack at the greatest title of all, the British Open at Muirfield. Together with his second wife Mavis, they flew with Papwa to Europe paying for all the costs that came along with this trip.

At the time that Graham took Papwa to the British Open, it was also a time when he was at the cusp of making Oil of Olay an international brand.

He couldn't really give as much of his time to Papwa apart from creating the enabling environment by providing the funding and the resources to do that.

There was also excitement among the local black golfers as the Natal Indian golf champion would get his big chance when he teed off in the British Open in Scotland, and as the first black golfer since Bambata Boodhun, he was showing the world that there were black golfers of quality from Africa. He represented them, so they would be ecstatic if Papwa made it through the qualifying rounds into The Open proper.

The Leader, March 13, 1959 newspaper quoted an anonymous sponsor saying: 'Papwa has equaled Player's scores in Durban. I think that Papwa stands a jolly good chance in the British Open. However, there are things like the intense English cold and the temperature to be considered.'

So, in 1959, Papwa's entry for The Open at Muirfield was

accepted but, as Wulff recalled, that was the easy part: 'He had no papers whatsoever, so we had to guess a date of birth for him, get him a passport. Since he had never been to school it was foolish to teach him each of the letters that constituted his name, so he was taught how to draw 'Papwa' simply by copying one I had written out for him'.

Papwa went on a special diet, clothing was bought for him to withstand the cold northern hemisphere weather, something which Papwa, coming from a hot all-year-round humid climate couldn't comprehend.

Clearly this trip to Europe must have been a daunting experience for Papwa. Before he left, Papwa had much to learn about European mannerisms. Cultural habits also needed mending. A Durban Indian waiter taught Papwa how to use a knife and fork, while he also learned which utensils to use for what meal course. Clearly this alone must have been an incredibly frightening experience for Papwa who was used to eating his food by hand.

At this time, Papwa had never set foot outside Durban, let alone flown in an aeroplane. Wulff was proposing that they fly through Africa in this small light single-engine aeroplane; it had a retractable undercarriage and was only capable of flying up to 1,000km at a time, meaning they had to plan to find multiple airports even in bad weather.

'A good friend of mine, Wolfie du Plooy, who was an airline captain with Rhodesian Airways and had recently flown a light aircraft to Europe from Durban, gave me lots of good tips, and I planned the trip very carefully before setting off,' recalled Wulff years later. 'As the Comanche did not have an autopilot, I would have to fly and navigate myself, so I planned to fly only in the mornings, leaving the afternoon free to do some business where possible and some sightseeing.'

On 27 May 1959, friends, family, and supporters arrived at Durban's Stanford Hill airport to bid farewell to their hero, a caddy of 16 years, sometimes earning as little as seven shillings and sixpence a week, who was off on the adventure of a lifetime which would change the world he lived in.

The day before, the Durban Indian Golf Club gave him a farewell party chaired by A. Naraidoo, and where, 'several hundred people turned up at this farewell event that was arranged by community

Chapter 4: The Papwa Story - A Challenge to Apartheid

leader Ram Chetty at the Sir Kumar Reddy School Hall in Rustomjee Road (now Uitsig Road, Durban North).'

He was presented with their club-blazer which he wore proudly, and whose pockets were stuffed with loose cash which they had collected. There were no so such thing as traveler's cheques, and it was time to follow in the footsteps of the great Ramnath 'Bambata' Boodhun.

Leaving for Europe with Graham and Mavis Wulff. Jack Lowe bids the threesmome goodbye (photographer unknown)

Dressed in his Durban Indian Golf Club blazer, 30-year old Papwa bade farewell to his family. He kissed Suminthra and each of his children goodbye. Jack Lowe was also there to see them off. Proudly waving goodbye, he Papwa mounted the narrow stairs of Wulff's private aeroplane, circumventing the need to stand in a separate queue for non-europeans for ordinary commercial flights and the petty laws making him a second-class citizen.

The aircraft lifted into the air, and suddenly the full horror of what he was doing scared the living daylights out of him. He gripped the seat tightly, scarcely able to breathe. Suddenly there was no ground below him as the plane banked over the sea, and as the wings were gently buffeted by the breeze, the plane peeled away, rising higher and

Papwa

higher into the clouds. He squeezed his eyes shut and prayed.

Then they turned again and headed back towards the land, for Johannesburg and customs where the Afrikaner emigration officials examined Papwa's passport, conferring with one other before making a phone call. Then an Afrikaner captain appeared and questioned Papwa, reviewed the letter with the official letterhead, another reviewed his passport, and with a thump he stamped the passport, and in broken English wished them a pleasant journey.

They hurried back to the plane before any official could change his mind, and readied for take-off. Would he ever see Suminthra and his children? Why had he agreed to come?

From Johannesburg, they flew to Beira, Mozambique's second largest city, which is located on the banks of the Pungue River near the beautiful palm-tree lined beaches of Pemba, already a diving mecca known only to the locals, and where they were able to get in a round of golf with a five-handicap golfer – the manager of the hotel into which they'd been booked.

The luxurious Grande Hotel in Beira was Papwa's first experience of indoor plumbing and having a room all to himself – only five years old, a palace of unlimited luxury where glamorous Hollywood starlet Kim Novak had recently been a guest.

At that time, it was the 'pride of the nation' but fell into decay after its owners failed to secure a casino license, and later served as a Frelimo military headquarters and jail, and then as a refugee centre during the Mozambiquan Civil War from 1977 to 1992. (At present it is occupied by over a thousand squatters who use the famous Olympic swimming pool overlooking the Indian Ocean to wash their clothes.)

The exterior of the Grande Hotel was done in the Art Deco style that was popular in Portugal during the 1930s and '40s, while the interior had an eclectic style with the use of modern materials. Of course, Papwa had never stayed in a hotel – the room seemed huge – and Wulff recalled how he entered Papwa's luxurious carpeted room where 'Papwa had a huge double bed to himself, and when I went to see him, he was chipping across it'. This was certainly a far cry from the 'shack' that Papwa called home.

Chapter 4: The Papwa Story - A Challenge to Apartheid

Given that Suminthra did all the washing, Wulff had to show him how to wash his clothes and how to use the various gadgets in his room, including the bathroom to have a good wash.

Back then it was spectacular, with red earthen floors, an overhead fan in each room to circulate the tropical air, and where dining included mangoes and other exotic fruits, while the waiters hovered with big smiles and white gloves.

Dinner that evening was another eye-opener. 'He was quite bewildered with everything, especially the meals, and did not know why we each had three knives and three forks to use when we could use our hands.'

Taking off was exciting but also terrifying. Next stop was Dar-es-Salam, Tanganyika's (Tanzania) former slave trade stopping-off point, with palm-clad beaches and rolling surf, with the three again staying at another beachfront hotel. Being a Hindu, Papwa was vegetarian. As a result bananas and biscuits became his favourite foods.

Then they flew past the Ngorongoro crater to Kenya and the Rift Valley, soaring over the herds of elephants and wildebeest, swaying giraffe and antelope. They flew past the snow-capped Mount Kilimanjaro (Africa's highest); the first time Papwa had seen snow.

By now he was getting quite used to flying and, excited by everything, it was wonderful. 'The whole flight was a tremendous thrill, especially as it was at a comparatively low altitude, and we were at the best advantage, as we were able to see all the features along the route,' said Wulff.

Then a night in Nairobi where Karen Blixen's farm featured in 'Out of Africa' ('I have a farm in Afrika' – Robert Redford and Meryl Streep) had already been turned into the premier Karen Golf Club, and on to Entebbe on the Lake Victoria peninsula, as the Royal Mail Ship MS Victoria steamed towards the port laden with passengers for a further fuel stop.

This was where in 1976 Idi 'Dada' Amin would hold the Palestinian-hijacked Israeli aircraft hostage until Israel flew a daring Mossad commando raid, 'Operation Thunderbolt', and freed 102 hostages with only one elderly hostage (Dora Bloch) having been taken to hospital, was later killed as the world watched and held their breath. There was only one Israeli casualty, their commander Lt. Col. Yonatan Netanyahu, the older brother of Benjamin Netanyahu, the Prime Minister of Israel.

There were further stops at Juba, a river port of 35,000 people on the banks of the Nile in Southern Sudan, a strategic location and focus for much of the fighting during the first Sudanese Civil war, then 1,200 km to Khartoum.

Khartoum, at the confluence of the White and Blue Niles had also been a slave trading hub where in 1884, the British army led by General Charles Gordon was wiped out by the forces led by the Mahdi. Then over the deadly Sahara Desert and nothing, just shifting sand and more sand dunes, and every now and then a few herders with their 'ships of the desert', a few camels.

Wulff often let Mavis fly so he could rest his eyes and have a short sleep. "Just keep this needle parallel on this dial, on that mark, so we are going in the right direction". Flying this plane is like driving a car except there is no road beneath you, and hardly ever any traffic, so it is easy to lose concentration and see the needle drop below parallel.

One afternoon Wulff was woken with a start because of turbulence over the desert. They were surrounded by storm clouds, Then a bolt of lightning, followed by the crashing thunderclap. With a shout of alarm he grabbed the joystick and pulled it down, dropping the aircraft to a low altitude so that the plane could fly out of danger.

Lightning flashed continuously about them as rain battered the light plane. Mavis was white with shock, and Papwa had his eyes closed tightly, praying, hoping that the danger would pass. After 20 traumatic minutes, which seemed like forever, and during which time the plane was buffeted from side to side, Wulff saw a break in the dark clouds and headed for safety.

Now the challenge was how to navigate without instruments which had been knocked out by the lightening? 'Look for the Nile,' Wulff instructed, 'it will be our only guide for the route north.'

Anxious moments passed before they spotted the river. With a sigh of relief, they followed it across the parched landscape, the best navigation beacon of all, all the way to Cairo, where Julius Caesar had taken Cleopatra, the Queen of the Nile, as his bride.

Chapter 4: The Papwa Story - A Challenge to Apartheid

Here they spent a week visiting the pyramids, and viewing the recently discovered god statue of the boy king, Tutankhamun, and posed for photographs sitting on camels in front of the Egyptian pyramids, another exciting first for Papwa.

Papwa also had the thrilling experience of riding a camel and could not wait to regale his children and friends with the story when he returned home.

It was easy to believe that this was all one long dream, Papwa thought, marvelling at his changing fortunes. All he'd wanted to do was play golf.

He'd never guessed how much golf would open up the world to him, a simple man from Riverside. Once the trip had been confirmed, Ma had told him that it had always been his destiny, set out before him by the gods, and that he should do her and his late father proud.

Sometimes Papwa felt that it was not only Ma and Pa, Suminthra and their little ones, his brothers and sisters and friends who were relying on him to do them proud. He carried the hopes and dreams of all of Riverside on his shoulders – of all Indians who'd been told that they were nothing more than Coolies, worthy of their second-class status in a country that only grudgingly accepted them.

There were days when Papwa missed home badly. He missed Suminthra's cooking and faced with all the foreign food, including beef and pork, which he would not eat, Papwa continued to stick to what he knew – bananas and biscuits – to the Wulff's great amusement.

In such close quarters, Papwa discovered that not only was Master Graham a generous man, he was something of a joker too.

"Papwa, don't you think it's wonderful that we don't get lost?" he'd ask, at least once a day.

And always, Papwa would answer: "Oh, I think the master's been this way before."

Graham had not in fact flown that way before and had relied heavily on a friend, who'd flown from Durban to Europe in a light aircraft the previous year, to help plan his journey.

There was another ritual they observed. Before setting off, Papwa would ask whether the Comanche contained enough petrol to get them to their next destination.

Papwa

Graham had found the question hilarious the first time Papwa had asked. To humour him, Papwa continued to ask the question and the joke never grew stale. Other times Graham would pretend that he'd lost his way or that the plane was indeed about to run out of fuel, just to see Papwa's reaction.

The final leg of their epic journey took them to Benghazi, and then on to Tripoli in Libya, where 18 years earlier most of the SA Infantry Division had faced General Rommel's Panzer tanks at Tobruk, and where many SA soldiers were taken prisoner and marched across the Sahara Desert to prisoner-of-war camps.

Despite the losses, General Montgomery regrouped, and in 1942 secured a key victory at El Alamein, and by May 1943 the entire North African region had been cleared of German and Italian troops, causing Hitler to order Rommel to take his own life.

Many of the Italian prisoners-of-war were brought back to camps in SA, including Cape Town, where they were put to work building Chapman's Peak, chiselled out of the mountainside from Hout Bay.

After crossing the Mediterranean, there were further stops in Tunis and Rome before heading to London, shortly to be regarded by young people as the music capital of the world with the advent of 'Beatlemania' in 1963. They had navigated across Africa and Europe, that was the easy part, but now in the mist they could not find Gatwick Airport.

'I crossed the coastline at what I thought was Brighton after flying north from France over the Channel. We should have been at Gatwick in nine minutes. There are no real landmarks in that area, with numerous towns, railway lines, roads and rivers all looking the same."

By this time the tension and animated conversation up front at the controls between Wulff and Marvis was palpable. Papwa was really panicking, mumbling a Hindu prayer, then he shouted that we were all going to die, which did not help my nerves, so Mavis told him to shut up, and then gave him her hand to hold.

I could not spot the airport, and then I found we were approaching London, so I called 'Mayday' on the emergency frequency, the static whistled and shriek, then the RAF station answered. Suddenly I saw a

Chapter 4: The Papwa Story - A Challenge to Apartheid

huge aerodrome below, and as my fuel was running low, I decided to land and radioed Gatwick accordingly.'

The aerodrome turned out to be the Royal Air Force (RAF) fighter base Biggin Hill, the famous fighter airfield that defended London and won the Battle of Britain in 1940 by shooting down over 1400 enemy planes. This was where the famous World War II ace, Douglas Bader had been posted to command as Squadron Leader in the WW2 Battle of Britain despite having lost the use of both legs: 'and we received a wonderful reception.'

Bader was then playing golf off a scratch handicap despite his artificial legs. He had just returned from Cape Town, where after climbing the stairs up onto the stage, with whispers circulating around the hall, he turned to the young SACS Junior School boys, and with a smile said: 'I bet you thought I was going to fall.'

"After taking on some fuel, and after nearly a fortnight's worth of travelling, we arrived at Gatwick, where again we had a wonderful reception from air traffic controller, customs, and immigration, especially when we told them we had flown all the way from SA to play in 'The Open', which at that time was a South African domain with Bobby Locke winning in 1949, '50, '52, and '57. 'From there we caught a train to Victoria Station, and we were on our way.'

The city was alive with reconstruction work following the war, and tourists were pouring through Piccadilly Circus. Their accommodation at 30 Craven Road, near Paddington Station was basic but interesting, as there was a brothel across the road.

The first thing they did was go to the West End Prince's Theatre, where the original production of King Kong, uniting audiences of all races in SA had opened – a direct challenge to apartheid – it was billed at the time as an 'all-African jazz opera.'

The musical King Kong portrayed the life and times of a heavyweight boxer, Ezekiel Dlamini, known as 'King Kong' or the 'The Spice Smasher' because of his size and strength. After a meteoric boxing rise, fighting out of the Bantu Men's Social Centre – a den for the hard hitters, he won the SA Non-European Heavyweight title in 1956 with a victory over Joe 'Foxy' Mtambo.

King Kong loved the attention and was often seen doing his

roadwork carrying dumbbells and wearing weighted boots and shadowboxing in the busy Marshall Street in the Johannesburg city center. Crowds would run behind and alongside him ala 'Rocky' and chant his name.

An icon to millions of blacks, a year later his life degenerated into drunkenness and gang violence. He knifed his girlfriend, asked for the death sentence during his trial and instead was sentenced to 14 years' hard labour. He committed suicide at Leeukop Correctional Prison where he drowned in a dam, and a legend was born. He was 36.

The song 'Sad Times, Bad Times' was considered a reference at the time to the infamous SA Treason Trial in Pretoria in 1956, which lasted for more than four years before it collapsed with all the accused acquitted. Among the defendants were Albert Luthuli (African National Congress president), secretary Walter Sisulu, Oliver Tambo, and Nelson Mandela.

'King Kong' launched the international career of Miriam Makeba, who played the shebeen queen of the 'Back of the Moon', a popular shebeen of the time in Sophiatown, as well as Hugh Masekela who led the brass section.

Everything was new to Papwa, and he had to catch himself greeting everyone as 'master'. People walked on the same side of the street as he did, and engaged with him as if he were one of them and not a person of colour. It felt so different not shrinking back when a friendly police 'bobby' passed him by, and the shops, so rich and full of everything.

Papwa spent a few days with the Wulffs in London before Graham flew his 'bewildered' passenger to Edinburgh and made arrangements for Papwa to practice golf at Gullane, North Berwick, and at Muirfield, where the British Open was to be played.

Gary Player was also in Papwa's corner at the tournament and lobbied for him to be able to practice on the course before the championship started.

Since most of his business was in London, Wulff was unable to remain in Edinburgh for long. He booked Papwa into a hotel and explained he would have to get a train and then a taxi to get to his practice sessions.

Chapter 4: The Papwa Story - A Challenge to Apartheid

Because Papwa could not read, Wulff found a stationary shop and bought up their stock of postcards, while Mavis spent time cutting up magazines such that the pictures of where Papwa had to go were glued onto the postcards – flash cards with pictures of the train stations, the golf courses and the hotel – for Papwa to carry with him. Graham made sure to include the address of each, so Papwa could consult passers-by if he got lost.

This worked for a while until a misunderstanding resulted in a hefty taxi bill, when Papwa neglected to discharge his driver after being dropped at one of the courses for a day's practice.

After that Graham hired a university student to take Papwa around and moved him to a hotel closer to the course.

He couldn't sign his name on the entry form, which he now wrote hesitantly, regarding it more as a picture than a signature, but he had arrived on the international stage, reverse grip and all, and from then on he would never look back.

Given that he was in a foreign country, where people spoke with a thick Scottish brogue, it was with great relief that Papwa encountered a fellow South African during one of his first visits to Gullane.

That man was Player, and the meeting was the beginning of a friendship between a poor boy from Riverside and a poor boy from Lyndhurst, Johannesburg.

One had lost a father at a tender age, the other his mother. Likewise, both had discovered a passion for golf while young, haunting golf courses during their teens. Their careers however, would take two very different trajectories.

Seven years younger than Papwa, even at 23, Player was by far the more experienced and worldly golfer. He had already started to make a name for himself in the international golf standings. Since winning the Egyptian Match Play event in 1955, he'd gone on to win several tournaments – in South Africa, Australia, the USA and the United Kingdom.

That year in South Africa alone, Gary had won the South African Masters, the Western Province Open, Natal Open, South African PGA and Transvaal Open. He'd won both the Australian PGA in 1957 and the Australian Open in 1958. The USA was where the big money was to be found in golfing, and in 1958 Gary claimed his first US victory – the prestigious Kentucky Derby Open – and was the runner-up in the US Open played at Southern Hills Country Club in Tulsa, Oklahoma.

With successes such as these, it was not surprising that Gary was highly tipped to win the British Open, and was closely watched by the press.

It seemed there would always be this question around Papwa. Was he a talented amateur or did he have the ability to turn professional and vie for titles with the world's best?

Denied professional status by the South African PGA, there was little way of knowing into which category he belonged until he played outside South Africa. "To be a champion, you need to compete with champions," Wulff had always said. Despite Sewgolum suffering from culture shock in the rarefied confines of Muirfield, he adapted quickly.

At this stage of Papwa's career, the competition offered by the contenders in the non-European championships wasn't enough for him – not when he regularly trounced competitors.

One of the highlights of the week building up to The Open was that he was able to play a practice round with Player and, despite not being able to sign his name on the tournament entry form, became a minor celebrity.

Papwa found a worthy opponent in Gary. During their first practice round, Papwa set off to a spectacular start, scoring three birdies within the first few holes. He reached the turn in 30 shots, but only managed 38 strokes over the next nine holes to finish on 68.

Gary had a good second half to finish on 70, losing to Papwa by two strokes. The next round went to Gary with a score of 70 to Papwa's 74. Then the third round went to Papwa, who scored 70 against Gary's 78, although in essence Player was preparing for The Open and not competing with Papwa.

Player was approaching The Open with his customary determination. He careful studied each hole, and the possible wind conditions, such that he would deliberately play short to some greens to prepare for a change of wind during the championship proper.

Of course when the tournament started it was a completely

Chapter 4: The Papwa Story - A Challenge to Apartheid

different story. Nevertheless, the fact that Papwa could compete after shooting a practice 68, and even beating Player, confirmed his belief that he could qualify to play in The Open proper.

Edward Johnson-Sedibe

While Papwa got through the qualifying rounds, into the Open proper, Gary Player went on to win the British Open.

News of his practice round and his trip stimulated substantial interest, with a report on the 26th of June, including a photograph of Papwa coaching some mesmerised Scottish youngsters on how to putt with his back-to-front grip.

Golf courses did not have yardage indicating the distance to the front or middle of the green from the fairway, at best they had a white, yellow and red stake signifying 200, 150, and 100 yards to the green, and Papwa had one big advantage over the field, he was a caddy. His depth perception was excellent, and he had learnt to estimate the exact distance to the hole. Although players were given booklets showing distances from various trees and bunkers to the green, which of course he could not read, he did not need this additional information.

Papwa also received his share of attention as he was the talk of the town early in the week; 'Papwa Sewsunker Sewgolum, of Indian origin playing out of Durban, South Africa, who shot a 71 in the qualifying rounds using a cross-handed grip.'

Papwa

Henry Longhurst wrote in *Sports Illustrated:* 'Papwa, like Sam Snead, reckons he plays his best in bare feet. He holds the club with his left hand below his right and in the first qualifying round went round in 71 in a downpour. So much for those of us who write books on how to play golf.'

And they referred to the irony of Papwa being able to play in international tournaments, while his own country denied him the right to play in their decreed white-only tournaments.

With his sub-standard golf clubs – other professionals had their clubs fitted for them – no previous practice on SA white courses, no coaching, and no the ability to read coaching manuals, his scores in The Open under the circumstances were none too bad. In the qualifying rounds he breathed a huge sigh of relief when he sank a long putt for a birdie 3 at the 18th at Gullane for a second-round total of 147 (71 76) to be on the cut mark for the championship proper with 59 others.

Scores of enthusiasts following his progress congratulated him. 'I am so happy now. I will not be able to sleep tonight. The other caddies back home would never have forgiven me if I had not qualified.'

Edward Johnson-Sedibe who started out as a caddy (often caddying for Otway Hayes), and who won the 1951 and '52 SA Non-European Open championships also tried to qualify to play at Muirfield, but missed the cut shooting 88 80 – 168, and then told anyone who listened that he liked being there so much that he planned on sticking around, especially if someone would give him a ride to London.

Johnson-Sedibe didn't give himself any chance at all as he only arrived the night before the championship, and then borrowed strange clubs, which were either too heavy or too light. Nevertheless, he was the first indigenous African to take part in The Open championship.

'The journey from SA to Edinburgh was certainly more daunting and expensive than a trip to the same destination from New York. If Johnson-Sedibe, a player who didn't even have his own clubs, understood what just having a chance to compete in The Open should mean to anyone who loved the game, why were America's best players dismissing The Open?' wrote Longhurst.

Round One proper and Papwa was among the last to tee off in the lingering hours of the afternoon. Luck of the draw, the morning had

Chapter 4: The Papwa Story - A Challenge to Apartheid

been calm, now the conditions were terrible – in the sleet, wind, and biting cold – he struggled, not relishing the strong west wind as heavy rain lashed the course and had many big names in trouble. Papwa, used to the Durban tropical heat, opened with a 79.

Round Two and an incredibly strong wind howled over the course for the early starters and then died bringing heavy rain. Papwa shot a creditable 73 (one-over par), but with a score of 79 73 – 152, he failed by four shots to make the cut for the final two rounds.

After 36-holes, Peter Thompson was the leader by two over Player, 137 to 139, but Player went on to win the 'Claret Jug', his first Major victory, beating Flory van Donck.

Papwa was proud and happy for Player. He would not forget how Gary helped him navigate the Edinburgh transport system, often arriving at his hotel so the two could travel through the damp and mist to their practice sessions together.

'The best player won. I regard Gary as a friend and I am proud of him. Still, I look forward to challenging him on various courses in the future. Who knows, possibly even in South Africa... Who knows what the future holds?'

Player was equally impressed with Papwa. 'I practiced with him on Gullane where the qualifying rounds were played, and he had a 30 for the first nine holes, returning in 38. Any player who can do a 30 on Gullane must be very good.' He went on, 'Neither Johnson-Sedibe or Papwa were likely to do well on a course like Muirfield without being experienced on courses like that. You only find this type of course, a real seaside course in Britain. Also given that it was cold, neither of them was acclimatised coming from Africa such that the course requires at least ten practice rounds because of the conditions caused by the varying winds.'

Years later Gary would recall the mistiness of the Scottish golf courses that year, the rain and the damp wind that had chilled Papwa to the bone, even though he was dressed in waterproofs, which, Gary conceded, restricted his friend's play.

Both failed to make an impact. However, in the July 1959 issue of *Sports Illustrated,* Henry Longhurst describes their appearance: "Colour was limited to the qualifying rounds by two gentlemen named

'Papwa' Sewsunker Sewgolum and Edward Johnson-Sedibe, both from South Africa".

But it was also a significant championship for South African golf in that Papwa and Johnson-Sedibe's participation was to inspire a number of black golfers to try and compete in The Open, just like Bambata Boodhun had inspired Papwa.

Victory

Open was a stepping stone to other tournaments in the UK and on the Continent, and here Papwa did not disappoint.

Wulff conceded that the expectations back in SA must have been 'a tremendous strain on Papwa's nerves', but at the same time, he believed the experience had been invaluable and that it would surely be a launch pad for other victories.

The South African-born Indian was subsequently entered for the French (which he missed) and German Opens where he performed 'reasonably well', but it was at the Dutch Open at the Haagsche Golf and Country Club in The Hague, one of the loveliest courses in Europe, where he made his mark.

Traveling from The Open to the French Open, Papwa was harassed by the SA Secret Police wanting to know why he was in the UK. This caused a delay such that they arrived late in Paris and missed the French Open due to 'crossed lines in planning', that had anyway taken place a day earlier than anticipated, but they reached the Haagsche Golf & Country Club at the Hague well in time for the Dutch Open commencing 16 August, where both South Africa champions, Sid Brews in 1934 and '35, and Bobby Locke in 1939 had previously won.

The publicity that Papwa received on the European tour brought him recognition back in South Africa, with articles recording the support of his caddy friends at Beachwood, whilst a black teachers' conference was informed of his opportunity to aim for the stars due to the generosity of a white sponsor.

More of an oddity because of his colour and grip, and the fact that he was not allowed to compete in his own country, he came across in a humble, soft-spoken manner as a good sportsman, making him a favourite with fans.

Chapter 4: The Papwa Story - A Challenge to Apartheid

This dream landscape of a golf course with man pitted against nature on a grand scale set on rolling sand dunes was designed in 1938 by the famous golf course architect Harry Croft (who dominated golf in the Netherlands) and C.H. Alison – the latter's influence could be seen with the slightly longer bunkers. The course is still counted as one of the finest Colt designed courses in Europe.

The design of the course made use of the naturally undulating dune landscape. Each hole offered a completely different view and a new surprising challenge. Driving was both difficult and adventurous, iron play demanding and all sorts of shot-making were necessary to conquer the green complexes. A roller coaster fairway ride, up and down, from side to side, dips and valleys, leaving the golfer with breathless wonderment, as thick lush high seaside foliage flanked the fairway on both sides, and with no other hole visible.

The ground provided the challenge, so not many man-made hazards or bunkers, with only one fairway and 23 greenside bunkers, playing golf through rousing sand dunes.

Finally tee-off on the 18th with the green in full view and the impressive clubhouse as the background.

Entrants included players from England, Scotland, Wales, Ireland, Australia, Belgium, France, Italy, Germany, Portugal, Spain, the Netherlands, and SA.

Papwa stood on the tee as the excitement mounted, crowds congregated around the tee-box, and his name was called out representing the Union of South Africa. With his heart beating rapidly he gazed out over the course, much like Durban Country Club, with the first hole, a 3-shot par-5 descending from one of the course high points to a very low one, and then straight back up the hill, with the green tucked away behind the dunes, and where a poorly struck ball was shed away.

Round One, displaying nerves of steel with an exceptional temperament, he opened with an outward half of 35, and then five threes in an inward half of 32, coming home for a 67, a new course record beating the 1954 course record of Ugo Grapposani by one shot, to take the lead.

He followed with an equally impressive 69 in the second round and, with a three-shot lead over Dutch champion Gerard de Wit (three-time runner-up), the Durbanite was in the driving seat. Those who witnessed his upside-down grip marvelled at his accuracy.

From off the green where most golfers were playing it safe with a putter, Papwa used his trusted deep-faced pitching wedge, spinning it as it hung in the air, trying to hole the shot as it dropped. It was all about 'feel' and making sure he did not decelerate.

A wobble in the third round saw him shoot a 74. He began the fourth and final round with a two-stroke lead over De Wit, and by the fourth hole he had extended this lead to five strokes. At this stage, Papwa felt comfortable reverting to safety first golf, sensible, but he would soon regret his decision, as the Dutchman rallied to wipe out the deficit scoring an eagle at the 5th, a par-5, 448m hole, followed by four successive birdies from the 6th to the 9th hole, to go one stroke ahead at the turn with nine to play.

The crowds were cheering every shot De Wit played, and the scoreboards revealed the bad news to Papwa. He realised he was starting to panic as his caddy kept reminding him of his diminishing position.

Playing safe had not paid off, and so Papwa changed his tactics and went on the attack. On the 11th, a par-4, 377m dog-leg to the right, with a small green, he recorded a birdie, but De Wit matched it with a long curling putt from the edge of the green.

The 12th is played from high-point to high-point across a shallow valley, while the green epitomises the requirement posed at Haagsche for crisp, accurate iron play. Past the lone front right deep bunker is an eight-foot swale with the largest green on the course. The green is the high point of its surrounds and its pronounced back to front left tilt made a recovery from any shot missed right particularly problematic.

This was where De Wit's charge faltered when he hooked his tee shot at the short par-3, 153m 12th, one of the easiest holes on the course, and he was bunkered, dropping a shot. A turning point!

The predominantly Dutch crowd was stunned into silence as Papwa birdied the par-4, 378m 13th, and the par-4, 389m 14th hole to retake the lead. But now the partisan gallery started shouting encouragement for their man.

Chapter 4: The Papwa Story - A Challenge to Apartheid

They matched each other in par for the next three holes. Now he held a slender two-shot lead over De Wit with one hole to play, a hole some critics nominate as the best closing hole in continental Europe.

Papwa's uncanny temperament seemed to be carrying him to victory when more experienced players would have wilted away. The strain of knowing what one has to do is something that often twists the nerves of the stomach into painful sensitiveness and swings burn out, as players lunge desperately at the ball. Nothing of the sort was happening to Papwa.

The 18th is a par-5, 436m (now 499m). First, the golfer actually sees the clubhouse as it acts as a backdrop for the entire hole. Second, lined with trees left and right all along the narrow fairway, with out-of-bounds down the right, it is both more enclosed and sheltered than the previous 17 holes. Third, this is the flattest fairway on the course, and the golfer finally enjoys a level stance on back to back fairway shots, and the green is protected with two bunkers in the front right with another bunker just short of the green to the left.

He looked down the length of the fairway that was alive with 5,000 spectators, and calmly considered how he would squeeze out a par-5.

Then, for the first time, with his stomach churning and his heart beating faster, he stumbled, as the wind changed direction blowing strongly across the fairway from left to right just as he was about to tee off. He pulled his drive into the rough on the left-hand side, while De Wit's effort was rhythmic and 216m straight down the fairway.

With 220m left to the hole, and the ball lying perched high up on a tuft of grass, Papwa pondered for a while, discussing the options with his caddy, his hand moving over clubs as he changed his mind. Eventually he chose his favourite club, a brassie (3 wood), but felt himself tighten on the backswing, his hips came through too fast for his hands which lagged behind, as he snatched and blocked it, fading long and left onto an adjacent fairway behind a row of trees which blocked his path to the green. De Wit's second landed safely on the green to cheers from the local gallery, a possible eagle opportunity which he missed, and settled for a birdie.

Papwa

Papwa's third shot presented even greater difficulties as he now had to judge the distance and still clear the trees, then stop the ball on the green. With the wind shifting constantly he changed his club repeatedly. He settled on a pitching wedge – leaving the face wide open – he cleared the trees but overshot the green settling in the rough again beneath a tree with low-hanging branches.

For his pitch, he opened the deep face wedge – a dangerous shot if there is any hesitation or body movement, as the spectators held their breath.

His fourth shot never left the pin and plummeted down, safely five-feet short, checked, then rolled on another foot. Papwa lifted his cap to acknowledge the applause. His punchy putt was perfect, and the ball disappeared down the centre of the cup.

In front of a total attendance of 17,863 spectators, and a radio and television audience of three million, Papwa, who had never previously journeyed outside Durban, and who had never had a lesson, had beaten the Dutch star De Wit[7] by one shot scoring 67 69 74 73 (283), third was the well-known Belgian star, Donald Swaelens on 287, a five-time Dutch Open winner (wins 10 including the 1966 Woodlawn tournament, 1967 German Open). Papwa's final score of 283 was the 6th lowest in the history of the Dutch Open.

The world returned, and he blinked back tears, hugged his caddy, and took off his cap. Papwa amazingly had made history by winning the Dutch Open and a cheque for £200, the first time that a golfer of colour had won a major national tournament in Europe.

De Wit grasped his hand warmly, and the television cameras focused on his smiling face, while media cameras clicked, with images beamed across the world. South Africans of colour rejoiced, especially the Indian population – Papwa had shown whites that in the land of the forefathers of the Afrikaners those of a darker hue could compete on equal terms and win!

Later he told the press that he only practiced once or twice a week, and that he had imagined for a moment after playing the 12th that his blind mother, Parvathy, was calling to him across the ocean saying:

---

[7] The fourth time De Wit had finished runner-up, and five times in all – never to win the Dutch Open.

Chapter 4: The Papwa Story - A Challenge to Apartheid

"My son, are you alright?"

Donald Swaelens, Sewgolum Papwa met diens Londense vriend Sugden en wedstrijd-secretaris De Haan

Donald Swaelens, Papwa Sewgolum with his London friend Sugden and match-secretary De Haas.

Receiving the trophy for his win at the 1959 Dutch Open photographer unknown).

Clutching his replica trophy (the original stayed with the Open in Holland) he said; 'I am so happy to have won a championship here that I can hardly think straight,' Papwa told an interviewer. 'I'm only sorry that I did not have better scores on the final round, but my putting went off.' In response, the chairman of the organising committee said, 'We enjoyed your golf, and we hope to see you back here to defend the title.'

'Tell the folks back in Durban that this is the greatest day of my life. I am proud to have won this championship, not only for myself, but for SA.' Across the Indian Ocean in SA, Papwa's victory was banner-headlined in the Indian and black newspapers, and begrudgingly in the white.

So Papwa, had become the first man of colour, and the only player ever with a cross-handed grip, to win a significant overseas national title in Europe, and the third South African after Sid Brews (twice) and Bobby Locke to win this tournament. He attributed his success to his trusty putter. 'I would not change it,' he said. Papwa was now a role model.

Other winners of the Dutch Open include Payne Stewart, Sergio Garcia, Jose Maria Olazabal, Colin Montgomerie, Miguel Jimenez, Steve Stricker, Lee Westwood, Darren Clarke, Paul Casey, and other Southern African stars Bobby Locke (1939), Brian Wilkes (1961), Retief Waltman (1963), Hugh Baiocchi (1975), and Harold Henning in 1981. Sid Brews was the only player who won the trophy twice– in 1934 and 1935. Papwa was to win it three times in all and be runner-up.

'To win a tournament in the first year on tour is phenomenal,' stated Ryder Cup player Tommy Horton.

His name made the headlines in the press across the world and, like all great figures in sport he attracted controversy wherever he went. As the *Cape Times* of July 19, 1959 trumpeted: 'Indian ex-caddy from Durban wins the Dutch Open.'

The Dutch Open had attracted a first-class field, and to beat the seasoned De Wit on his home ground took a great deal of doing.

When asked for comment, Gary Player replied: 'Papwa has done very well. His grip restricts his follow through and therefore his length, but he has good nerves and a great short game. He is not only a fine man but also a fine golfer.

Chapter 4: The Papwa Story - A Challenge to Apartheid

| 1960 | Sewsunker Sewgolum (2) | South Africa | Eindhovensche | 280 | 3 strokes | Denis Hutchinson |

Fresh from his victory, Papwa travelled to the German Open which Bobby Locke had won in 1954. He however opened with a 76 putting him 9 strokes behind the leader and he was unable to make up the ground on Ken Bousfield who won despite a closing 68 in the last round for a total of three under par 285.

The publicity Papwa received on the European tour brought him to the attention of the media in South Africa. Articles mentioned caddy support and Dr A.D. Lazarus[8] told his audience of Indians about Papwa's success and that not only whites could succeed at sport, and the government took notice.

The news spread like a cheerful mist, and when the president of the Durban Indian Golf Club (later renamed the Durban Golf Club) received the news, he announced that he would recommend Papwa as their club's first full-time professional. Problem – the club however was still without a course although there was talk about the Durban Corporation building a course at Springfield, on the banks of the Umgeni River.

On his return to SA, he cradled his replica of the Dutch Open trophy – too precious to be stowed away as cargo. As *'Zonk'* newspaper headline screamed: 'Hero comes home – Former Durban caddy puts non-white golf on the world map.'

He was swamped by wildly cheering crowds, mainly Indians, at both Johannesburg and an estimated 2,000 at Durban airports, where he was welcomed with garlands and flowers, and carried shoulder-high from the tarmac so that Papwa was almost overwhelmed by the excitement as he also placed a garland over Wulff. Now a 'role model', Papwa's victory made people proud to be Indians.

Among the photographers was a man in a long brown overcoat from the government security establishment. He did not compete with the press corps for a close-up of the returning champion and his photographs were not intended for the front pages of the newspapers the next day. Instead they were filed for future use in a manila folder[9].

The white press, though, totally ignored his achievement. Papwa would make it harder for them the following year. South African golf would never be the same!

---

8   Dr A.D. Lazarus was the "Doyen of Indian Education" nationally and Internationally.

9   Christopher Nicholson: Papwa Sewgolum from Pariah to Legend.

Chapter 4: The Papwa Story - A Challenge to Apartheid

Lining the streets cheering Papwa their garlanded hero home.

From the National Party government however, there was a steely silence as it tried to fathom the feat's significance. *'The Leader'* newspaper noted that the racial barriers the Nationalist government had implemented in sport were backfiring badly: 'Papwa's success in the home country of the original Voortrekker, the birthplace of Dr Verwoerd, makes the embarrassment even more unbearable for the apostles of apartheid.'

And the *'Golden City Post'* noted the irony in that Sewgolum's own government didn't recognise him as a full South African, and that 'back home, the winner of the Dutch Open wouldn't be allowed to take part in a white tournament except in a menial capacity'.

Papwa had become a symbol of liberation to an increasingly beleaguered people virtually overnight was the way journalist Philip Galgut described Papwa's new status in the *Compleat Golfer.*

Papwa received a hero's welcome to the port city as his motorcade made its way from the airport. The streets were a splash of colour with thousands of women dressed in saris, and the air was thick with the fragrances of incense and spices of India. The roar of huge crowds lining the streets sounded as if the 'heavens had opened up'.

He was escorted by a cavalcade of cars as the convoy accompanied by well-wishers inched towards his small wood-and-iron shack where he lived with his blind mother and family.

Papwa Sewgolum stands alongside his family members outside his modest home in Durban. Picture courtesy of LLA.

Along the route thousands of cheering supporters went wild, while many jumped on his car and tried to shake his hand as he was

Chapter 4: The Papwa Story - A Challenge to Apartheid

greeted by crowds estimated to be 100,000 in number.

The plan was that the tired sportsman should return home as soon as the aircraft touched down. But this was not to be. A cavalcade of cars and buses followed his car after he had been chaired shoulder-high from the tarmac airstrip. At Clairwood, the motor convoy was mobbed by residents. Many onlookers clung to his car, stood on the sides and even held on to the roof as it crawled along – The Daily News

So, this celebrated Indian sports hero returned home after winning the Dutch Open and qualifying for the British Open to a welcome which he never dreamed possible in the days when he was learning golf as a caddy in Durban. First at Jan Smuts Airport and then at the Louis Botha Airport, Durban, thousands mobbed the man who had overnight become a world class golfer. This double triumph once again shifted the spotlight onto his troubled homeland.

A victory party was held at the Lotus Club later that evening where Papwa was congratulated by a host of signatories including Durban City Councilor Jimmy Bolton, as well as Mr Kalideen, president of the Durban Indian Golf Club, whose blazer and badge Papwa had worn so proudly throughout this trip.

Later he kicked off an inter-racial soccer match at Currie's Fountain between the Natal Indian XI and Coloured XI watched by 17,000 spectators, which the Indians won 5-1, and also saw him hit four autographed golf balls from the centre of the field to each corner of the ground. The spectators excited to see their champion clamoured for the golf balls as a souvenir.

Then he was the crowning of the new Miss India South African, Isabel Prince.

Papwa could hardly believe how far he had come since winning his first title here in 1945 as a 16 year-old, but his most important question to his friends was: 'Were the fish biting?' He was keen to get down to the Umgeni River to see.

He was full of praise for his employers who had sponsored his trip overseas and made his triumph possible. He said that while playing in overseas tournaments, great crowds had followed him to see his unorthodox grip.

Papwa

Advertising money started flowing – one advert showed Papwa enjoying a refreshing cup at the ninth hole, with the caption, "I like peppermints good and strong; that's why I go for Wilson Three-X Mints ...they're my favourite," says Sewsunker (Papwa) Sewgolum.

Natal Furniture Products, an Indian-owned store, presented Papwa and Suminthra with a new bedroom suite and he was asked to endorse Success cigarettes. Aside from these perks, it wasn't long before life returned to normal, although a number of new acquaintances now pitched up in the evening to discuss golf.

For white South Africans who were relishing the successes of Bobby Locke and Gary Player at home and abroad, Papwa, with that upside-down grip, remained something of an enigma.

The golfing establishment regarded him with amusement and mild embarrassment, while to the apartheid officials he was a black trouble-maker.

However, for hundreds of thousands of Indians living in South Africa, (SA has the largest population of Indians outside of India), he was a giant, a homespun sporting hero. Like Tiger Woods decades later, he was responsible for taking what was almost an exclusively whites-only sport to a much larger audience. Every youngster now wanted to hold his club like Papwa. Meanwhile, he was snapped up to promote 'Success Cigarettes'.

Wulff was frequently asked why they had helped Papwa: 'People are constantly asking us what we are getting out of this. The answer is: nothing. We simply felt that anyone with great skill, regardless of colour, deserves a chance.

Wulff's generosity was to support an underprivileged competent black golfer in a time when this was unheard of.

Nevertheless, once the euphoria died down, the Dutch Open champion found himself back on the production line at the Oil of Olay factory in Umgeni Road placing caps on the endless line of bottles.

The fact that he was barred from competing in 'white' tournaments meant that the victories he continued to notch up didn't pay the bills.

Following his return home, he had further success, setting a new Beachwood course record with a 65, winning the Natal Midlands

Chapter 4: The Papwa Story - A Challenge to Apartheid

Non-European Open, and succeeding cricketer Basil 'D'Oliveira as the *Golden City Post's* 'Sportsman of the Year' for 1959'.

Papwa's success overseas came at a time of increased repression by the authorities towards Indians. As a first step in 1960 towards reducing the Indian population, it was decided to cut down the political leadership by banning the entire Natal Indian Congress.

When this did not have the desired effect, the government used the Group Areas Act to move Indian traders to less favourable sites in the city.

But now the government was also facing serious problems with blacks living in or being in white areas save for employment. At the time black men had to carry a deeply resented identity document pass at all times allowing them into white areas. This law was now extended to black women.

International approbrium was also being heaped upon the increasingly out-of-touch South African government, when in February, 1960, the British Prime Minister, Harold Macmillan told parliament in Cape Town: 'The wind of change is blowing through this continent. Whether we like it or not, this growth of national consciousness is a political fact.'

Macmillan's Cape Town speech also made it clear that he included South Africa in his comments and indicated a shift in British policy in regard to apartheid.

A month later, passes were burnt in public and protests held, including a march of around 7,000 on Sharpeville Police Station on 21 March 1960. Within a few moments the police opened fire, and there was a massacre, leaving 69 unarmed protestors dead, serving notice that there were grave problems with the country's race laws, and international antagonism towards apartheid regime continued to gather momentum.

Although the Pass Laws were temporarily suspended, the African National Congress (ANC) and the Pan African Congress (PAC), both perceived to be behind the march, were banned and a state of emergency declared, while political activists were detained without trial, and the government clamped down on all opposition.

It was a time of severe pressure on the National Party government, and the White Football Association was suspended from Fédération Internationale de Football Association (FIFA) in 1961.

Now playing on golf courses reserved for whites, Papwa's magnificent game escalated and gained 'white' support – not the kind of thing the apartheid government enjoyed.

However, not even the close relationship with the influential Wulff would see Papwa participating and competing in white tournaments. The times were reminiscent of the Ghetto Act which reduced Indians to menial labour. Now added to this were the Separate Amenities Act, the Group Areas Act, and so many more heinous laws that took away opportunities for blacks.

Weeks later, with the Dutch Open trophy on the table, Louis Nelson, a former caddie turned union leader and an acquaintance, came to greet Papwa. He was ambitious and politicised, who liked the limelight, an avid golfer and an able organiser.

Sumithra shaking her head regretfully slid a letter with the SA PGA logo across to the visiting Nelson. "Mr. Wulff's right. If they won't take Papwa now, they never will."

"With all due respect Papwa", interjected Nelson, "the man's a factory owner. There are moves that can be made that he –". "Then what are you waiting for?" interrupted Suminthra before Papwa's glance caused her to withdraw.

Nelson continued, "All I'm saying is – this Wulff fellow …he's a white factory owner, a racist, what's his agenda? Everybody has one, huh? You're a hero to the black people. It's time you had a real manager…Me!"

They said Papwa couldn't handle a golf club 'right', but he kept collecting the titles. Now he added his first 1960 SA Non-European Open to his list. Shrewd judges of golf who saw Papwa battling his way through a near gale force Cape south-easter to a brilliant victory in the SA Open championship on January 1 and 2, reached a unanimous conclusion; this is a golfer who is on his way to becoming great.

While in Europe, Papwa played alongside greats such as Bobby Locke and Gary Player, playing with them in tournaments in Britain, France and Germany, and with fans from all over following his career including SA whites, in SA the race laws were intensified.

Chapter 4: The Papwa Story - A Challenge to Apartheid

Recognising that Papwa had little or no opportunity to compete on the SA professional circuit after his application for membership of the South African Professional Golf Association (SAPGA) was rejected on the basis of race, the British Professional Golf Association (BPGA) offered him membership and opened the way for him to play in all tournaments in the UK, Europe and beyond.

Funding remained a problem. Wulff had simply been too busy following his dream of setting up his worldwide business, to set up the 'Papwa Sewgolum Trust Fund' with the aim of raising funds for international travel.

Oil of Olay's international expansion had taken off into new Markets of England and Ireland, France, Italy, Germany, and the Netherlands. With a packed travel schedule and added responsibilities, Graham was unable to provide Papwa's career with the necessary nurturing. He'd set him on his way, now it was time for someone else to take over.

After his pitch to Papwa and Suminthra, Nelson, the former caddy and now a trade union leader in the Liquor and Catering union took over the management of the rising star. Soon thereafter, the Natal Golf Association was formed with Louis Nelson on the committee.

Recognising what he had achieved and how he was influencing the community, Nelson who was a strong and determined manager, started by having Papwa officially confirmed as the professional of its yet-to-be-built course at Springfield on the 3rd of November, 1959, although the club was only able to get a course in December 1961.

In November the 'Papwa Trust Fund' was formed under Nelson's chairmanship. The committee comprised of Louis Nelson (chairman), R.S. Govender (secretary/treasurer), E.I. Haffejee, G. 'Pumpy' Naidoo and T. Lutchman and was aimed at raising enough money for him to travel to the Netherlands to defend his Dutch Open title. They were confident of a generous response being made by the public. A cheque for £25 was also received from Papwa's employers.

The problem was being able to afford to get to play in Europe.

To raise money, the Trust published the 'Dutch Open Champion' book at two shillings and sixpence (R4,50) as the Trust aimed at a target of £1000.

It was a bit of a battle, but finally, the goal was reached after a few months, and in 1960 Papwa was able to make his second trip to the UK and Europe for three months, albeit using a more conventional flight, but now without Graham Wulff.

Once again he played in the centenary Open Championship at St Andrews (won by Australian Kel Nagle). It proved to be a repeat of the previous year. Papwa opened with a 70, followed by a 74 (144), but he again failed to make the 36-hole cut, with Gary Player leading the qualifiers on 137 – 67, 66.

This time 'native' Johnson-Sedibe opened with a 77 together with Brian Wilkes, followed by a 75 for 152, a much better effort than the previous year, but he too failed to make the cut for the championship proper. He would try the following year again, starting with a 76, but would not qualify.

Then on to the Dutch Open as the defending champion, whose main point of interest to people outside SA was that he played cross-handed.

Papwa's movements were being carefully monitored by a pair of Special Branch operatives who trailed him wherever he journeyed, ever concerned that he would bring SA into disrepute. Papwa was not a political man and had never been one for pronouncements, but the fact that he was competing on an international stage, and won tournaments, did not sit well with apartheid elite.

'The Leader' headline shouted out: 'A nerve-wracked despondent Papwa does it again.'

Suffering from 'serious neurosis' and having lost 9kg in weight after his failure in the Daks Tournament, and his disastrous British Open, Papwa became very despondent and kept repeating that he had let everyone down in SA. But he somehow managed to pull himself together in the Netherlands, as memories of his success in the previous year's Dutch Open came flooding back. This time, though, he didn't play on the lovely course outside of The Hague and the championship venue was at Eindhoven.

The Eindhovensche golf course was ranked in the top 20 of the world's leading Continental Europe Courses. Designed on heathland near the town of Valkenswaard by Harry Colt in 1928, the two

Chapter 4: The Papwa Story - A Challenge to Apartheid

huge 9-hole clockwise loops each return to the lovely thatched-roof clubhouse, and consist of excellently crafted holes with each hole individually routed through the tranquillity of this large and impressive woodland area. Blessed with sandy soil, it has one of the most beguiling starts thanks to the deft and deceptive mounding Colt employed to the left on the short par-4 2nd and right of the green on the par-3 3rd.

The fairways were wide, some flat, others more undulating, and the greens well guarded by large and deep bunkers. The most demanding holes were the 3rd, 7th, 10th, 13th, and overlooking four holes the historical natural 'swimming pool', a large pond, which especially came into play on the 10th and 17th holes.

Staying out of the trees and hitting the putting surface in regulation was the key to Papwa scoring well. Nicely elevated tee-boxes on several holes provided him with an excellent view of the challenge ahead.

Several golfers had won the Dutch Open more than once but to win it twice in succession is a feat accomplished only by golf's immortals. What stood against Papwa doing the trick? Well, when he stepped on to the first tee and wound up that long swing of his, he was under the whip from the start. He was the champion and in the eyes of the rest of the field became the pacemaker.

Above all, he was fighting against the thought that in the last 23 years since Flory Van Donck (others were Sid Brews in 1935 and Henry Burrows 1921) no champion had retained his title. They said that to win the Dutch Open was difficult, but to defend the title was well-nigh impossible.

Determined to retain his title and to justify the faith everyone had in him, Papwa heard his father's words 'reach for the stars Papwa'. He opened with a beautiful first round 69 and took a three-stroke lead from Belgian Arthur Devulde. He had another good round of 71 but found himself in joint leadership with Devulde who went round in 69.

He was back in front after a third-round 71, two strokes ahead of Brian Huggett and Denis Hutchinson (1959 SA Open champion), and with a final round of 69 and with scores of 69 71 71 69 (280), he romped home, beating fellow South African Hutchinson 72 71 70 70

Papwa

(283) into second place, followed by Ryder Cup star Bernard Huggett and Gerard de Wit, for a three-shot victory.

| 1960 | Sewsunker Sewgolum (2) | South Africa | Eindhovensche | 280 | 3 strokes | Denis Hutchinson |

Chapter 4: The Papwa Story - A Challenge to Apartheid

Edward Johnson-Sedibe

But Papwa wasn't the only South African of colour making waves. His compatriot from the 1959 Open Championsip, Johnson-Sedibe was carrying his relatively good form in The Open qualifying, and eight years after winning the 1952 South African Non-European Open (and the year before), 'Eddia' Johnson-Sedibe headed for the famous Wentworth golf course (home of the 1953 Ryder Cup and 1956 World Cup, and where Ernie Els has his home), and the Ballentine Bigger Ball tournament.

This was the first tournament in Europe where the American 1,68 inch (42,67 mm) and not the smaller British 1,62-inch golf ball, which had always been in use, was now compulsory.

Why? A 0.06-inch difference in golf ball diameter doesn't sound like much. But the smaller ball provided around ten per cent more distance and was more workable in the wind. However, it didn't sit up quite so well on the grass and was, therefore, slightly harder to hit well, while the larger ball made putting easier and had more weight to fall into the hole.

Source: Christopher Meister

Papwa

Eddia opened with an astounding 65 to take the first round lead at the East course. He certainly had no reason for complaint as he beamed over his card, which was easily his best effort so far in a British tournament. He had a good homeward half of 32 including twos at the 10th and the 12th. Bobby Locke opened with a 69 and Harold Henning a 70.

Here was Eddia leading the best of Europe, only allowed to play with his friends on their pick-up golf course in the bush, not allowed to play on a white course back home, denied membership of golf clubs or the ability to play in a white tournament.

What would Simon 'bra Cox' Hlope (now 36) and already the winner of the SA Non-European Open titles in 1955, '57, and '59, have achieved if he had been let loose on the European fairways? Meanwhile, Edward Johnson-Sedibe had arrived.

Source: Christopher Meister

And England, Europe, and the World thought we had no black golfers, let alone quality players. Certainly, those playing in Europe had no idea there were black golfers in Africa, as Eddia became the first African to take the lead in a major tournament in Britain.

After Round Two, Bernard Hunt had taken the lead on 132, followed by Christy O'Connor Snr on 135 (69, 66), then came R.M. Jacobs 136, John Panton 138, all Ryder Cup players, and then Eddia after a 74, but still in the hunt, together with Peter Thompson (five-

Chapter 4: The Papwa Story - A Challenge to Apartheid

time British Open champion), and Eric Brown (Ryder Cup player).

The tournament was eventually won by Irishman O'Conner Snr on 277 by two-strokes over John Patton. Sadly Eddia fell away with an 84 and 78 (301), but this gave him the encouragement to persevere, eventually becoming the leading golf coach in Germany. In SA, he would not have been allowed to coach or enter a clubhouse. What talent had apartheid SA driven from its shore!

Eddia also finished 26th in the 1960 Italian Open, and 30th in the Portuguese Open; and in 1961 he finished 26th in the Spanish Open. He also won some minor tournaments in Portugal and England.

In 1962, Eddia had his first employment as the assistant professional to the Royal Winchester Golf Club Golf, and in 1965 he was the professional at Hamburg-Ahrensburg GC in Germany, which at the time consisted of mostly of beginners, and where, as the lead singer, he formed a pop band, and taught golf for 20 years.

Meanwhile, Papwa played in a number of tournaments with varying success, his best finish being 5th on 281 in the Yorkshire Evening News Tournament seven shots behind the winner Peter Thompson, and 12th in the French Open.

So Papwa had carved a niche for himself in golfing folklore when he won the Dutch Open in 1959 and 1960 which caused the government to reconsider their ban as they deliberated allowing him to play in some white tournaments. He was already aged 32, just starting out, at an age when many golfers reach their peak.

Against high calibre opposition, Papwa was accorded the respect and courtesy befitting a top-class sportsman wherever he played abroad. But when he came back to the country of his birth, he had to revert to a sporting life of second-class status and needed official permission to compete each week against white golfers against whom he was more than a match.

With the country seething with political dis-content, dissent and repression, the Natal Golf Union received Sewgolum's application to compete in the whites-only Natal Open Championship in 1960, and it became a political hot potato. The issue was referred to the SA Golf Union (SAGU) – the country's governing body – attention was drawn to a statement by the Minister of the Interior, Jan de Klerk that 'entry of Non-Europeans into national and provincial tournaments would be a departure from customs and traditions', and the request was turned down.

The South African Non-Racial Olympic Committee (SAN-ROC), headed by Dennis Brutus took up the cudgels and urged the British Professional Golfers Association to reprimand the SAGU.

It wasn't long before Brutus was arrested after being shot in the back, and where he had to lie in the street bleeding after a white ambulance was waved away.

CHAPTER 5: BREAKTHROUGH

A loophole

For years Papwa had been forced to pursue his game only in 'non-European' tournaments. He applied for permission to enter numerous 'white' tournaments, and the government turned each one down.

But there was ambiguity in the law: Was it really illegal for a 'non-white' to 'occupy' a white area if that area was, say, a cinema, or a golf course? The question centred round the meaning of 'what constitutes occupation'? Must it be permanent or temporary?

The Olympia bioscope in Kalk Bay, Cape Town, for instance, had coloured folk sitting upstairs while the whites sat downstairs. For fun those sitting in the top tier would hurl water bombs onto those down below. But after the show they departed. They were temporary occupiers, and no longer occupied the premises.

This question had already been raised in 1957 where it was found that occupancy, the cornerstone of the promulgated Group Areas Act, required permanent occupation, such that the Act was broadened and changed in three instances: restricting attendance for entertainment, partaking in refreshments, and being a guest of a member of a club.

Meanwhile, Papwa continued to be watched – and sometimes directly threatened – by the secret security police. He lived in two worlds: on the golf course he was equal to those against whom he played, while off of it he was a second-class citizen.

Papwa applied to compete in the SA Open in March 1961 (Nelson: 'We have to keep on challenging them, or accept that we can't change a thing'), and SAGU approached the government for authorisation. In terms of the Group Areas Act – one of the cornerstones of apartheid – different 'races' were required to live in separate areas.

Nevertheless, there was a senior advocate's legal opinion, a loophole in the law that was open to interpretation. So if for example, a golf tournament that permitted all races was held in a so-called white-only area, then 'non-whites' would be allowed to compete and spectators watch – with restrictions.

The next hurdle was to circumvent the Group Areas Act by securing a permit enabling Papwa to travel from Natal to East London, where the tournament was staged. On the eve of Dr Hendrick Verwoerd's departure to a Commonwealth Prime Ministers' Conference, where SA was to withdraw and set up a Republic – a permit was granted under the Group Areas Act signed by the Minister of the Interior, Jan de Klerk. Such permits were rarely granted, usually at the last minute, and always came with significant restrictions.

This loophole enabled Papwa to gain permission to play in a few white tournaments, starting with the 1961 SA Open, but in the convoluted logic of the day, he would be allowed to 'occupy' only the golf course, not any of the facilities, including the clubhouse, and the permit was just for the days of the tournament.

Permission to play would often arrive at the last moment. The fact that no practice round was allowed, was to become a feature of all future permits, such that he was always at a huge disadvantage as he would have to play the course 'blind', while other competitors had time to formulate their strategy.

The day before the tournament, Papwa slammed his hand in a door, gashing a finger. He was using the car as a change room and was treated by a doctor. That morning the hand was still throbbing and bandaged. He could only hope the hand would not affect his grip and swing, and he could play through the pain.

Barred from entering the clubhouse, he ate his vegetarian sandwiches caringly prepared by Suminthra, with a flask of tea and some painkillers while sitting in his car, but they did not do the trick. Meanwhile, the other competitors entered the clubhouse for their sit-down meal.

The press followed the event with great anticipation and recorded that history was being made as Papwa stepped up to the tee at 9:55 a.m. with Jinks Jones, a Cape Town amateur.

In his book *Gone to the Golf,* Ronald Norval wrote: 'Whether he

Chapter 5: Breakthrough

knew it or not when he stood on the first tee at East London in 1961, he was a trail-blazer for the non-European sportsmen and, illogical though it may be, all his colleagues' would be judged by his behaviour. How well I remember that East London tournament. Before he struck a ball there had been a tremendous hoo-ha about whether he would be allowed to play. There were solemn meetings of the South African Golf Union, lawyers' opinions were studied – some of them contradictory – and the matter was raised in Parliament.'

A few days before he played a rather bewildered Papwa told me with puzzlement in his voice: 'But sir, I didn't know I needed a permit to play golf'. For that was all the poor fellow wanted to do, and the political and social overtones passed clear over his head.

Papwa was nervous as he addressed the ball on the first tee. He especially didn't want anyone to notice his hands shaking, and just hoped he would be able to take the club back smoothly in one motion.

Journalists, photographers and spectators crowded around the first tee, all anxious to see the Indian maestro with his strange back-to-front grip and that rock-and-roll motion. He stood back, wiped his hands on his towel, took a deep breath, then settled again and launched his drive, pushing his tee shot slightly right of the fairway to the applause of the gallery.

That year another first-time winner came to the fore at East London, 22-year-old Retief Waltman (289). He won by eight shots from Free State amateur Barry Franklin (297), aged only 17 years, with Bobby Locke (298) a shot back in third place.

Papwa was given every support by the East London GC, its members and fellow competitors, but the tension of not knowing whether he could play or not until the last minute for every tournament affected Papwa's game and left him emotionally exhausted, taking the edge off his game.

Papwa failed to mount any challenge during the tournament. His hand was hurting, and he finished way down the field (76 77 75 79 (307)) in 16th place. He departed feeling disappointed that he had let down his army of fans, friends, and the caddies at Beachwood, but more important than his score was the fact that he was able to play at all. The political and social overtones passed clean over his head.

Papwa

Money was always a problem, and the Papwa Trust Fund did not have enough in the kitty to send Papwa back to Europe in 1961, so he was unable to defend his Dutch Open title.

By July there were murmurings concerning the Trust Fund's lack of accounts. Various businessmen had dug deep into their pockets to fund Papwa. Nelson replied with the documents as evidence, but contributors were not satisfied, and suspicion continued.

Papwa, of course, could not read, he could not check or verify any of the entries, nor could he follow the vigorous debate in the Indian press and became the victim of rumour mongering. This left a sour taste as the press galvanised public opinion without presenting Papwa's side.

One article reported the misgivings of the donors about the trust fund paperwork. Mention was also made of the failure of the fund to sponsor other non-white golfers, like Hlapo and Chowglay despite the fact that the fund was ear-marked purely for Papwa.

Meanwhile William Manie, an East London caddy, worked his passage to take part in the British Open at Birkdale, but alas, he too did not make the qualifying cut.

Sharpeville was a thing of the past, a 'mistake'. South Africa was now a republic, and the Commonwealth could no longer dictate policy to the nationalist government, and this included the Indian golfer and his horde of unruly Indian fans.

The Indian golf club at Currie's Fountain had been closed for a number of years and there was no golf course for those of colour other than the Southbroom lagoon which had become a makeshift golf course, with sticks positioned around the lagoon as holes.

Finally, the Springfield Golf Course was opened on 16 December 1961, by the Deputy-Mayor of Durban Jack Forsdick, this being the new 'home' course of the future Durban Golf Club.

At Springfield, the Durban Corporation agreed to level the land, turf and drain the grounds with the necessary amenities to be undertaken by the members, a gigantic task. Once again the course consisted of nine holes with no clubhouse facilities. Players and officials conducted their own affairs from their vehicles.

Chapter 5: Breakthrough

Papwa, Censer Skakarie, Fred 'FM' Paul and the legendary R.T. Singh (the most dominant player from around 1937 and still featuring in tournaments as late as 1961) were the very first four-ball to tee off on the new course. Later a temporary clubhouse was officially opened by Papwa on 30 August 1969.

Past President, Hassan Mall wrote in 1975: 'Given that the Durban City Council spent little or no resources on the Springfield Flats Golf Course, such that the course was maintained by members of the Durban Golf Club. Broken tractors, burst water mains, weeds, collapsing grass mowers and blunt green cutters were a few of the nightmares experienced, but the Club managed each week to turn out a golf course of pride.'

The year 1962 was a disappointing one as form started turning against Papwa as far as participation in tournaments in SA were concerned. Ismail Chowglay beat him to the national SA Non-European Open title with a score of 297 to secure the trophy and the winner's cheque, 2nd Percy Mazibuka, 3rd Johannes Semenya, 4th PL Paul, 'Cox' Hlapo and Ronnie Ditsebe, with Papwa languishing in 8th position.

He also lost the Durban Indian Golf Club championships, and then rediscovered a semblance of form by winning the insignificant Naidoo Brothers Trophy at the Springfield golf course, setting a new course record of 1-under.

At this stage there were many who thought Chowglay was the better golfer. A Kroonstad businessman together with the SA(N-E) GA funded Chowglay to play in the British Open, but he did not make the cut.

Insofar as white tournaments were concerned, limited chances to play restricted the family's income. The Natal Golf Union now sanctioned Papwa's entry for the Natal Open, but the government refused to allow him to play, citing that his application to play on the white Royal Durban Golf Course was received too late to put the necessary permissions in place.

Even the Transvaal Non-European Open was cancelled by the government as it was to be played on a white Irene golf course in Pretoria. Chowglay and others had already travelled there at great expense, but fortunately Papwa was yet to arrive when the government stopped the event. The Minister of Bantu Administration Michel de Wet Nel stated: "Participants would be insulted by being disallowed clubhouse facilities, furthermore it would lead to mixed sport between Coloured, Blacks and Indians registered to play."

Not even the support from the top ranks in the golfing world could persuade the authorities to allow Papwa to enter national tournaments, nevertheless his performances in the non-European competitions remained riveting.

After a long break due to a family tragedy following his youngest son's death after a short illness in November 1962, he won the Natal Non-European tournament for the fifth time smashing Harold Henning's course record with a five-under-par 67 which was recognised now that he was a member of the British PGA. It was a title he successfully defended the following year.

Out of the blue, Papwa received an offer to play in the famous televised series, 'The Shell Wonderful World of Golf', where he was to join 21 other leading players to compete for a winner's purse of $3000, with a guarantee of $1800 plus travel and living expenses. The letter was signed by J Edward Carter, the former director of the American PGA. This would be Papwa's chance to be exposed to millions of viewers, and where attempts would be made to get him onto the USA golfing circuit, the most lucrative in the world.

"This is perhaps the big break he's always been looking for", commented Nelson. With a population of 439 million, Papwa had become a hero to the masses in India, and there was much speculation as to how their new Indian hero would perform against the best in the world.

Months later after signing the contract, Louis informed him that the organisers had changed the structure and India had now been eliminated from the competition, such that his selection had now been cancelled. Gary Player nonetheless was featured playing against Peter Thompson in Australia.

Chapter 5: Breakthrough

Permission

The most important quality in a champion golfer is your mind, and the power to remain positive – Gary Player

In 1963 Natal Open with R2,000 in prize money staged at the Durban Country Club was the tournament that would put 'Papwa' on the map for various reasons. Like many other exclusive clubs around the country, it selected its members by race and religion, so, at various times, different ethnic groups, such as Afrikaners and Jews were excluded, and, of course, there were no people of colour.

The 'whites-only' club attracted some of the most affluent and successful businessmen and other personalities of the time, where they were served by Indian staff. Indian doormen would welcome them, Indian chauffeurs parked their cars, and Indian waiters served them food and drinks, even the caddies were Indians. But there were no Indian golf members.

Finally, in 1963, the SA government together with the Natal Golf Union and the local Durban Country Club executives buckled to international pressure, and a subsequent decision by Judge-President Sandy Milne on a similar matter, and eventually allowed Papwa (now 34) to compete in the 1963 Natal Open, having been satisfied that apartheid laws would not be broken, thereby making sporting history of one sort and political history of quite another.

A Hindu who lived with his large family in a corrugated steel shack, not a mile from the magnificent exclusive Durban Country Club built in the Cape Dutch Style, the site of the tournament he would compete in. This country club with its bowling greens, swimming pool, and tennis courts which admitted no members of colour, would now see two worlds colliding.

He would have to change in his car, nibbling sandwiches and sipping Thermos-flask tea prepared by Suminthra, because he wasn't allowed into the Country Club's changing rooms, and as he couldn't enjoy lunch in the clubhouse, he likewise could not order a beer at the bar.

Meanwhile white golfers ate food prepared and served, ironically by Indians, in the luxurious clubhouse. For his ablutions, he would join the caddies in their segregated facilities round the back. Same old shit, different day.

Now Suminthra took charge preparing him for the tournament by keeping him to a strict diet, preparing his food, carbohydrate-loading just before the event, and ensuring that he did his daily exercise and roadwork. During the tournament, after each round, she was the masseuse, rubbing in oils and creams into his tired muscles. The rest was up to Papwa, his ability to focus and concentrate, and let his clubs do the talking.

When Durban Country Club course was constructed by Laurie Waters[10] in the early 1920s, with a combination of lush vegetation, sand dunes, and a stunning view of the Indian Ocean, the art of architecture as we know it today had not seeped into the consciousness of golfers. His adventurous layout instinctively followed good basic principles such as very little interference with the lie of the land, and the player was not shown everything at a glance but was given a thrill of anticipation and uncertainty.

The holes fell into one of two categories: those that played in and

---

10   Inducted into the 2009 Southern Africa Golf Hall of Fame

Chapter 5: Breakthrough

out, and over the dunes, such as holes 1–5, 8–13, and 18, and those that were farther removed from the dunes and ocean. The remaining seven holes, 6, 7, 10 and 11, and 14–16 played across the flat land where the high to low point was less than seven foot. The dunes and holes were full of allure, given how distinctive the landforms were and how they were captured within the holes.

One could point, for example, to No. 18, only 253m, as being technically weak – too short for a four. But this hole had character and 'personality', a teasing hole with its own 'Valley of Sin' (like St. Andrews) off the front of the green, snaring either tee-shots or approach shots that were a shade too weak, sending them well back onto the fairway. While a tee-shot that faded down the left of the fairway took the left-to-right fairway slope, bounding past the depression at the front right and onto the green.

A great finishing hole of real risk-reward, where anything could happen, eagles or double-drops if the golfer decided to go for the green with his tee-shot, while the bushy vegetation masked the seaside road gave a feeling of isolation from the outside world. It had a spice of danger and was memorable – Sam Snead once asked, 'Where is the other half of the fairway?'

The right side favoured the tee-shot as the fairway sloped left to right towards the green if you have a go at the green with your drive. But for the over-cautious or fearful, flinching from the out-of-bounds, and blocked too far left, left the player unsighted from a hanging lie, and the hollow in front of the green backed by a massive dune.

In the field were the South African big-boys, Bobby Verwey (playing on the US PGA tour), Bobby Locke (previously banned from the US PGA tour for being 'too good'), Cobie le Grange (just prior to beating Jack Nicklaus), Denis Hutchinson (previous SA Open champion), and Harold Henning (playing on the US PGA tour) the favourite.

It was a four-round event of 18-holes a day, with the last 36-holes being played on Saturday (Sunday was the religious day of rest – no sport or entertainment).

Let's have a look at their playing records:

Harold 'The Horse' Henning (wins 50)
- Inducted Southern Africa Golf Hall of Fame 2009
- ☐ S.A. Open 1957, 62.
- ☐ Canada (World) Cup 1965 (playing with Gary Player).

Bobby Verwey (wins 25)
- Inducted Southern Africa Golf Hall of Fame 2019
- ☐ PGA Tour wins (1), 43 top 10's
- ☐ South African circuit (5)
- ☐ Other victories (13) including the 1962 German Open
- ☐ European Senior Tour wins (6) including the Senior British Open.

Arthur D'arcy 'Bobby' Locke (wins 74).
- World Ranking 1 (1949 unofficial).
- 'The greatest putter ever'.
- Inducted World Golf Hall of Fame 1977
- Inducted Southern Africa Golf Hall of Fame 2009
- 1949 – 1952 PGA Tour: Banned for being too good
- ☐ Major wins (4), 2nd or 3rd (4)
- ☐ PGA Tour wins (15)
- ☐ South African circuit (40) including SA Opens (9)
- ☐ Other wins (19)

Cobie le Grange (wins (16)
- World Ranking 15
- Inducted Southern Africa Golf Hall of Fame 2011
- ☐ European circuit (5) including British Masters 1964, 69
- ☐ Australian circuit (3) includes beating Jack Nicklaus head-to-head in the Australian Masters
- ☐ Sunshine Tour (8)

Denis Hutchinson (wins 15)
- Inducted Southern Africa Golf Hall of Fame 2009

Chapter 5: Breakthrough

- Sunshine Tour (5) including 1959 SA Open, SA Masters (3), SA PGA
- Other (10) including French Open

Others included

- Hugh Inggs (wins 2)
- Bruce Keyter (wins 3)
- Terry Westbrook (wins 5)
- Barry Franklin (German Open 1968, 67 2nd, SA Open 1961 2nd)

Harold Henning opened with 68 at the end of the first round. Henning seemed to have a liking for the Durban Country Club, particularly in damp conditions. Two years previously, he had won the Natal Open in a play-off against Alan Brookes after a devastating last round in the pouring rain.

It was not raining but the course was still saturated, and the greens slow after 36 hours of continuous rain. Hugh Inggs also joined him on 68 which included four 3s, while his card showed seven birdies (3rd, 6th, 7th, 8th, 10th, 16th, 18th) and two dropped shots, as they took the lead.

They were three strokes ahead of Mike Finney and Phil Ritson, close behind in third place were Denis Hutchinson and Springbok amateurs, Barry Franklin and Murray Grindrod.

Sewgolum was on even par-73, a modest start in eighth position, together with defending champion Stewart Davies, Cobie le Grange, Terry Westbrook, Peter Leighton, and Taff Evans (the Natal Amateur), then followed Retief Waltman, Cedric Amm and Bobby Locke[11] (who was applying a sticky ointment to his hands to help his grip as he played without a glove).

Papwa was just a little unlucky in the round, but he took it all on the chin and remained quite unperturbed outwardly. He had, however, made up his mind that no one would ever see him play like that again during the tournament. He was happy to still be in the running in spite of everything.

---

11 In 1958 Locke had virtually lost the sight of his one eye in a horrific train accident.

1963 Natal Open – Papwa was very popular with the Indian community and everyone came out in droves to watch him

Source: Peter Sauerman

Eagles were on the cards at the signature 468m par-5 third hole, rated the third-best hole in the world. An elevated tee gave the golfer an extended carry from the tee and a windless day brought the green in reach in two. However, the fairway took on the appearance of a narrow ribbon winding its way past thick vegetation along the entire length on both sides, and a well-placed bunker on the left-hand side cut into the dunes, made it tricky but reachable making it one of most popular holes on the course.

Papwa had one of the biggest galleries of the day made up mostly of Indian caddies as well as those that didn't even know golf, and he did not disappoint. In charge of both his golf and the crowd – He rebuked them sternly if their whispered chatter interrupted his concentration – he played solid golf to gain birdies at the possible eagle 3rd hole, the 12th, and 18th, but short putted the 4th, 11th and 17th to lose the advantage.

His best shot and the one that drew most applause was at the 18th green, a 45-yard nine-iron chip that landed 15cm short of an eagle 2.

After opening with a lacklustre 73, he 'bared his teeth' in the second round with a brilliant 70, which saw Papwa tied with Barry Franklin, just a shot behind the leader Cobie le Grange. His best shot

Chapter 5: Breakthrough

was on the long 8th where he slammed a wood off the fairway to only 8-foot from the pin and then sank the putt.

Papwa played golf as if in a complete world of his own. Nothing ruffled him. He could play in the wind and believed everything followed the sun. Putting with a bent shafted putter (like Tommy Bolt), he brushed the grass with his putter to see which way it lay. In the morning he putted lighter, and in the afternoon he putted harder. He said the grass followed the sun.

On Saturday, the last day, the car park, with dilapidated cars and even some horse-drawn carts, was bursting at the seams. Papwa, the crowd favourite, was paired with Cobie le Grange. Wind and rain was interspersed with fine weather. It was one of the most extraordinary scenes in SA sport.

After the third round, he still shared second place with Bruce Keyter, both 217, Hugh Inggs (68) having taken the lead. The leaders after the third round: Hugh Inggs 215, followed by Papwa, and Bruce Keyter 217, next came Denis Hutchinson 218 and Cobie Le Grange on 219.

Papwa went into the last round in the driving rain that fell in the late afternoon, two strokes behind Hugh Inggs after a morning round of 74, one-over par, and when all those in with a chance crashed about him over the 18, he dealt with the conditions much better than his nearest rivals, playing steady golf.

'We were wet, our grips were wet, and we could hardly stand up, but he played like there were no problems,' said Cobie le Grange, and his grips were leather, and when wet could easily slide out of his grasp.

Such was his gallery that the only way individuals got a chance of seeing him was by putting their heads down and rushing from one vantage point to another.

There were dropped shots at the 2nd and 4th, both short holes. His clubs seemed to be a natural extension of him, swinging smoothly, and the ball obeying his instructions, another at the 14th. Miracle shot at 15th!

Papwa

Cobie le Grange

Papwa, drenched by rain, was forced to eat in his car because only whites were allowed into the Durban Country Club.

Once again, as in the earlier rounds, it was his immaculate work around the greens that set the seal on a grand victory. His chipping was near perfection, and few in the gallery of over a thousand Indians and Europeans would forget his masterful chip at the short 15th, only 177m, but playing a little longer than expected.

This shot could well have won him the tournament for the bush telegraph tom-tommed news informing him that he had to par the next four holes to beat Bobby Verwey who was already in the clubhouse.

Verwey's performance was magnificent, but it was only an excuse for Papwa to produce a further display of his brilliance allowing him to prove once again that he had control over every club in the bag and his own temperament. He knew what he must do and proceeded to do it, and this showed once again why his Indian army of supporters believed that there was some old black African magic in his swing.

His tee-shot drifted to the right of the green and landed in a water-filled bunker. Taking a free drop out of the bunker, the ball settled on to one of the dew patches, as smiling, he asked for his sandwedge and

Chapter 5: Breakthrough

proceeded to explode with water spraying into the air while imparting a reverse spin on the ball.

Today it is normal to see backspin like that, but in those days with those golf balls, it was unusual. The ball pitched about five foot past the pin, stopped momentarily, and then to almost everyone's amazement spun back as though bewitched, finishing eight inches from the hole, and giving him a most-needed par-3 at a time when he had dropped three shots and reports had filtered back that he needed a final round of 76 to win. It was such a romance!

In his final two rounds, Papwa made only two birdies; that was in the morning when he got a three at the 338m 7th, and at the 453m 14th. For the rest he played 29 holes in regulation figures, dropping shots at only five holes. It was remarkable golf under any circumstances, and more so considering the wind and driving rain in the late afternoon as he took control of the elements as if it was a clear day filled with sunshine.

And while Papwa was working towards a possible victory, there was high drama among the remaining professionals who, in their own words, did not play good enough golf to win.

Hugh Inggs was one player who twice had the tournament in his grip. He had two rounds of 68, in the first and third rounds, and sandwiched in between them was a 79 and an 80, the same as Bruce Keyter. The tall, handsome Harold Henning found the touch that had deserted him for so many months when he opened with a 68, but then blew up with a 78.

Then Bobby Verwey almost stole the title from under the noses of the leaders as he posted a brilliant 70 that included six birdies including the 5th, 8th, 13th, 14th, and 18th.

Cobie le Grange started 73 69, and as the overnight leader, he was drawn with Papwa over the final 36 holes but found the tension just that too much for him as he blew out with 77 78 to finish on 297.

Papwa needed level par on the last three holes to win the tournament. He duly parred the 16th and the 17th, then strode confidently to the last hole.

Watched by a surging legion of Indian supporters shocking the conservative white bastion Country Club members, and with squalls of tropical rain passing through, Papwa kept his game on track as he now arrived at the par-4 18th tee. He needed just a par to beat Bobby Verwey (Gary Player's brother-in-law following Gary's marriage to his champion golfer sister Vivienne) and Denis Hutchinson.

The 18th has the Indian Ocean to the left, and a deep steep bank to the right leading to the practice tee. Marshalls struggled to hold the gallery at bay as many wanted to touch Papwa to inspire him. Excited, Papwa could feel the adrenalin as he focused his mind.

He nailed a solid drive, but it caught the breeze, veering right, tumbling down the bank towards the rough and ended up deep on the right-hand side, below the fairway green. Had disaster struck just as he was going to make history as the first man of colour to win a 'white' tournament in South Africa?

Down the steep slope, Papwa could not see the flag. Back up the bank he strode and took a fix on the east side of the clubhouse. His eyes surveyed his bag of clubs, then spoke softly to his caddy, he drew out his club, opening the club face, a practice swing, then he addressed the ball, and without hesitation planted the clubface into the ground with a thud, connecting crisply with a full pitching wedge, dislodging the turf, as the ball rose to land on the edge of the plateau green. The crowd gave him no chance to see where the ball had finished.

Two putts to win! His first putt, delightfully struck, narrowly missed the hole, and he tapped in the winner for par, a one-shot victory, and the purse of R800 ($1,120).

Pandemonium broke out as ecstatic followers swarmed cheering across the green and chaired blue-jerseyed Papwa shoulder high away from the pin – becoming the first person of colour to win a professional golf tournament in South Africa, a new icon for any person of colour in this land of apartheid. Every caddy, waiter and labourer in Durban stood a little taller that day.

Although there were complaints from some competitors that his gallery was unruly, Cobie le Grange was more objective and said that he thought the crowd was particularly well-behaved.

History was thus made at Durban Country Club when, with scores of 73 70 74 76 (293), Papwa finished one shot ahead of Denis Hutchinson and Bobby Verwey. Playing the game with his characteristic serenity and a strange upside-down grip, the man they called 'Papwa',

Chapter 5: Breakthrough

had overcome some of the best SA professionals of the day to win the tournament, and in so doing became the first person of colour to win a professional golf championship previously set apart only for Europeans in SA (the 1937 caddy victory by Nathan/Sewpersadh over British professionals Padgham/Dailey 2/1 was not a championship).

It was an astonishing victory, which made not only golfing history but sporting history. To the large Indian community in Durban and to observers around the world, Papwa was a revelation, a homespun hero, a dark-skinned 'David' in a world of white golfing 'Goliaths.'

That Papwa deserved his victory cannot be denied. He played well with every club, but as ever, his chipping was again his strongest point, and it may be that his 'reverse' grip had something to do with his success in this department. That left-hand-under-the-right on the grip kept the club on the line long after impact compared to the normal grip.

Papwa had done the seemingly impossible; he had beaten 103 white golfers including the favourite Harold Henning, as well as Hutchinson, Le Grange, Locke, and Verwey, and won the 'white' open tournament.

Firestorm

But with Papwa's first local victory came the first backlash in what was to be a series of injustices that would tarnish his short-lived career.

A closing ceremony that turned into an internationally publicised event caused Papwa to be thrown into the limelight in a very harsh and degrading manner.

The event gained notoriety and is perhaps most often remembered **as the championship where Papwa was presented with the trophy on the 18th green in the rain, with the other white golfers looking on from inside the clubhouse.**

The legend of the ensuing prize-giving has been handed down through the decades like folklore. Papwa, surrounded by hordes of Indian supporters who were clamouring to touch him and shake his hand, made his way back to the car park where he changed in his manager's car and combed his hair.

What followed went down as one of the most shameful incidents in South Africa's sporting history. As the rain swept across the course, the

Papwa

laws of the land kicked in, and the white competitors, their supporters, and club members made their way to the clubhouse. The planned outdoor ceremonies would have to be moved inside, into the clubhouse.

Papwa remained waiting outside the clubhouse because he was a man 'of colour' and, therefore, under apartheid laws, prohibited from entering the building for fear of the club losing its liquor license. And it was raining!

And so it was, in a game of fair play and integrity, Papwa was barred from attending his own prize-giving. Instead, drenched in a downpour, he was quickly presented with the trophy beside the 18th green. The evening was lit up by smiling Indian faces, by photographers' flashbulbs as he held the trophy aloft, and as if in benediction, by forks of lightning in the sky that highlighted that moment – the rain, sweat, and tears on his face as he received his trophy and a cheque for R800 under an umbrella.

'There is no time for a formal speech, but I would like on behalf of all of us congratulate the 1963 Natal Open Champion, Papwa Sewsunker Sewgolum.'

A fierce wind suddenly blew and the sky blackened ... then came the rain in pounding tropical torrents.'

Then as the whites sought refuge in comfort inside the clubhouse, where the celebrations got underway with Indian waiters serving them, the remainder of the prizes were presented half-an-hour later in the lounge, while Papwa and his fans made their way home.

It was not the choice of either the Durban Country Club or the Natal Golf Union that this differentiation was made. Just because there was a risk that under the Group Areas Act it was possible that if Papwa had gone into the clubhouse he might have been guilty of a crime under this act.

Pictures of Papwa standing in the pelting rain being handed his trophy were published across an outraged world and gave impetus to the international movement to boycott apartheid sport.

Chapter 5: Breakthrough

27 January 1963: Natal Open, Durban Country Club, Papwa finishing the 72nd hole in the rain. Photo courtesy of LLA

27 January 1963: Durban Country Club, Papwa Sewgolum receives his R800 Natal Open cheque and the winner's trophy as it starts to rain from Mr. RA Bell (Gilbey's). Behind the microphone is Louis du Plessis, President of the Natal GU, and on the far right Felix Fielding, chairman of the Durban CC. Picture courtesy of LLA.

Papwa

Whatever the truth of the conflicting details of the prize-giving, the incident was just one of countless apartheid assaults Papwa endured. But as a potent symbol of exclusion, it turned into a firestorm, starting with press commentary at home and abroad.

'In any normal land the treatment of this fine player would be considered an insult to him and an acute embarrassment to everyone else,' said the defiant *Rand Daily Mail* the day after the event.

'Papwa wins the Natal Open', and the 'GLORY and the SHAME' screamed the POST newspaper headline, and none of the players spoke out!

The local and international media devoured the story. Images of the prize-giving were flashed around the world and played a significant role in cementing the sporting boycott against SA.

The headline of *The Daily News:* 'South Africa is a land of perpetual mid-summer ideology madness'. And the London's *Daily Mirror* smirked: 'Here's a story to warm the cockles of your heart – that is if you are bigoted, prejudiced and vicious racialist'. While the SA state broadcaster, the South African Broadcasting Corporation's (SABC) planned airing of the tournament was suddenly cancelled for the final round at the last minute, and they failed to announce the result.

The SABC said no coverage was given to the Natal Open (during the final round) because 'We do not broadcast multiracial sport. We have separate programmes for Bantu, Indians and Coloureds in which we cater for the broadcasting of sporting events of the various race groups. On the English and Afrikaans service coverage is given to sport in which whites compete.' An official confirmed that results of the Natal Open were not included in the Monday morning national news bulletins.

Reg Taylor (SA's all-time leading amateur) praised Papwa's victory insofar as it would keep SA golf free of the expected onslaught from the outside world when golfers plied their trade overseas. Prophetic words for the future boycotts and demonstrations yet to be unleashed on SA white sportsmen competing abroad.

Allan Henning, who won the 1963 SA Open, and who played against Papwa on many occasions stated; 'it was an absolute crime,

Chapter 5: Breakthrough

I could cry about it.' Henning went on to say: 'This guy was a phenomenon and he had a massive support base. When he played in Durban, the place would swarm with his supporters. It was an unbelievable experience.'

The incident further highlighted Papwa's potential and, at the same time, marked a new low point in the failed experiment of racial segregation. The issue was addressed in parliament when Helen Suzman, the lone parliamentary representative of the opposition Progressive Party noted: 'Papwa receiving his trophy in the rain will do more to establish our true image abroad than all the glossy sunny SA pamphlets issued by the State Information sports department.'

The Minister of the Interior, Frank 'Bunty' Waring, conceded that the incident had caused the country considerable harm, but blamed the opposition parties and the media for fueling the flames. The question now was could they turn down his request to play in the SA Open?

Minister of community development PW Botha (the future President of South Africa) claimed later that Papwa did not have permission to compete. "No permit was issued to him authorising him to take part in the tournament, and the question of what steps should be taken is under consideration."

Of course it was alright for an Indian to caddy for a white golfer – that wouldn't destroy the *volk*. But Papwa cannot play golf with whites because 'mixed-sport' was *verboten*.

Papwa's low-key response to the saga was: 'There would have been no fuss if it hadn't rained'. He remained silent about the snub – and about all the indignities to which he was subjected. He did, however, reveal that he only practiced once or twice a week, whereas other golfers playing at this level practiced for four or five hours a day.

'I've read so many stories about what happened, and nobody's ever got it right,' says Bobby Verwey, who finished tied second. 'Papwa was a friend of mine, the loveliest guy you'd ever know. In those days they gave out prizes to the top-five finishers. And the five of us got together and decided to have the prize-giving outside because Papwa wasn't allowed inside. It wasn't just Papwa – we all got our prizes outside. There was no prize-giving inside. And it was barely even raining. I don't think we even had an umbrella.'

However, in the photo below, it would appear that Bobby Verwey received his prize indoors, and probably in the lounge as not only is there a woman in attendance, but she is seated, and there is a bottle of beer on the table. Further, Colonel D.W. Geddie is now presenting the prize as stated in the newspaper caption, whilst Papwa received his prize from Mr R.A. Bell.

Colonel D. W. Geddie, secretary, Natal Golf Union, presenting Bobby Verwey with his prize as joint runner-up in the Natal Open.

E.S. Reddy, a former director of the UN Centre Against Apartheid, wrote in 1998: 'The photograph of 'Papwa' receiving his trophy in heavy rain outside appeared in many newspapers around the world and greatly helped the boycott of apartheid sport.'

Although he was non-political, Papwa had unintentionally become the figurehead of the anti-apartheid sport movement, and a symbol of liberation to an increasingly beleaguered people.

The government, already under scrutiny, received even more criticism, and this gave impetus to the international movement to boycott apartheid sport as a number of countries reacted by imposing sports sanctions on South Africa.

Images of him being presented with the Natal Open trophy under leaden skies were flashed around the world, serving notice that something had to be done to address the scourge of apartheid, and International action against apartheid sport began in earnest.

A Committee for International Recognition was formed by non-racial sportsmen in 1955, and was succeeded by the South African Sports Association (SASA) in 1958, and the South African Non-Racial Olympic Committee (SAN-ROC) in 1963 – to fight against racism in sport and press for international recognition of the non-racial sports bodies in South Africa. Their leadership was largely from the Indian and Coloured communities as Africans were not participating in many of the codes of sport with international affiliations.

Since SAN-ROC was prevented from sending representatives abroad, the British Anti-Apartheid Movement sent appeals to Olympic Committees and other national sports bodies to exclude apartheid sport from international competition. Abdul Samad Minty, honorary secretary of the movement, lobbied delegates at the meeting of the International Olympic Committee in Baden in October 1963 on behalf of SAN-ROC.

The IOC adopted a proposal by the Indian government led by Jawaharial Nehru[12] which led to the exclusion of South Africa from the Tokyo Olympics in 1964. It was formally expelled from the IOC in 1970.

Clearly, Papwa was now a catalyst for the movement that brought about bannings from international sport.

Although he did not participate in this Natal Open, Gary Player's career was from here on intertwined with that of Papwa Sewgolum, now a worldwide symbol of the country's hated race laws.

Apartheid thorn

The response of the authorities was repression against the non-racial sports movement.

The Afrikaans daily *Die Burger* was critical of what was termed 'petty apartheid', and said that it was better handled with common sense. Although the government was against mixed sport, it did not want incidents such as the prize-giving in the rain to happen, as they could be (and were) strongly exploited by its opponents.

---

12 India's first Prime Minister

Papwa

Papwa put the government in a spot. The administration was in a dilemma over the Indian golfer. It didn't want him to play in multiracial golf tournaments – but he was apparently not committing an offence by doing so.

Nor was the government keen to introduce legislation to stop him from doing so. This would shatter the international image it had been cultivating of trying to create, an image of being flexible and reasonable. 'The situation was plain crazy.'

Meanwhile, the general feeling was that nothing was more calculated to bring SA's name into disrepute among influential circles overseas than the Papwa incident. Golf had become the aristocrat of games played by men of high positions all over the world – men like Britain's Premier Harold Macmillan and American President General Dwight Eisenhower.

To these people, it would bring home the meanness of apartheid more than anything else. It would make a particularly bad impression in the USA, where golf was a game played by the influential and the rich.

Clearly with continued practice over good courses, a player like Papwa was bound for the top places. Already streets in Chatswood were named after him, as was an open space called the 'Papwa Green.'

Shortly after his win in the Natal Open, Papwa solidified his growing reputation when he was given permission to play in the SA Open at the very last minute. The tournament was the next day, and around midnight Nelson got a call to say Papwa could play the following day as the permit had just been issued. The entry of another non-european player, William Manie who had played in the British Open Championships, was refused.

This was to motivate William Manie to emigrate, and he became the assistant professional at the Royal Winchester GC, and later the club professional at Richmond (UK).

In the light of the statement made by the Minister of the Interior that, if the SAGU accepted Papwa's entry, the government would consider legislation to prevent racial mixing on the sportsfield, and they requested that the SAGU reconsider the conditions of entry for future championships.

Chapter 5: Breakthrough

The SA Open Championship is one of the oldest national open golf championships in the world. In 1903, the first formal event was contested following a series of exhibition matches held over the preceding ten years. The championship was initially contested over just 36 holes until 1908 when it was extended to become a 72-hole tournament.

In the field was the new potential superstar, Afrikaner Retief Waltman. Waltman started his career as an assistant professional at the Pretoria Country Club. He showed promise as a teenager and, at the age of 18, he beat Bobby Locke in the first round of the 1957 South African Professional Match-Play Championship.

His victory was referred to as "one of the greatest surprises in South African golf for several years". Waltman was an unknown teenager and Locke was considered one of the best golfers in the world who would go on to win his fourth British Open four months later.

Waltman won his first big tournament, the 1961 South African Open, by an extraordinary eight shots.

The Indian gallery had only one Indian to represent them, and despite not being allowed to play any practice rounds, Papwa took the lead after the first round, opening with a 70, one-shot ahead of Bruce Keyter and George Farmer, followed by Harold Henning and Stewart Davies a further shot back, with Locke and Hutchinson not far behind.

After round two, and a 71, Papwa was still leading on 141 followed by Farmer a shot back. Three-shots behind on 144 followed Keyter, with Retief Waltman lurking a further shot back.

Round three, and moving day, saw Waltman shoot a magnificent 67 climbing the leaderboard to share first place with Papwa who shot another 71 – 'Papwa dipped his knees and chipped the ball into the hole at the 18th' – both on 212. They were leading from a group of players, Keyter, Farmer, and John Hayes the amateur (Dale's brother) who shot an excellent 69, all on 216. Denis Hutchinson also shot a wonderful 68, but he was too far back.

Papwa was aiming to become the first person of colour to win the SA Open Championship as he and Retief Waltman battled it out all the way playing together in the final round.

Papwa

By the 14th, many people were running to get to the next tee-box after Papwa had putted out, and Waltman had to request that they halt to allow him to putt out. Papwa needed a 5m putt on the last green to tie. It just slid by the hole, and he was eventually beaten by a single shot, 70 71 71 70 (282), to Waltman's 74 71 67 69 (281), but it could not dim the brilliance of his fighting display. Papwa was the only player to score under par in all four rounds.

Once again, however, the photograph that circled the globe was not of Papwa driving, putting, or even of his obscure grip – it showed him having his lunch in the car with a friend.

Retief was 24, Papwa now 34, a new generation of youngsters were now coming through, yet Papwa had only been allowed to play his first 'white' tournament in SA three years earlier, aged 32, and then only sporadically.

Retief Waltman

Source: Rajen Sewgolum

The leading scores were

R Waltman   74 71 67 69 – 281
S Sewgolum   70 71 71 70 – 282
S Davies   72 75 70 70 – 287

Chapter 5: Breakthrough

J Fourie *	78 73 70 67	– 288 (Freddie Tait Cup)
B Keyter	71 73 72 73	– 289
G A Farmer	71 71 74 75	– 291
D Hutchinson	75 76 68 73	– 292
A D Locke	76 71 74 72	– 293
P Oosthuizen	76 74 72 73	– 295
H R Henning	72 75 74 74	– 295
J Hayes *	73 74 69 79	– 295

Papwa's second-place finish to the brilliant Retief Waltman by one-shot needs to be put into perspective.

From humble beginnings, growing up as an awkard shy crew-cut boy from an unhappy home with a deep hurt in my sou, to become a champion in one of the most difficult professional sports.

By now, Waltman had won the SA Open twice and six professional events in all, which also included the 1963 Dutch Open, whilst he had represented South Africa twice in the Canada Cup (together with Gary Player).

The whole world lay before him. He was a potential 'superstar'. Consider that Bobby Locke and Gary Player won the SA Open ten times between them from 1950–1969, and at the age of 24, Waltman had already won twice in that era.

At this time, Retief Waltman was the brilliant young heir apparent to Gary Player, for which he believed in his own case, he received 'divine help and guidance'. For him the meaning of life lay in the Bible and not birdies.

In 1964, Waltman narrowly missed the cut at his first Masters (won by Arnold Palmer) after rounds of 72 and 78. And that, he decided, was enough. "I wanted a purpose for my life. I was devoting my whole life to a game. Being so involved in golf limited me. Man is his own biggest enemy."

Longhurst wrote of Waltman: "The whole world lay before him. Perhaps if he had not been so good and so dedicated he would have settled down happily as a club professional in his native land. Ambition, however, took him further afield and drew him into the rat-race of tournament golf. Gradually the sheer materialism of this form of life and the unceasing emphasis on money began to sicken him, as it must have done so many before him. The difference was that he did not threaten to give it up. He just gave it up."

Consequently, shortly thereafter, aged just 25, Retief Waltman walked away from golf at the top of his career in 1964. He simply packed up his bags, gave his clubs away, said goodbye to the circus, and walked out on the game, found 'God' and engaged in missionary work retreating from the world of news and celebrity, and occasionally holding church services for black golfers prior to their events. It is a job he has nearly given his life to on more than one occasion having survived three knife attacks during the course of his missionary work.

In a recent interview with Mark Reason he stated: "Ben Hogan was my hero. He was the greatest. I played with him in the Dallas Open. He shot 67, I shot 72." Waltman isn't certain what he shot, but he has no problem recollecting his score the day that he played with Hogan. Waltman's own hero was and still is Ben Hogan. He even wore a flat white cap in tribute to the great man although Waltman says that it also kept the sun off his ears.

Chapter 5: Breakthrough

Retief Waltman found his God and it turned out not to be Ben Hogan. He gave away his clubs to Dave Thomas and his life to others. The question is, and I ask it in no flippant sense, who will die the happier man – Retief Waltman or Tiger Woods?

At the Masters of 1964, Waltman was billeted in the same house as Henry Longhurst and many years later he inquired if Longhurst was still alive. He was saddened to discover that Longhurst had, in fact, died in 1992, a mark of how far Waltman's missionary work had taken him from the world of news and celebrity.

And somewhere in South Africa, Retief Waltman is thinking of publishing a book about his strange and wonderful story, immune from all the fuss and folly of the outside world.

Waltman says: 'I have no regrets about the decision I took. To live is Christ. To die is gain. That is grace alone.' Henry Longhurst would have nodded at those words, wished Waltman well and padded off for a beaker of something soothing.

He was a hero at home. A good five years after Waltman had handed in his golf shoes, a boy from Pietersburg was named in his honour. The young Goosen was christened Retief.

So a single stroke decided the title and with that Papwa's chance to play in the 1964 US Masters. It also thwarted his hopes of playing in the prestigious Carling World Cup tournament in Detroit.

Initially after winning the Natal Open, Papwa had been advised by the SAPGA that he would be the first alternative if one of those chosen to represent the country – Trevor Wilkes, Bobby Verwey and Cedric Amm – in the Carling tournament dropped out for some reason. However after Allan Henning won the 1964 South African Open in Bloemfontein, actually played in December of 1963, he replaced Trevor Wilkes in the team, and Wilkes became the first alternative with Papwa now relegated to second alternative.

Unconfirmed media reports cited that the organisers were unhappy with the selection process. It said the organisers had instructed the SAPGA to select players based on the results of the 1963 Natal Open and the first SA Open that year, and the media and public was left discussing this in the press.

Meanwhile, Papwa took back his title when he won the 1963 SA Non-European Championship coming from a shot behind after two rounds, to win going away by 13 strokes at Walmer CC over the defending champion, Ismail Chowglay.

Papwa's one consolation was that the Papwa Trust Fund had enough money to send him overseas on his European tour, but only after Papwa had played numerous exhibition matches around Durban, while his friends went door-to-door to collect money from his supporters in Riverside and other Indian communities. Even the school-children helped with their pennies.

"You are an inspiration to children," commented Nelson, "they look up to you and dream that one day they too can compete internationally against the whites. Don't forget that."

Papwa making his speech in the Feather Market Hall, Port Elizabeth, after his victory at Walmer C.C. for the 1963 S.A. Non-European Championship. On the left is Louis Nelson and on the right Des Durow, area manager, Gordon's Gin Co., who sponsored the championship.

Chapter 5: Breakthrough

This time only a small crowd of family and his caddy friends saw him off. His popularity was clearly waning, and as usual two men from the security branch with short shaven hair watched from the edges of the gathering.

Now a seasoned traveller, he finally returned to Europe where he had become friends with the other South Africans playing there. On this occasion his trip met with mixed success.

Further validation of Papwa's golfing prowess came when he finished 13th in the British Open played at Royal Lytham & St. Anne's Golf Club in England, won by Bob Charles (the most successful left-handed golfer that century) with a score of 277 (-7) in a playoff with Phil Rodgers, with Jack Nicklaus a stroke behind.

In coming 13th Papwa beat Arnold Palmer, one of the big three and the defending champion, with his Arnie Army of supporters. Among the many South African golfers at the event (including Harold Henning, Bobby Locke, Denis Hutchinson, and Brian Wilkes), Gary Player was the only one to score better than Sewgolum, beating him by three shots.

With respect to this, golf writer Herbert Warren Wind wrote; "I have an idea that it will be only a matter of time now before a major title falls to the world's greatest cross-handed golfer Sewsunker Sewgolum."

That year's Dutch Open played at The Hague was won by Retief Waltman, now the new darling of white South African golf, on 279. Papwa disappointed the Dutch crowd, who had come to watch their 2-time winner after his ignominious prize giving at the Natal Open had reached their ears, as he finished down the field on 289.

Next came the German Open where Papwa overslept (Louis was supposed to have woken him) and was disqualified for being late on the tee. In truth, he was not well and only too happy to return home.

After two months he returned with only R300, most of which was for his placing in the British Open. Of this R50 was spent on medical treatment, and the trip cost R2,000. He was met at the airport by a large crowd, but they were not there to see him, rather his manager, trade union leader, Nelson, who was also returning from successful meetings at the International Labour Organisation.

Papwa

Later in that year, the decision was taken to dissolve the 'Papwa Trust Fund' – it had served its purpose. The remaining R1,000 was allocated to Papwa to buy a new family home.

However, from a management point of view, Louis Nelson had failed Papwa.

A manager is supposed to source sponsorships and place a management team around his man to allow him to concentrate on his golf, and not only apply to participate in tournaments and travel arrangements (it appears as if that was all he did). All Papwa had to show as far as sponsorship was concerned were golf balls from Dunlop and a set of clubs every five years.

At the same time, Nelson should have either invested some of Papwa's winnings, or at least mentored and instructed Papwa on how to do these things.

With some money in the kitty, Papwa would continue to generously spend the majority of his winnings on his friends and liquor, bringing home only a minor portion.

By this time Nelson was becoming politically vocal and tried unsuccessfully to also persuade Papwa to speak out against the apartheid regime, which he would not do, which irked Nelson.

But it was Papwa's living and Papwa's neck, not Nelson's, which would be on the line. It was obvious that Nelson was too busy to manage Papwa's affairs. And so it was that Louis Nelson, now also the President of the Durban Golf Club, jumped ship, opting for a higher leadership role in the labour movement.

It was now time for the modest Fred Paul (or FM as he liked to be called) with his trademark moustache, to step forward in Nelson's old role. Although 'FM' had no previous managerial experience he was – Bhai (brother) to Suminthra and Matie (a corruption of the Afrikaans word maat) to Papwa.

At least Paul had a car and could drive, which was not yet on Papwa's resume, although they were followed by the security police wherever they went.

It took Paul a while to get used to Papwa's style of preparation for a day of competitive golf – it usually involved an evening of partying, for no sooner did Papwa arrive at his host's home, than a

Chapter 5: Breakthrough

crowd invited them to a party back in the city. Despite Paul counseling otherwise, Papwa was keen and the locals insisted. Surprisingly he would somehow perform the next day and sometimes set course records. But when Paul took it on himself to lock Papwa inside, he ended up posting a horrid score.

While there was always the veiled threat that Papwa's participation in open competition was contrary to government policy, nevertheless permits to play were mostly granted and the summer of 1963/64 was a busy one for Papwa.

A series of three Grand Prix sponsored tournaments were schedule to be held in Durban, Cape Town and, finally, Johannesburg. Papwa played in all three, and in November 1963, he won the prestigious Richelieu Grand Prix Series 1 at Royal Durban CC with scores of 71 72 73 70 (286). Once again, he received his trophy in the rain outside the clubhouse, but this time, runner-up Gary Player also received his outside.

Papwa was proving to be a thorn in the side of the National Party and the invincibility of white sportsmen, but they still had their white champion in the second event of the Richelieu Grand Prix Series. Papwa was runner-up to Gary Player, at King David Country Club, Cape Town.

He had opened with a 72, which placed him two strokes behind Player, and he had the second largest mixed-race gallery of 2,000 following him. They drew reverberating applause when he recovered from behind a tree for a par-4 at the 17th after his drive, instead of drawing over the mound, continued straight down the left side of the fairway into the rough. His curious upside-down grip continued to fascinate the gallery, and his courtly manners made an excellent impression.

He finished 12th in the third leg at Kensington GC, and tied for 8th place on 289 in the 'Open 5000' sponsored tournament held at the same venue.

At the end of 1963 the political correspondent of Dagbreek – the National Party's Sunday mouthpiece – indicated that the government was tiring of Golf Unions allowing Papwa to play in their tournaments and that the time had come for legislation.

A few days later he was told that his application to play in the 1964 SA Open, along with that of Ismail Chowglay (now 31 and playing in his first SA 'white' tournament), had been accepted, but no practicing, and only for the four-day duration of the tournament, this time in Bloemfontein in the OFS, where Indians had been barred since the 1890s (it would take until 1972 before an African was allowed to play).

Participants included Gary Player, Bobby Locke, Cobie le Grange, Retief Waltman, and Harold Henning, but let's have a look at some additional competitors' playing records:

Bob Charles (wins 79)
- Major (1)
- PGA Tour (5)
- Others (49) including World Matchplay Championship 1969, SA Open 1973
- Senior Major (1)
- Champion Tour (23)

Allan Henning (wins 16)
- Sunshine Tour Order of Merit (2)
- PGA Tour Qualifying School 1966 3rd
- South African circuit (5) including SA Open 1963, SA Masters
- Sunshine Tour (7)
- Other (4)

Ismail Chowglay (wins 16)
- Inducted Southern Africa Golf Hall of Fame 2019
- TPA Tour (16) including SA Non-European Open (2), 2nd (5)

The event in Bloemfontein presented fresh challenges for the two players of colour and the National Party government. In terms of the laws of the Free State province at that time, Indians were not permitted to spend more than 24 hours at a time inside its borders.

As a result, the two Indian golfers would be forced to commute from Kimberley every day, but at the last minute they received a reprieve and were allowed to stay in Bloemfontein, but only for the

Chapter 5: Breakthrough

days of the tournament, and they had to keep the authorities updated as to their place of residence and movements. At the tournament, they were provided with a standing-room tent, pitched a few metres from the clubhouse, in which to change.

The evening before the commencement of the tournament, Papwa and Chowglay were barred from the golfer's reception for the visiting 300 golfers playing in either the SA Amateur or the SA Open championship as municipal regulations did not allow social fraternisation with non-europeans.

Meanwhile, during round one, a foreign television crew focused their camera on their provided bell tent where they could be seen eating sandwiches, and their coming and going, and then panning back to the luxurious clubhouse with the white players entering, thereby causing the organisers much embarrassment, such that the following day they replaced the tent with a caravan. Supporters of both players were now entertained, but still separated from the white players and their supporters.

Papwa opened with an eventful 69 in round one, only one shot behind Bobby Locke and Bruce Keyter who both shot 68s, and one shot ahead of Retief Waltman and Allan Henning.

In round two, Papwa found himself tied for fourth place on 140 (69, 71) together with Keyter, five behind the British Open leader, left-hander Bob Charles who had shot a brilliant 66, and one behind second-placed Trevor Wilkes and Bobby Locke.

Chowglay failed to make the cut, and it would be a number of years before he was again allowed to play in a 'white' tournament.

Having shot 71 in the third round, Papwa was right in the mix on 211, now only four shots behind Charles and young Allan Henning who shot an outstanding 67, and one shot behind third-placed Keyter and Trevor Wilkes. Graham Henning was on 212, followed by Player, Locke, and Waltman on 213. All to play for...

Another first-time winner of the SA Open emerged when no one was able to mount a challenge to Henning, although Gary Player shot an excellent 68, as the 19-year old won the title with a final-round 71. He was followed by Bruce Keyter on 280 and, tied for third place on 281 Sewsunker Sewgolum, Gary Player, and New Zealand star Bob

Charles, followed by the maestro Bobby Locke.

Bob Charles had a four-shot lead after two rounds and was tied with Allan Henning after the third round, but he finished weakly with 74. Three Henning brothers were in the field, Allan, Harold and Graham. Papwa was again under par in all four rounds.

Leading scores were:

A Henning	70 70 67 71 – 278
B Keyter	68 72 70 70 – 280
S Sewgolum	69 71 71 70 – 281
R Charles (NZ)	69 66 72 74 – 281
G Player	74 71 68 68 – 281
A D Locke	68 71 74 69 – 282
T Wilkes	72 67 71 73 – 283
G Henning	71 69 73 71 – 284
R Waltman	70 75 68 71 – 284

Henning Brothers

Source: Barry Cohen

There was a lot of talk that Papwa would not be able to beat Player with his regular sub-standard golfers, compared with the fitted clubs the others were playing with, and his lack of practice on 'white' golf courses. Then there was the fact that he was illiterate such that he

Chapter 5: Breakthrough

couldn't read instruction manuals, nor had he had any lessons.

But Papwa reminded reporters that he had honed his short game whilst a caddy waiting for a bag when they would wager as to who could chip closest from just off the green. This wager may be their entire days caddy fee, so this was real bread-and-butter tension. And whereas many professionals would putt the ball from just off the green, Papwa thought nothing of taking a deep-faced club and flicking it to within inches of the hole.

Another criticism was that he was lazy as he didn't like practicing, but he saw no point in practicing, and preferred the real cut-and-thrust of tournament play.

Papwa was back overseas campaigning, playing in a number of tournaments in Britain, including the Open Championship, then a 15th place in the German Open, and returning to Holland where amazingly, for the third time, he won a magnificent 3-stroke victory in the Dutch Open, once again over a top field of international golfers including South African stars in Harold Henning, Brian Wilkes and Denis Hutchinson.

| 1964 | Sewsunker Sewgolum (3) | South Africa | Eindhovensche | 275 | 3 strokes | Ted Ball |

Source: Rajen Sewshanker

Papwa

This was again played at Eindhoven, and his outstanding scores were 67 71 66 71 (275), giving him a three-shot victory over Australian Ted Ball.

Ted Ball (wins 50)

☐ PGA Tour of Australia (4) including the Australian Open
☐ Australasia other (13)
☐ Asian Tour (2)
☐ Other (31)

Papwa was lying second at the end of the first round two shots behind Harold Henning. But he took a two-stroke lead the following day, and almost made sure of winning with a 66. At this stage, he was five strokes ahead of Ball. In the final round, Papwa carded a 71 while the Australian returned a credible 69 to reduce the final deficit to three strokes, with Hutchinson fourth and Henning fifth. Papwa's win gave SA their fifth success in the championship in six years.

This victory received less publicity in Durban than his previous two triumphs in Holland as he was now an established name in world golf.

'The record books don't lie, three Dutch Opens, I repeat, three Dutch Opens in four attempts in six years,' said Ken Schofield, Executive Director European Tour.

To put this into perspective, in the modern era, the only other players who won the Dutch Open three times were Seve Ballesteros (wins 90), Bernhard Langer (wins 133), and Simon Dyson (wins 10), and their victories were after a number of attempts.

Once again Papwa was having problems with his health and, in spite of 'enjoying the best of my four trips overseas', this 1964 tour had to be curtailed when his struggle with jaundice proved too much.

He was once again mobbed by thousands of supporters at Durban airport, and it clearly shook the government.

But Papwa was denied entry for the Dunlop Masters, the Natal Open, the Transvaal Open, and the Western Province Open. 'The door was not permanently open'.

Golfers, however, came to Sewgolum's support with some commonsense remarks as both Sid Brews (eight-time SA Open champion and British Open runner-up) and Reg Taylor (SA's greatest

Chapter 5: Breakthrough

amateur inducted into the 2009 Southern Africa Golf Hall of Fame) came out in support.

Papwa has earned the right to be classed as one of the best players in the country, and the idea of an 'Open' is to allow the best players to compete against one another," said Brews, a view wholeheartedly echoed by Taylor.

Still Papwa was denied entry to the Western Province Open, forced to withdraw from the Transvaal Open, and initially refused entry to both the SA Open and Natal Open. He finished 11th in both the PGA Championship at Germiston CC and the SA Masters at Zwartkops CC. The SAGU now instructed him to apply directly for his own permit.

Similarly in 1964, it must have been difficult for Ismail 'Boy' Chowglay, the 1962 SA Non-European Open Champion, and Clovelly Country Club caddy master, now in his prime at the age of 31, to just watch Retief Waltman win the Western Province Open with a record breaking last round of 65 from Gary Player, followed by Harold Henning and Bobby Locke, at his home Clovelly Country Club course where he would regularly shoot sub 70s. With his local knowledge he would have been one of the favourites had he been allowed to compete. Permission still denied!

Player on the other hand had a fallout with rules official, Cecil Goldberg and club captain, Manfred Salomon after getting a negative ruling on the difficult par-5 9th hole in the final round, such that he indicated he would never again grace the Clovelly fairways (however he recently played there where his half-brother Chris Goldsbury is a prominent Clovelly member).

As a sideline, for years Bobby Locke would visit and play almost daily at Clovelly during the summer months, residing in Fish Hoek where he also owned Bobby Locke Motors. At no time did he invite Chowglay to join him for a game of golf. But then Chowglay was not supposed to play on a white golf course without a permit.

Of some interest were the measures that had to be taken to accommodate Papwa during the playing of the 'white' tournaments. At Houghton, he had a special flatlet at the back of the clubhouse with bed-sitting room and separate shower and toilet, and to allow the gallery to be mixed, a special permit was obtained.

Insofar as the other tournaments where he could participate, he won the Cock 'o North Tournament at Ndola in Zambia against a strong 'white' field.

Papwa mesmerised the black SA opposition, and when he moved on to defend his SA Open title there were few who looked further than him for the winner.

He duly won the 1964 SA Non-European title at Glendower by a margin of 21 strokes when he retained the title, winning R200, with scores of 71 72 70 75 for 288, a new record for the Open, and cemented his position at the top of the golf ladder (his 27-stroke win in the Western Province N-E Open merely confirmed this). Ed 'Otto' Lee and Johannes Semenya on 309 were 2nd sharing R150, Chowglay 4th and Hlapo 5th.

Colourful Otto Lee playing with Papwa, entertained the gallery with his antics after hitting the ball as he twisted and swerved his body as if piloting the ball in flight. There was also 'Cox' Hlapo, the Transvaal champion, with his characteristic enormous beard, wearing a multi-coloured woolen headgear that looked like a beret, and then 'Goli-Goli' Mdeni, another fancied player.

On the whole, participants were more accustomed to the grass-veld courses in the townships and were somewhat disadvantaged when it came to the greens, as they simply 'cracked' when facing the pin. That's where Papwa, now seasoned in playing on proper courses, capitalised.

1964 SA Non-European Open, Glendower. Mrs F W. Pitman handing the trophy to the winner, 'Papwa' Sewgolum. Picture courtesy of LLA.

Chapter 5: Breakthrough

Had Papwa any real opposition among the non-european golfers in the country? The answer was simple – he was unbeatable at this stage, and it would be many years before he would be ousted from that top position. Once again, Papwa was honoured as *The Leader* newspaper's Pepsi Cola 'Non-European Sportsman of the Year.'

Meanwhile, Papwa became the first golf professional at the new Springfield course on the banks of the Umgeni River, not more than five kilometres from where he had grown up. An article in Drum magazine showed Papwa teaching teenager Leela Moodley the art of putting.

Despite offering his services there was a sparse uptake such that after a month the funds set-aside for his salary was depleted and his job ceased.

Meanwhile, SA was banned from participating in the 1964 Olympics, whilst FIFA suspended South Africa, despite Sir Stanley Rous, president of the International Soccer Federation, urging the lifting of South Africa's suspension.

More pressure was brought to bear on the SA authorities (and the public) when in January 1965, Hayden Banda, the Zambian Minister stated: 'This territory is to cut all sporting ties with South Africa. We will have no dealings with them as far as sport is concerned. South African teams cannot play here, nor will Zambian teams be allowed to compete there.'

The 1965 Springboks faced stern criticism for their refusal, as on all previous tours of New Zealand, to play against a Maori representative team, and doubts were raised about the English cricket tour scheduled for the end of the decade.

In 1963, Nelson Mandela had been arrested for conspiring to overthrow the state and sentenced to life imprisonment in June 1964 in the Rivonia Trial. Mandela served 27 years in prison, split between Robben Island, Pollsmoor Prison, and Victor Verster Prison.

For the next 14 years, while Papwa challenged white sports superiority, Mandela and his comrades would only hear whispers concerning Sewsunker Sewgolum, the man who unwittingly became the symbol of the anti-apartheid sports movement.

However, Papwa's next big achievement happened in 1965 as he was set to rock the world once again.

CHAPTER 6: THE SHOWDOWN

Papwa vs Player

At the end of 1964) Papwa lost the Natal Non-European Open which he had dominated for the last eight years to 22-year-old, former caddy, Raydmuth Rajdaw (whose brother was the equally well known 'Anooplal').

The news of Papwa's defeat poured from the sports pages to the front pages of the Indian newspapers saying that he lacked the fighting qualities needed for competing on a professional level and called for opportunities for other black golfers to play overseas such as Rajdaw and Hlapo. But other newspapers saw it differently: 'His defeat will make him shake off his complacency. Up till now, he has been having it, more or less, his own way.'

Other critics were inclined to suggest that the champion was on his way out. That of course, was ridiculous. But it did show that Papwa was human, and his defeat was a tonic to his brother professionals who had become supreme pessimists when there was talk of beating Papwa. Now they said, 'If Rajdaw can do it, so can I.'

Papwa was in a slump, and his defeat had also smashed the myth of his invincibility, and there was now a growing contingent of black golfers eager to beat the master at his game. Chowglay was widely believed to be the equal to or better than Papwa. Vincent Tshabalala, a 23-year old furniture-store delivery driver for Dlamini, was another, and during the January 1965 SA Non-European Open, all three came together on the East London Golf course in a thrilling battle for ascendancy.

The temporary setback made Papwa all the more determined that he would preserve his near-unbeaten stroke-play record on the SA fairways.

Papwa

While waiting for his train from Bloemfontein as he travelled to East London, Vincent Tshabalala placed his suitcase down next to another, near a bench. When the train came in, nobody claimed the other suitcase, so Vincent told a railway policeman about it. The cop immediately took him and the case to the station charge office.

'That's what scared me,' said Vincent. 'I remembered the Johannesburg station suitcase bomb incident, and I thought I was being arrested. I was so upset I nearly caught a train home.' It was just as well that Vincent went to East London as he played sparkling golf.

Ramphal Tiney took the lead, equaling the Alexander CC course record with a 69, followed by Percy Mazibuko on 70, Hlapo 71, Ranjith 72, Tshabalala and Lee 73, with Papwa languishing behind with a 77.

After Round Two, it was Tiney 69 73 (142) with Papwa 77 74 (151) nine behind. By lunchtime on the last day, Papwa had a one-stroke lead over Tshabalala, with Chowglay and Tiney following close behind him.

Vincent took the lead between the 10th and 15th hole; however, he 3-putted the 16th, and they were once again tied. The mixed crowd of spectators cheered every stroke played by the leaders, and by now the hot money was on Vincent. But Papwa was playing brilliantly, as was Vincent, with Chowglay breathing down their neck. Vincent was on the green for three within a foot of the pin on the final hole and then sunk his putt.

Now it was Papwa's turn, he was ten feet away, and the gallery was silent as he stalked the hole, and settled himself knowing full well that the shot would determine the tournament. Nerveless, he potted it. They were tied, and players and spectators rushed over to congratulate both players.

Papwa had done it again, with Chowglay, having equaled the course record 69, following one-shot behind, and Hlapo scoring a hole-in-one at the 14th.

As they had only been allotted a three-day permit for the event, there was no chance of a play-off, and the result was declared a draw.

Papwa received a total purse of R160 for coming second in the Natal N-E and tied first in the SA Non-European Opens. But his

Chapter 6: The Showdown

application to play in the Natal Open was turned down.

Gary Player, a previous winner in 1958, '59, '60, '62, said he was disappointed with the ruling that Papwa could not play, declining to comment on the political aspect of Papwa's situation.

Despite their disappointment, Suminthra was not willing to let Papwa become despondent, telling him to fight this and not put aside his dreams. 'You will triumph. I have confidence in you. You are a brave and determined man, and you my hero!'

This time round, the authorities decided to look the other way. They had been embarrassed by the photos (syndicated around the world) of Papwa receiving his trophy in the pouring rain after winning the 1963 Natal Open and were determined not to be shown up a second time. The ruling was reversed, Papwa could play, and one of the greatest duels in world golf was allowed to commence.

With Papwa beating Gary Player in the 1964 Richelieu Grand Prix Series 1, and Player turning the tables on Papwa in Grand Prix Series 2, followed by his tie for third with Player in the 1964 South African Open, this was the showdown everyone was waiting for. The caddy against the world champion, superseding even those of the legendary Ouimet-Vardon and future Nicklaus-Watson battles, not just in terms of golf but insofar as the worldwide impact on black-white politics.

Player could muscle his ball further down the fairway but Papwa, with his quick hands, was impeccable in his approach play. If the rain held off and the humidity didn't become too draining, they had three days (a double round was scheduled for day three) of potentially brilliant golf to look forward to.

The year 1965 was a big one for the king of SA golf, Gary Player, his 'golden year', when he was probably the 'Number One golfer in the world', and over this period together with Jack Nicklaus, Billy Casper, and Arnold Palmer, one of the top four golfers in the world.

That year together with Harold Henning, he won the Canada Cup (later called the World Cup) including the individual title beating the Americans for the first time, as well as the US Open to complete golf's Grand Slam of Majors. He took his third SA Open, his fourth Australian Open, and notched up wins in the World Series, World Matchplay (legendary comeback win over Tony Lema), and the NTL

Challenge Cup – he was clearly at the top of his game!

Gary Player was now at the peak of his career, he was 'walking on water', the National Party's white champion, and with a record that by then included three Major wins (1959 Open Championship and the 1962 Masters and PGA).

Aged 29 in 1965, Gary Player became only the third golfer in history to win the Career Grand Slam. He accumulated nine major championships on the regular tour and nine Senior Tour major championship victories, and 165 tournaments on six continents over six decades.

If that was impressive, you need to understand Gary Player's lifetime record:

- 1965 he was the World Number 1 (unofficial),
- Major Grand Slam wins (2),
- Major wins (9), second and third (8), Professional wins (165) – ranking 3rd most,
- PGA Tour wins (24),
- South Africa Tour wins (73) including South Africa Open (13),

Chapter 6: The Showdown

1963 Cassius Clay (Mohammed Ali) knocking out Sonny Liston for the World Heavyweight Boxing Title.

- Australian Open (7),
- Other wins (18) including the 1965 Canada Cup, World Cup Individual (2), World Match Play Championship (5),
- Senior Major wins (9),
- Champion Tour wins (19),
- Other Senior wins (14).
- 1974 Inducted into the World Golf Hall of Fame,
- 2000 S.A. Sportsman of the Century.

Player was finally due to compete in the 1965 Natal Open, alongside Papwa, and despite his achievements, there was enormous speculation about how he would fare.

As the world watched one of the most controversial fights in the sport's history, the re-match between the former underdog Cassius Clay (Muhammad Ali), the 'The Louisville Lip', and big bad Sonny Liston for boxing's World Heavyweight Championship. In SA, sports lovers waited for the duel which had all the ingredients of a heavyweight match for the four-round golfing championship of SA!

To win you need four commandments: consolidate, dominate, subjugate, and annihilate – Danie Craven

In the white corner, the champion, standing 1,67m tall, weighing in at 69kg, age 29; the white 'Black Knight', a heavyweight giant of the fairways with three Majors, three SA Opens, and four Australian Opens having once again been victorious in the SA Open, and a previous winner of four Natal Opens.

In the black corner, playing out of Durban, the Indian contender, standing 1,66m tall, weighing in at 65kg, aged 37, classified non-white, the only person of colour in the white field, the heavyweight of non-European golf with three Dutch Opens, five SA Non-European Opens, one Natal Open, and 19 Provincial 'Non-European' Open titles.

The hot money was on the white guy. But who would win and be the champion golfer?

This was 'war', a chance for blacks to prove that the black sportsmen were the equal of white sportsmen and break down the government's perception of invincibility. Prime Minister Hendrik Verwoerd was confident that finally Papwa would be put in his place.

Papwa's supporters told him that he could win despite not being able to practice on the course prior to the tournament. Speculation abounded, and the fans held their breath.

Papwa, unlike Player, did not like the rigours of practicing and hitting hundreds of golf balls as he did not have to concentrate in the absence of competition. So with Player pounding away on the practice range, he donned an old t-shirt and grubby khaki pants and went fishing to relax.

Once again he would have to change and eat in his car and use the caddy facilities for his other needs. The stakes got even higher when Papwa returned to his vehicle in the car park before the tournament, and found a dead Indian mynah bird, its neck broken, placed under one of the windscreen wipers.

The common 'mynah' bird, whose plumage is dark brown, with

Chapter 6: The Showdown

yellow head ornaments, is derived from the Hindi language *mainā*, and is a bird of the Starling family native to India, although several species had been introduced to SA. Disturbed, Papwa tried to wipe out the memory as he focused on what he had to do.

The Durban Country Club, established in 1922, overlooking the Blue Lagoon estuary and the Indian Ocean, saw an astounding feat that week. For three days, Gary Player, Harold Henning, and Papwa Sewgolum went head-to-head as their supporter bases swelled and became increasingly vocal and animated rejoicing in their representatives' performance, and in Papwa's case showing him to be the equal of the whites in this respect.

The first five holes were considered among the games most taxing starts. The appealing ripples found down the first fairway already lined with spectators, a 351 par-4, had the hole swinging left around the dunes with a hint of the glories that were to come. The approach shot to the green sat atop a dune with a swale in the front of the green, while behind the green the views highlighted how close the course was to the Indian Ocean.

Denis 'Hutch' Hutchinson took the round one lead shooting a 70, followed by a group of players on 71 including Player after an eagle 2 on the 18th. Papwa, also on 71, was still a distinct threat and like Bobby Jones, he preferred someone else to set the pace in the opening rounds. He played against the course, conservatively in round one, never against the field.

During round two, a stiff southerly wind sprang up late in the morning, and the late starters faced difficult conditions. Papwa wasn't putting well and holed nothing of significance, however he 3-putted only once – at the 7th.

He dropped shots at the 1st hole, and another at the 7th, but picked up one at the 10th, 13th, and the 14th, then again lost shots at the 12th, 15th and 17th for a 73, and now trailed Player by one shot.

His impassive face showed nothing of the turmoil inside, knowing that a mishit shot might mean the loss of hundreds of rands. After he had finished the second round, he was more content because he felt that he now had the measure of the course and himself.

As the sun came out for the beginning of the final 36-holes,

Papwa's game brightened too. With every stroke he played he seemed more certain as his golf became a thing of graceful, effortless beauty. All the old confidence was back, and there was an uncanny air of finality in the way he paced himself.

Sensing a battle between the white's favourite sporting son and their hometown hero, Durban's Indians flocked to the white-only course in droves. If Papwa was to beat Gary and win the title once more, his loyal fans wanted to be there to witness it.

Many of Papwa's supporters were unaware of the strict rules governing ones behaviour on the golf course. But a small unruly minority were indifferent to these rules and this created a problem.

Papwa's army of Indian supporters among the gallery consisted of black, coloured, Indian, and white, was growing into thousands, swarming across the fairways, most having never been onto a golf course, let alone knowing the rules of golf. They were unruly, kicking balls around and making a lot of noise, even while the players were playing their shots despite the marshals' attempts to control them, and as soon as Papwa had played, they were off, not waiting for Player to finish putting.

Papwa had edged up the board to be one of the tournament leaders, as he burned the course from tee down the fairway and even scorched the greens. He and the 'Black Knight', Gary Player, were paired together for the last two rounds on Saturday, with Papwa one-shot behind. It was more like match-play between Papwa and Player.

The day was perfect – there was no wind or rain that had disrupted the championship two years previously as spectators jostled for a better view, tempers flared and muttered curses of 'coolies' were heard betraying the titanic battle they were watching, a match between races and cultures – between the darling of the white supremacists and the living hope of the oppressed.

Off the course, Papwa, like many of his supporters, was severely disadvantaged. The golf course was the one place that allowed him a chance at equality, and he was determined not to let his 'army' down as the word filtered through the township and more and more came to support him.

Chapter 6: The Showdown

The only shot that matters is the next shot. Focus 100 per cent on the shot in hand. What's happened is history. You don't want to get too excited or start thinking ahead. Stay in the present. One shot at a time!

Then Harold 'the horse' Henning blitzed the field with a brilliant 69, pulling level with Player and Papwa, shooting 72 and 71 respectively. All three were in the running going into the final round, and the knowledgeable money remained on Player.

Player was the first to tee off at the beginning of the fourth round. Never an easy start, the famous architect Robert Grimsdell had deliberately ensured the slope of the hole could present some very unpleasant situations.

The green is set into the side of a huge sand dune and Player immediately picked up another shot after a magnificent drive saw him birdie the first. Papwa was now two shots behind Player and equal second with Harold Henning after they both dropped shots at the first. The spectators snaked their way between the marshals to the second tee.

Player, dressed in his traditional last-round black shirt and trousers (he had always been a western fan and these were the colours the hero wore) and his caddy walked ahead of Papwa. There was no talking as they focused on what lay ahead. Tension gnawed away with both spectators and players, despite the brilliant sea views. They understood what was at stake.

Player immediately picked up another shot. Now three behind, the occasion was clearly too big for Papwa, as the white members of the crowd cheered loudly while the Indian army was quiet.

Dare the 7,000 Indians, who packed the fairways overlooking the azure Blue Lagoon estuary hope that their man would win?

The seething gallery knew that he was closer to defeat than he had ever been in his short playing career. He was not only playing against the skill of his opponents, against years of experience, but never for a moment did Papwa change his tactics.

These enthusiastic and partisan supporters contrasted with Player's reserved white gallery. Well-dressed whites, many wearing their short khaki pants with long socks, and the colourful flowing saris

Papwa

of the Indian women streaming down the fairway after their 'man'.

There was something inhuman about Papwa's play that afternoon. He churned out a stream of perfect strokes from the production belt that was his swing. He was hitting his drives further than he had been doing for some time, but the foundation of his score was the straightness of his second to the flag and his short game.

Then trouble found Player on the par 5 third hole, a possible 'eagle' hole, when he cut his ball landing in a small stand of bush and thick tropical trees as the sun's rays streamed through the undergrowth, and small black faced silvery-grey vervet monkeys chattered in the treetops.

The spectators piled into the bushes in search of Player's ball. An Indian man picked up a ball and took it to Player: 'Is this your ball?' Player rounded on the man for picking up the ball, and there were mutterings among the Indian crowd, but it was not his ball.

After the mandatory five minutes spent looking, the ball was declared lost. Even if found, it would have been unplayable, nevertheless Player was a little upset when it was reported that an Indian spectator had pocketed the ball, and so Player returned to the tee with a two-shot penalty, clearly rattled, such that he signed for an eight to Papwa's par-5, a turning point of the tournament. A huge swing – now they were even as they matched each other stroke for stroke.

Player muttered; the vervet monkeys in the treetops muttered with him. He regained his composure, but now Sewgolum was on the charge.

By the 14th they were both one shot behind Henning, and the pressure began to build. This was after Player had shot three birdies in a row to draw level when the word filtered back that Henning now had the lead, and they only had five holes to play. This was where champions kick in. Papwa seemed to be playing as if in a trance.

Inspired, Papwa mopped his brow and replied with an eagle three. His supporters, who had swelled to a few thousand, erupted, running over the green before Player had completed the hole. Player countered with a long putt, sinking it for birdie, then commented: 'If this goes on I just cannot play in these tournaments anymore.' Clearly the pressure was on.

Chapter 6: The Showdown

Mutterings from Player's supporters included the fact that Papwa had taken too long to play his third shot, but it was that eagle at the 14th in the afternoon round that finally clinched the title for Papwa, the second turning point, and Papwa must have thought that this par-5 442m – 14th, was his Eldorado.

In the morning round, he gained a hard-earned par-5 when everything pointed to him dropping at least two shots. He had driven into the rough, saw his iron to the green kick left and back into the rough, played a weak third, and then chipped his fourth over the back of the green. But to everyone's surprise, he calmly chipped the ball into the hole as if he was doing it every day.

The afternoon effort was even more amazing. A good drive was followed by a magnificent three-wood to the back of the green, and then he sank the 15-footer for his two-under par eagle 3. Player sank his for a birdie.

They matched each other with pars over the next two holes both missing makeable putts – pressure, and Papwa missed a 7-foot (2m) putt on the 17th followed by audible groans and worried looks. Other spectators looked knowingly at each other, but then Player also missed – the atmosphere was electric.

Papwa was being followed by hordes of enthusiastic fans, noisily rooting for their hero. 'Come on Papwa,' yelled a young fan as the marshals' tried to take control as they moved to the 18th tee – the same hole where Papwa nearly lost the 1963 Natal Open.

Crowd control was not the best, 'If we didn't have ropes to keep back the crowd today, we would be dead,' was one comment, and Player was unnerved by Papwa's jostling fans, as he again complained about being 'put-off' by the over-enthusiastic Papwa Army when he was lining up a vital putt.

Admonished by Player, they informed him that they were there to watch their hero, Papwa, not Player, while Player's supporters were willing him to pull a rabbit out of the hat and win again. Was it too late to save the game? And the government took notice.

The 18th, Papwa held a two-shot lead over Player, and one ahead of Henning. The two golfers strode to the par-4 18th in silence while the marshals rallied the spectators behind the ropes and urged them to be silent as they attempted to navigate the devilish par-4 closing hole, where a skillful tee shot that is favoured with a couple of fortunate breaks can sometimes reach all the way to the green.

The sun was shining. Monkeys were playing in the trees, and a breeze coming off the nearby Indian Ocean filled with tropical suggestions of exotic fruits and spices, and forgotten sultry afternoons.

Just then some spectators ran across fairway, whilst up ahead, others encroached onto the green, refusing to heed the marshal's warnings when confronted to get a better spectating position. Seven thousand were lining both sides of the fairway.

Papwa's body felt tight but strong, pumped up, heart pounding, grimly focused. He had the honour and launched his drive, but he came up on it rather quickly, and the ball faded – far right, gathering momentum as it rolled down a slope which had been trampled by the spectators, well below the green. Player needed an eagle to tie Papwa.

Had the 'Black Knight' left his legendary charge too late? Player went for broke, as he drove the green and now he had a 10-foot putt for an eagle two, and a possible victory!

Papwa had an awkward up-hill pitch to play and instead of being in a position to win outright, now he was battling for a tie.

His wedge pitch flew into a greenside bunker to the right of the green. Was this the opening Player was waiting for? Player would win if Papwa dropped a shot, and he made his putt.

Ignoring the muttering from the crowd, as in anticipation they held their breath, he calmly exploded from the sand, and the ball sailed up over the lip of the bunker, landing with a thud, released and rolled a few feet from the pin. It would require another superb putt for him to avoid a tie given that Player had driven onto the green and was lying handy to repeat his eagle two of the first round.

In silence Papwa walked up and down the line of that vital putt. A cine-camera whirred. Papwa motioned to the offender and there was complete quiet. Again he surveyed the line. There was a nasty drop from the top of the hole. It was so easy to be short, yet too much strength and the downhill slope would carry the ball off line. Fred Paul, standing together with Louis Nelson, was scarcely breathing as the ball, as if guided by a magnet, never left the line of the hole.

Chapter 6: The Showdown

Papwa dropped the putt for his par-4.

In the enormous cheer echoing over the course, Player heard the death toll of defeat. He was now faced with a 10-foot (three metre) putt to force the play-off. His caddy crouched next to him, holding the flag, then whispered his read of the putt. A fly settled on the ball, and Player waved his hand over the ball.

The tension was unbearable. Finally Player's putter moved rhythmically back then clipped the ball in total silence, making a popping sound as everyone held their collective breath. It rolled, gathering pace straight for the cup, it encountered a stud mark, a miniscule direction-changer – then slackened losing momentum, taking the slope and at the last moment veering left, catching the lip of the cup, and peeled away.

Papwa, despite all the indignities and challenges, had stared down the champion and become the finest golfer in all of SA (for that day at least) with scores of 71 73 71 70 (285) he defeated the great Gary Player 71 72 72 71 (286) head-to-head and Harold Henning 73 73 69 71 (286), both by one-shot to take his second Natal Open in three years.

For the first time in those grim holes, Papwa allowed his face to ease into a boyish grin of delight. Then Player walked over to shake Papwa's hand.

The Indian community had their man who could embarrass the government, and delirious, they mobbed Papwa, chairing him off the green as he waved to the crowd.

'You're a symbol. And when you beat Gary Player, beat the best golfer in the world, you sent out a message, the message that maybe whites aren't automatically better than you and I,' said Louis Nelson. 'They can't stomach it. Gary is their blue-eyed boy. Now they will see you as a troublemaker. They just don't understand. How can it be that a nobody from Riverside can beat their man?'

Once again the SABC refused to broadcast 'mixed sports' news of Papwa's win, despite 'David's' victory over 'Goliath', although it filtered back onto the Riverside streets, so that they were ready to cheer him on his way home, as friends and neighbours started to throng outside his home in a mood of defiant revelry.

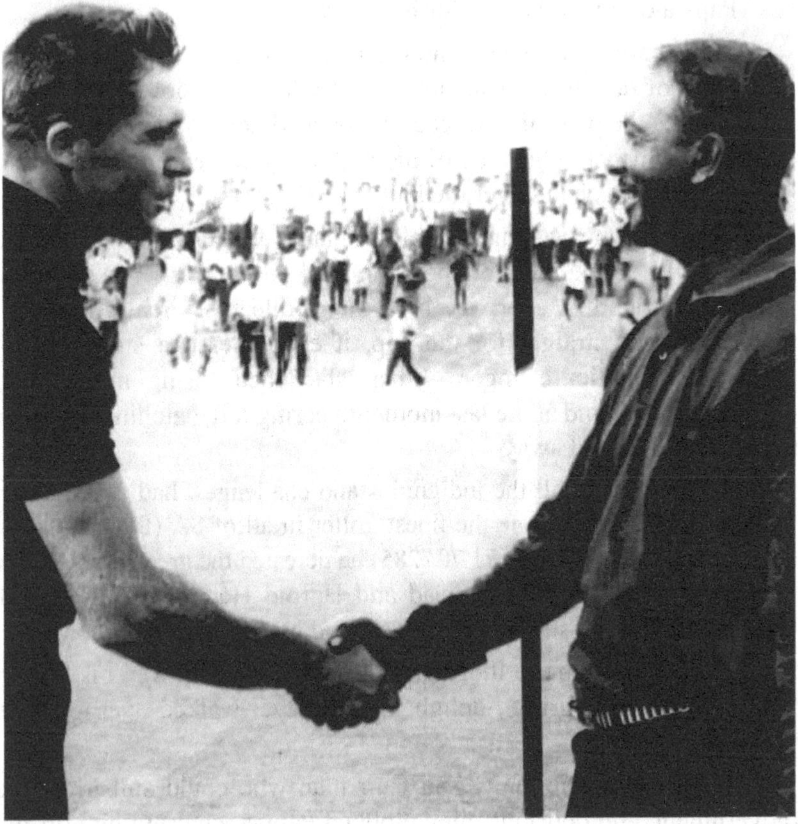

Source: Getty Images

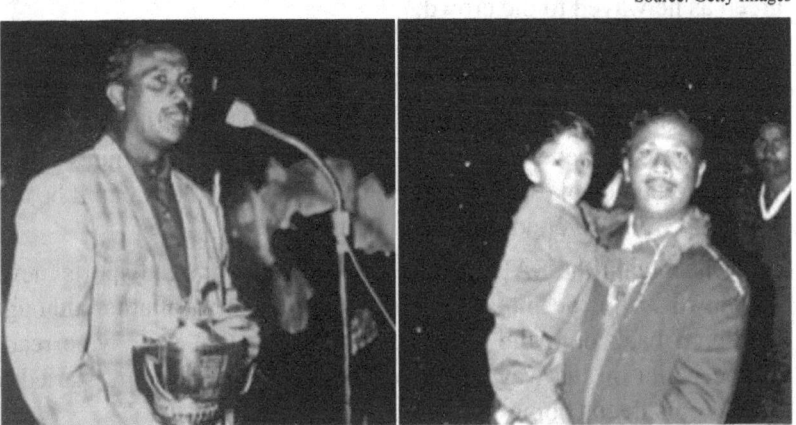

Papwa holding his trophy giving his prize-giving speech; then holding his son for photographers.

Chapter 6: The Showdown

Gary Player was in scintillating form making Papwa's feat all the more remarkable. This time it was not raining, only drizzling, and a red carpet was laid out on the 18th green where all the players received their prizes. But they forgot to hand Papwa his cheque which they had to do through an open window, such was the excitement.

Afterwards, Gary Player sportingly commented that he had no excuse and that Papwa: 'On today's showing Papwa deserved his victory, he chipped like a genius. Every time I thought he was in trouble, back he came to pull one out of the bag.' The press however reported the 'disgraceful behaviour of the crowd'.

Subsequently discussing this with Rajen Sewshanker, Papwa's son, Player said: 'It was a big thing your father beating me then because I was the champion. He beat me when I was playing very well. His mind was outstanding, and he was one of the greatest gentlemen.'

Despite not winning, Player was happy for him as they stood to receive their prizes – with Papwa's remaining Army of 1200 supporters looking on, as it meant Papwa could now go and play in Australia.

When interviewed after the victory as to how he found playing with Player: 'I have found Gary to be very friendly although one might think he is not so while he is busy.'

Papwa won because he was the best golfer in the field, and the best tactician. He knew that accuracy was needed above all else and, except for the second round, his play was straight and true from tee to green.

This victory should not be taken lightly as Player would go on to win the US Open later that year and complete his Grand Slam.

There were no celebratory drinks at the club – and no champagne sprayed over the winner as it would jeopardise the club's liquor license, so Papwa went home to enjoy a sumptuous curry meal, with the trophy on the table, and a bottle of Cane-spirit to fill the glasses. He retold the story of his victory hole by hole to the children late into the night – he had achieved the impossible!

When the family celebrations were over, FM and Papwa travelled into town where they joined their friends and an exuberant crowd of supporters to celebrate his victory. Pretty girls hung on his every word, whilst others asked him to dance, with Roger Miller's 'King of the

Road' playing on the jukebox. Others insisted on buying him drinks. This was how you should celebrate! A memorable evening, their dignity restored, and amongst his own people, Papwa was indeed 'King of the Road'.

Chapter 6: The Showdown

Slazenger, the sponsor of his clubs, sent R60, and Dunlop provided an additional 150 free golf balls for the year and money for expenses. The Castle Wine and Brandy Co. (Pty) Ltd sponsored him to the tune of R150, well wishers sent cash, and the Indian community of Greytown presented him with a radiogram, while Coca-Cola sponsored him with R200 for the following three years.

This happened at a time when there was deep depression amongst blacks, as the Indian Congress had been banned, and all the black leadership jailed, with Nelson Mandela, Andrew Mlangeni, Govan Mbeki, and Elias Motsoaledi, joining Robert Sobukwe on Robben Island (Denis Goldberg was sent to Pretoria Prison). This was the vacuum into which Papwa stepped unintentionally. Now they had their champion who was going to embarrass the national government which maintained blacks were inferior to whites.

This was just too much for the apartheid government; the bubble of invincibility of their white sportsmen compared to black sporting heroes had burst. His victory was seen as a symbolically threatening event by the apartheid leaders. Papwa was regarded as a man looking for trouble instead of an athlete passionate about his game. An illiterate man was beating a white icon to boot.

Although Player retracted and denied some of his beliefs later on in his life, at the peak of his career, he was an apartheid-sympathiser and identified with the regime. Despite this, Papwa considered Player a friend and they both shared a common interest in their country.

'My father was never bitter despite all the things that happened to him. He was very humble on and off the course, and he always controlled his temper. He was a good man,' said Rajen Sewshanker.

This was Papwa at Germiston, playing under the threat of banning. He was very quiet, the strain often showing. Official efforts at separating the races soon collapsed and possibly with them, any hope of Papwa getting Government approval for the next tournament. These smiles could have been the fatal blow.

Papwa playing with Denis Hutchinson at their following event at Germiston GC, with a mixed gallery of supporters looking on. (Photos Drum magazine)

'Papwa's win may have widespread implications. There is a danger that any ban may result in the world blackballing SA sportsmen,' stated the *Cape Times*, whilst Sewgolum's performance received worldwide attention and was covered by *The New York Times*.

Within two weeks of this magnificent feat, the National government, concerned about the ramification of Papwa's progress, saw it necessary to further restrict 'non-white' audiences from attending certain sporting events decreeing that mixed sport would not be permitted (except by permit), and in so doing, effectively blocking Papwa's army of supporters from attending the SA PGA Championships.

This prompted an international outcry, causing a reaction from those blindly following apartheid who were determined not to make any 'concessions' and explicitly thwarted Papwa's chance of representing his own country in golf.

Prime Minister, Hendrik Verwoerd then took matters further by warning the New Zealand All Blacks that they would not be allowed

Chapter 6: The Showdown

to tour SA with mixed-wrace Maoris in their squad. The world took notice, and a number of new boycotts were implemented.

Papwa still had permission to play in some tournaments, and after opening with a 71 in fourth position, he finished 12th behind Player in the SA Open at Royal Cape GC, and 3rd in the SA Masters at Royal Durban GC. He was 5th in the PGA Tournament at Houghton, 15th in the Liquidair '5000' at Kensington GC, and 5th in the Flame Lily tournament in Bulawayo.

In July *Golf Magazine* requested that Papwa contribute his opinion as to the nine toughest golf holes in Africa for publication in the September issue of the magazine which would serve as the official programme for the 1965 Carling World Championship.

Papwa was also in much demand to address school prize-giving and other community functions, lighting up the bright young eyes as to what was possible. Clearly, Papwa's performances placed a severe and very public dent in the government's fantasies of white supremacy. Papwa's success embarrassed them, and his play became a matter of national security. Permission to play in a string of other events was denied, and all appeals failed.

He continued winning the non-European tournaments by large margins, but this earned him a pittance, such that his average monthly income was around R35 in 1965.

At the end of all this period, and despite not playing in the Transvaal and Western Province Opens, Papwa nevertheless finished third on the South African Order of Merit for the 64/65 season.

Order of Merit 1964/5

Gary Player	12 rounds	70,25	R1 750
Harold Henning	28 rounds	71,03	R2 940
Papwa Sewgolum	20 rounds	71,90	R1 448

This result should have been sufficient for Papwa to be considered for selection, on merit, to represent South Africa and partner Gary Player in the Canada Cup, but instead Harold Henning partnered Player to a sensational eight stroke victory over the Spanish team of Angel Miguel and Roman Sota, followed by Jack Nicklaus and Arnold

Palmer, the first foreign country to beat the USA, with Player winning the individual low-player-of-the-tournament, two shots ahead of Nicklaus.

Chapter 6: The Showdown

Given Papwa's inability to campaign abroad, financially these comments spurred Paul to write to Mark McCormack, Player, Nicklaus, and Palmer's famous agent, to request financial assistance to play in America. Many months later, in March 1966 they finally received a short reply from W. Trollip of Gary Player Enterprises (Pty) Ltd stating that the 'board of directors unfortunately cannot accede to your request'.

1965 Record: Papwa Sewgolum vs. Gary Player

PAPWA SEWGOLUM		GARY PLAYER	
S.A Non-European Open	1st	US Open	1st
Transvaal Non-European Open	1st	SA Open	1st
Natal Non-European Open	1st	Australian Open	1st
Natal Thunderbird Classic	1st	NTL Challenge Cup (Canada)	1st
Griqualand West N-E Open	1st	Piccadilly World Match Play	1st
Natal Open	1st	World Cup & Individual Trophy	1st
SA Masters	3rd	World Series of Golf	1st
SA Open	12th	The Masters	2nd
SA PGA Championship	5th	Natal Open	2nd
Flame Lily (Rhodesia)	5th		
Carling World Golf Championship	6th		
1964/65 Order of Merit	3rd	1964/65 Order of Merit	1st

*despite being denied permission to play in the Western Province & Transvaal Opens

CHAPTER 7: REACTION

What goes up must come down

In January 1966, now aged 37, Papwa hoped the year would be his big one; after all, he was one of the few golfers in the world who had beaten Gary Player, and by so doing, he hoped to make enough money in 1966 to be able to play on the American circuit. With that in mind, in November, Papwa resigned from his factory job in order to dedicate himself entirely to golf, practicing every day on different golf courses to keep himself in trim, as well as doing strenuous exercises and regular 6 mile runs to keep his sometime ballooning weight in check at 145 lbs (65kg). At the same time, he entered a string of white tournaments where winnings added up to as much as R20,000.

As the lone 'darkie' on the white professional circuit, Papwa could enter their tournaments, but not the clubhouse. He gambled everything by giving up his job and going into strict training for full-time golf. On the parallel but unequal black TPA Tour, if he won everything – the South African, Natal, Transvaal, Western Province, Kimberley, and Port Elizabeth Opens, he could earn possibly R500.

January 07, 1966 and Papwa proved once again that he was still the top non-european golfer in the country when he cruised to an easy ten-stroke victory in the Natal N-E Open at the Maritzburg GC. He regained the title from holder R Rajdaw who finished in 4th place with a total of 307 – 16 behind the new champion.

There was nothing spectacular in the tournament itself apart from an incident in which one player was alleged to have clouted another after a dispute over the number of strokes.

Nevertheless, Papwa was aware the Carling World Golf Championship, sponsored by Carling Brewing Company of Cleveland in the USA, had evolved and extended to cities in which the rapidly expanding company was building breweries.

Chapter 7: Reaction

In order to differentiate from other US tournaments, their event now offered the largest purse in golf for the best professional golfers from all the golfing countries in the world. Entry would be decided on a points system.

Aware of South Africa's stance regarding mixed competitions, the organisers deemed it necessary to include the North African and Middle Eastern countries in Europe and to allow South Africa to form its own zone.

Again permission to play arriving so late created mental strain brought about by the uncertainty as he desperately needed to play in order to qualify for the Carling World Championship.

In terms of the regulations of the Carling World Championships Committee, five places were to be awarded to eligible players who earned the greatest number of point in five tournaments. The five tournaments were the General Motors, Dunlop Masters, South African Open, Transvaal Open and the Natal Open.

Points allocated for different places were 1st 60, 2nd 45, 3rd 35, 4th 26, 5th 20, 6th 16, 7th 12, 8th 10, 9th 8 and 10th 6.

The World Championship was due to take place in Lancashire later that year, and the SAGU and the PGA were authorized to select five players, amateur and or professional, to represent the African zone, with the selection based on the points system.

There was to be further bad news, despite Papwa's best attempts to start the year in a hurry. His application to participate in the 1966 Natal Open was refused.

Worse was to come: He and 'FM' Paul were brought into the Security Branch offices for 'a chat'. They were troublemakers, weren't they? Always applying for permits to play in tournaments reserved for whites! After hours of answering the same questions, they were released.

There was much consternation that Papwa's failure to be granted a permit for the Natal Open might lead to SA golfers being blackballed worldwide, and a special plea was made to the Minister of Planning to reverse the decision.

A few days later this decision was reversed, with permit permission for Indian and Coloured spectators approved, but not Africans. The problem was how to keep the Indian and white spectators apart.

Separate facilities were to be provided with a special change room reserved for him in the caddy facility. In addition, special entrances for white and non-european spectators would be erected.

White golf administrators feared that if Papwa was not allowed to play as one of the five, South Africa's standing with the championship committee could be endangered on the grounds that a qualifying contest was subject to race discrimination. This in turn could disqualify many South Africans from contests which were subject to international control.

And so subsequently allowed to defend his Natal Open title at Royal Durban GC, by the 11th hole on the final day, Papwa was on -3 with Gary Player and Cobie le Grange playing behind him only one shot ahead and both battling. But he dropped shots at the 12th and the 16th where a spectator trampled his ball into the ground, and that was that.

Nevertheless, he finished strongly with scores of 75 73 73 71 (292) for 4th place, losing to Gary Player's score of 286 followed by Cobie le Grange and Tommy Horton (wins 41 including SA Open) in second and third. Behind him were Tony Jacklin (wins 29 including 2 Majors), George Will (wins 20, Ryder Cup), Lionel Platts (wins 6), and Bobby Cole (wins 13 including two SA Opens, World Cup).

It was an excellent effort as he was 9 strokes behind at the beginning of the final round. There was a special cheer for him when he came off the last green and also at the prize-giving.

Nevertheless, it was not a particularly good tournament for Papwa who, despite improving each round, was not at his best and weak on his chipping that was usually very accurate, and perhaps the strongest phase of his game.

To complicate matters, given that Papwa was playing under the threat of banning, official efforts at separating the races soon collapsed and possibly with them, any hope of Papwa getting government approval for the next tournament.

The decision by the government was that Papwa could only play in events in which he had previously played up to the end of the previous year, and then still only subject to the issue of the necessary

Chapter 7: Reaction

permit, created anxiety due to the uncertainty over whether he would be allowed to play in the other tournaments required to qualify for the Carling World Championship, and his ability to amass points in the Natal Open.

He hoped this year would be his big year, but while playing in the first of these tournaments, the PGA at Germiston where he finished 11th with rounds of 72 70 76 72 (290), he was informed that he was banned from the following Western Province Open, and he appealed.

When Papwa was thereafter barred from competing in the Transvaal Open, it effectively prevented him from qualifying for the lucrative $200,000 Carling World Championships in Canada in September, given that selections were based on the important SA tournaments, in case he succeeded on the world stage and drew attention to the iniquities of his position.

It was clear the government did not want Papwa to qualify for the Carling World Championship which carried a prize purse of $200,000 and once again embarrass the government.

This raised the possibility of South Africa in turn being banned from the Carling World Championships in Britain later that year.

Selection, being based on the major South African tournaments. With Papwa not allowed to play in at least two of them, South Africa could lose her standing on the grounds that a qualifying contest was subject to racial discrimination.

Drum January 30, 1966 magazine headline put it: 'Is Sewgolum Sunk?', and 'Papwa – Ghost of Golf?'

A golfing ghost, a dark shadow drifting about white golf courses, among the white professionals, but not one of them...

As *Drum* reported: 'They, the best of them, led exotic lives pursuing golf balls halfway across the world. He, who ranked with the best of them, rented two rooms in a Durban shack for himself, his wife and four young children, and scraped around to find extra cash to support his blind mother.

IS SEWSUNKER SUNK?

Photographer: Alfred Kumalo

'Once he had a shack of his own, but that was swept away with the building of the new Northern Freeway. He holds unquestionably one record: the world's poorest professional golfer who has won three National Opens. As the lone darkie on the White professional circuit Papwa can enter their tournaments but not their clubhouses. Now, it seems he may be barred from all the major tournaments.

'Officialdom has him bunkered, without a niblick. The one-time barefoot boy, who first handled a club caddying to help support his mother could be back where he started.'

Worse was to follow. Upon his return home, Papwa was informed that Riverside, where he lived, had now been declared a 'white area'

Chapter 7: Reaction

under the Group Areas Act, and he had to relocate to Mobeni Heights. This was an area set aside for Indians in Chatsworth consisting of 11 neighbourhoods and a total of 20,000 sub-economic and low-cost houses reserved exclusively for Indian occupation; it was deliberately built as a buffer area between white and the black Umlazi township.

A newspaper article told of Papwa's removal. It described the shack in which he and his family lived, with its corrugated iron walls, holes in the roof and newspaper stuffed in the broken windows. The article recorded how he propped his golf clubs against his bed, whilst magazine cuttings of Papwa's victories adorned the walls.

In summer the corrugated tin roof radiated heat as the tropical sun beat down, adding to the humidity forcing them out of the shack. In winter the cold winds and at times driving rain squeezed through the cracks and onto their beds while they slept.

Costing R8 in monthly rates, his meagre golf purses from his wins and coaching hardly covered the cost of school uniforms and fees, as well as food, such that there were hungry stomachs.

This led to a spate of letters asking if Gary Player would assist, and why none of the white players were speaking out against Papwa's ban. A word of warning was sounded that in the long run, Papwa might not suffer alone, as any such ban could lead to similar bannings for Player, Henning and others when playing abroad.

Up to this stage Player's political utterances had been confined to meaningless platitudes and non-committal statements. But now he released his first book, Grand Slam Golf, wherein he declared his loyalty to Verwoerd and apartheid, defending segregation and denying he was living in a 'police state'. He further referred to Africans as still tribal, believing in witchcraft, primitive magic, ritual murder and polygamy, and where his wealth was seen in cattle not money. He went on to state that Africans were happy and better off than in the rest of Africa.

However Papwa's plight struck a sympathetic chord and donations came in such that he was able to obtain a 'dream house', as described by the press, situated at No. 1, Road 403, Mobeni.

Assassination

It was evident that any effort to compete in predominantly white tournaments was an exercise in futility. To add insult to injury, Papwa now discovered that the Security Branch, who had monitored his movements for some time, had a thick file on him, and this knowledge must have placed considerable pressure on him.

The security police knew Papwa was not a troublemaker and that he just wanted to play golf, but it was his followers who brought politics into the sport with their uncivilised behaviour which made the country look bad.

Now intelligence agents started moving into their area and began looking for any sinister things trying to dig up 'dirt' on Papwa, for instance, that he was an insurgent carrying mail to different underground 'terrorists'.

Still awaiting a response to his appeal, and while preparing in the hope of competing in the WP Open in Cape Town, burly security police burst through the door in District Six, hauling him out of bed in the dead of night while staying at the home of prominent activist Sissy Gool. They demanded to know what Papwa was doing in Cape Town and warned him that he had become an embarrassment to the SA government, threatening to do something about it if he continued to compete in white tournaments.

Papwa responded that he had come to play as the minister had yet to make his pronouncement concerning his appeal. 'You banned, boy. You not allowed to play! Didn't you know that? Have you seen all the trouble you make? We know what to do with troublemakers; Robben Island is just out there. Continue and we going to get you!'

Shortly afterwards, still shaken, Papwa and Fred Paul drove to Port Elizabeth for the General Motors Open at the Wedgewood Park Country Club, and for the first time, Papwa was invited to attend the mayoral reception at the city hall where Port Elizabeth mayor H.J. Toerien welcomed Papwa by name to scattered applause, while in the corner the Security Police hurriedly scribbled their notes.

The organisers had arranged a caravan for them on the course as well as two 'white' security guards whose presence suggested they were more likely to be security police, supposedly to keep them safe from agitators and fans.

When darkness set in, clouds rolled across the moon to blot out the moonlight. Papwa suggested FM take the guards some hot tea, but when FM peered out of the caravan, the guards were nowhere to be seen. They felt alone and in the eerie pitch-black night, FM's gut was sending him a message, especially as during the day they had also noticed some men with closely-cropped hair watching their movements and the caravan, such that their nagging fears persisted.

Still disturbed by their Cape Town experience and the chilling message from the security police, FM suggested that they quietly depart the caravan, especially given the isolation of the club. They checked into a non-european hotel in the city.

The next crisp breezy morning as the sun was rising, they returned showered and refreshed, feeling a little foolish, teasing each other about their stupidity and fears. The security guards were back outside the caravan, and for just a second, Papwa thought he saw a puzzled look on their faces as they caught sight of them.

Chatting on their way to change and retrieve Papwa's clubs, FM suddenly stopped grabbing hold of Papwa, he flung him to one side as he attempted to open the caravan door; and a strong wave of gas hit them. The caravan was reeking of gas! But neither of them had touched the stove, and surprised, they backed away rapidly, waiting for an explosion.

They strode over to the clubhouse and sought out the manager. Together they returned with the maintenance manager, who confirmed the strong smell of gas. On further inspection, they discovered that the gas pipe leading to the stove from the outside had been tampered with and cut during the night. Gas is a silent killer. The assassination had failed!'

By the time he teed off in the Dunlop Masters, Papwa was lying 7th on the world championship table after missing out on the Transvaal and Western Province Open. But his quest to make up points was not to be, as he finished 11th at Zwartkop CC in the SA Masters 74 74 69 69 (286) after injuring his wrist and out of the money (the top 10 received prize money). The tournament was won by Gary Player 273 by three shots from John Hayes.

Then late Tuesday afternoon, FM received news that Papwa had been granted permission to play in the South African Open at Houghton, Johannesburg the following week.

Papwa's performance in the South African Open, the last tournament on the circuit, was worse when he failed to make the cut, with Gary Player beating Harold Henning and Cobie le Grange by one stroke to retain the title, shooting 278.

This relatively busy, and one must add, lucrative schedule, clashed

Chapter 7: Reaction

with the SA Non-European Championship. Accordingly, he did not play in the 1966 Non-European Open held in Bloemfontein, which was won by David 'Bobby Locke' Motati. His winnings for the year on the SA Non-European circuit were a meagre R476.

The apartheid apparatchiks were determined not to make any "concessions" thereafter and explicitly thwarted his chance of representing his own country in golf.

So where did this leave Papwa's future? He intended playing in the three Rhodesian tournaments the following month, but he did not have sufficient money to venture overseas again.

The question doing the rounds was would his followers rally round and start a fund to sponsor him again?

The professional circuit in Rhodesia (that is the former Southern Rhodesia following the break-up of the Federation of Rhodesia (Southern & Northern Rhodesia – Zambia) and Nyasaland (Malawi), and the Unilateral Declaration of Independence (UDI) by Ian Smith) in 1966 and subsequent years consisted of three events, the Dunlop Tournament, the Bata Bush Babes Tournament and the Haig Flame Lily Tournament.

These were all open non-racial events and Papwa took the opportunity to play in all three, but he was the only black golfer to do so, as despite the term non-racial, Rhodesian black golfers were not allowed to participate[13].

There was a strong representation of South Africa's best professionals, and Papwa was able to compete with the best. In the Dunlop he finished 5th with scores of 71 75 71 71 (288) five shots behind winner Allan Henning. Papwa won the Bush Babes 71 73 72 69 (285) by three shots from Trevor Wilkes, and he finished 8th in the Flame Lily 72 69 75 72 (288).

An illicit affair

Whilst playing in the Germiston PGA tournament the white press reported in regard to Papwa that 'only a handful of Indians and

---

[13] According to Lewis Muridzo, father and coach to Lewis Chitengwa, and the first black Rhodesian golf professional to be allowed to play on the Rhodesian circuit in the 1980s.

Coloureds chased Papwa's shots – including his wife Isabel.' But Papwa's wife's name was Suminthra. So who was this? Was this Isabel the beauty queen?

Graham Wulff noted in his unpublished autobiography, *Olay Capers*, that Papwa had an affair with a beauty queen called Isabel Prince, and a relationship developed between them.

Fred Paul recalled Isabel being in Papwa's life when he started managing Papwa's career in late 1963. Isabel and Papwa occasionally travelled together when he was away from Durban, and frequently spoke on the telephone. Papwa was seldom away from her when he visited the 'Golden City' (Johannesburg) for golf tournaments, and where Papwa ingratiated himself with her parents who were impressed that such a celebrity was courting their daughter.

The first reliable confirmation that Wulff had of the relationship was when Paul came to see him and told him that Papwa was being sued for maintenance. Isabel had given birth to Papwa's child some nine months previously, and the case was to go to court the next day.

Paul asked Wulff if he could use his influence to stop the news from getting into the English press, but Wulff was not optimistic. His view was a practical one: to tell the newspapers the story was the best way to guarantee that it would receive publicity – 'keep mum', was his advice.

He was right, as the English press failed to sniff out the story. By contrast, the *POST*, which served the Indian community, tumbled to the affair and splashed the story over the middle section of its edition of the 8th of June 1966. The newspaper also carried a picture of a smiling Papwa with his wife Suminthra, wearing a colourful sari.

The *POST* article called attention to rumours that had spread during the previous year about Papwa's relationship 'with a woman' who appeared to be largely unidentified. 'When he played on the South African Circuit last year, there was talk about a "mystery woman" following him from course to course.'

Golfers log a lot of time on the road, away from families, ensconced in hotel rooms, sometimes doing up to 20 one-week tournaments a year. More important, there's no shortage of temptation.

Chapter 7: Reaction

It is quite usual for women to follow successful sportsmen, starry-eyed, hoping to gain their attention. It was lonely on the road and not incomprehensible that Papwa would fall for Isabel's charms.

Clearly the rumours would have reached Suminthra. How this was dealt with is unknown. But the Sewgolums were a close knit family with four young children. Papwa had to make a choice, and he chose his immediate family, whilst Suminthra chose to stand by her man.

When the *POST* reporter arrived at her house in Bristow Road, Isabel's mother was prepared to say very little other than: 'Papwa is a nice chap and we all like him. He still visits us and we don't want to give any interviews to the press.'

In the streets, *POST* billboards announce to passers-by: 'Unwed Mum takes Papwa to court.' The article started dramatically with the words: 'Eyebrows were raised when our national golf hero, Sewsunker "Papwa" Sewgolum, appeared on a summons at the Durban Maintenance Court.'

The fact that he had to appear at the Maintenance Court meant that Papwa had not heeded the pleas of the mother of his child to provide money in any adequate amount to cover the child's expenses.

As such, Isabel Prince would have had to show that Papwa was the father of her child, Nathan, born on the 27th of July 1965, and that, not only was she in need of maintenance, but that Papwa was in a position to pay such money.

Papwa was certainly aware of Isabel's pregnancy, and the birth of his child. Only after repeatedly asking him for money would she have gone to the police for assistance, and thereafter been referred to the maintenance officer at the Durban Magistrates' Court.

The maintenance officer no doubt asked her for all the details of the birth of the child and his father. Isabel would also have been required to establish her daily financial needs for food, clothing and accommodation for Nathan, which list of invoice expenses in caring for her one-year old child she would have had to present to the magistrate on her first appearance.

In the normal course of events, the arrival of mothers and fathers at the Maintenance Court provides no cause for comment, but on the 5th of June 1966 it caused a great stir. Papwa's renown meant that everyone in the crowded waiting room recognised him.

The newspaper report continued in the same dramatic fashion. 'Within minutes of his arrival word went around like wildfire and women gossiped in the waiting room and the precincts of the court.'

The article went on to explain that Papwa was soon joined in court by Fred Paul, his manager and friend: 'Papwa, who was dressed in a time-to-shine suit and a "Robin Hood" hat, was accompanied by his wife, wearing a colourful sari, and an attorney, Rabbi Bughwandeen.'

Bughwandeen was a prominent member of The Natal Indian Congress in its campaign against apartheid.

That this human rights lawyer represented Papwa should come as no surprise, given Papwa's prominence to the anti-apartheid movement following his victory in the 1963 Natal Open and the 'trophy in the rain' photo travelling worldwide, followed by his victory over Gary Player in the 1965 Natal Open. It was politically important to maintain his image as the underdog in the local and international media.

In 1960, Bughwandeen together with his 'Brothers of Cato Manor & Newlands', known as the diamond brothers, purchased the Moon Hotel, and ventured into the hospitality industry being pioneers of the hotel business in the Indian Community in Durban. Under apartheid the Moon Hotel was one of the most upmarket hotels of Durban in the "non-european" sector. It attracted all race groups, and featured many famous groups and artists with regular jazz and other musician line-ups.

Roopie Bughwandeen, the widow of Rabbi Bughwadeen, told author Christopher Nicholson[14] that her husband had asked Papwa if he acknowledged his paternity. On being given an affirmative he was insistent that Papwa should do the right thing and pay as much maintenance as he could afford. 'Rabbi felt very strongly that whoever the father was, irrespective of fame and fortune, he had to make sure his child was not without means,' was the way that she put it.

This was confirmed by the POST article that went on to say that after a consultation between his attorney and the public prosecutor the matter was settled.

'Papwa signed the consent order to support Nathan Prince,' according to the *POST*. The article stated that 'the complainant in

Chapter 7: Reaction

the case was Miss Isabel Prince, of Bristow Road, Mayville. She was also present, wearing an attractive dress.' Papwa agreed to pay R8 per month through the court, starting on the 3rd of July 1966.

'Papwa left the court in a jocular mood after cracking a joke with the clerk of the court,' reflecting that Isabel had insisted that payment be made through the maintenance officer. Clearly she had no faith in the payment being made without the threat of court action hanging over the golfer's head.

Were he to default, he could be charged with a criminal offence. If such infringement was repeated and the non-payment could not be justified, he could be sent to prison.

Every month Papwa had to and make this payment at the Magistrates' Court in Durban.

The newspaper also made mention of his imminent golfing trip to the European circuit: 'Papwa is due to pack his bags for the fabulous Carling World Championships to be played over the Royal Birkdale Course in England in September.'

No doubt, Bughwandeen would have discussed how he would manage his obligations when he was away later in the year, and he would have seen to it that Papwa left enough money to enable the payment of these monthly payments in his absence.

Bughwandeen did not charge Papwa for his services, instead he traded his services for free golf lessons and a pair of golf shoes (which did not fit).

Papwa, who had always been beset by financial problems, now found that his new obligation to support his child simply worsened his plight. He fell into arrears with maintenance on several occasions and had to reappear in court.

Clearly their relationship had ended, and little is known of what happened to his son Nathan, and Isabel could not be traced. The rumour is that they went abroad, and the Sewgolum family lost all contact.

Banned

Because of his success, and as part of an increasing clamp down on all forms of interracial sport, he found it tougher, to raise money to play overseas. Playing abroad was no longer as successful, and the 'Papwa

Trust Fund' was drying up.

Meanwhile, companies used his fame, getting him to promote their products, but in return, instead of cash payments, one prominent liquor company simply offered him a case of 'Cane spirits' every month as payment. No corporate sponsored a player of colour, no matter how famous.

Cracks slowly, appeared in the SA sports wall that kept black sportsmen out of the establishment. Pressure was brought to bear, both externally and internally, when in 1966 Senator Robert Kennedy (President John F Kennedy's brother, and the previous USA attorney-general prior to his bid for the USA Democratic nomination and his subsequent assassination) addressed UCT. His inspirational Day of Affirmation speech is widely considered as one of the greatest American civil rights speeches, where he spoke out about his belief that all people have a basic human right to participate in the political decisions that affect their lives.

"Laws can embody standards; governments can enforce laws – but the final task is not a task for government. It is a task for each and every one of us. Every time we turn our heads the other way when we see the law flouted – when we tolerate what we know to be wrong – when we close our eyes and ears to the corrupt because we are too busy, or too frightened – when we fail to speak up and speak out – we strike a blow against freedom and decency and justice."

On 6 September 1966, SA was rocked to its core with the assassination of the so-called architect of apartheid, Prime Minister Hendrik Verwoerd in the House of Assembly, who was stabbed to death by a court messenger Dimitri Tsafendas[15].

Verwoerd was replaced by Balthazar Johannes Vorster, who oversaw the abolishment of the Coloured's voters' role and escalation of SA's border wars, and further alienation of Sewgolum and other sports people of colour.

For inadvertently putting the bigoted state policy under the international spotlight, Sewgolum became a target of official harassment and machination. When he again won the Natal Open two years later,

---

15   Tsfendas of Greek-Mozambique extraction, a lifelong militant, was detained in a mental facility until his death in October 1999

Chapter 7: Reaction

apartheid directors were determined not to make any "concessions" thereafter, and explicitly thwarted his chance of representing his own country in golf.

Then finally the severest of all blows. After BJ Vorster was declared Prime Minister, he immediately announced that he would continue to implement apartheid as conceived by Verwoerd. Consequently, the new Vorster government announced it would be strictly enforcing the colour bar in golf, and that included Papwa. He would be excluded from all white tournaments in the future.

Papwa, still in his prime at 38, was effectively **banned**, and was not allowed to play in any white tournaments or enter any golf course, not even as a spectator.

Banned from playing in any more tournaments in South Africa in 1966, it was clear beyond doubt that this was the end for him as far as big golf here was concerned.

When asked for his comments, Gary Player said, 'I do not meddle in politics.' Later he did speak out in support of Papwa saying he should be allowed to play in SA golf tournaments.

The government, which had decreed that mixed sport would not be permitted, lashed out at the global community, but the country was now on its way to being wholly isolated during the 1970s and 1980s.

During this uncertain period, Papwa is lost between two worlds. He has gambled by giving up his job and going into strict training for full-time golf. On the Non-European circuit, if he won everything – the South African, Natal, Transvaal, Western Province, Kimberley, Port Elizabeth Opens – he could collecting maybe R500.

With no rich sponsor such as many White professionals had, and no private club to pay him, he could barely support himself and family on this, let alone find the cash to play on the big circuits overseas.

There were just a few tournaments for blacks, and although Papwa was good wherever he played, how could he be expected to be competition sharp? With his soul amputated, Papwa became very ill, depressed, and worried as to how he would make ends meet and support his family; he began declining.

The outlawing of Papwa clearly affected the standing of SA's ambassador-of-goodwill, Player. Player was a hero in America and treated with respect, yet the last thing he wanted was to have his name connected with a 'racial' incident. But this is what happened. Player's remarks that in SA, sport and politics were one and the same 'game', simply meant that black, anti-South African groups now targeted him.

Politics entered the SA sporting arena more forcibly and on a much larger scale than ever before: multiracial versus multinational.

Papwa had become a severe embarrassment for the National Party government, which faced growing international scrutiny, particularly in the wake of the 1960 Sharpeville massacre. However, instead of easing its race laws, it was determined not to give in to the growing pressure.

Papwa now took his plea to Vorster but never received a response:

"This humble letter is designed to bring to your notice the many difficulties I am faced with in order to play in the South African Golf Circuit. I am proud to be South African and I shall always remain loyal to my country. This banning order preventing me from playing golf for a living will indeed cripple me financially and as a result my family will be destitute. In this dark hour of crisis, I can only appeal to you to consider my plight and the plight of my family. I close this letter with the fervent prayer that my pleading will not go in vain."

Meanwhile letters started streaming into the newspapers asking why Player was not intervening to help Papwa. Was it because Papwa had beaten him?

'I don't know, John, what should I say?' Player asked his confidant. Hildyard suggested he just say that golf was his game and not politics. 'That should not offend anybody,' said Hildyard.

But the reply did offend or at least got caught in the crusader's craw of *Sunday Times* newspaper's woman columnist, Molly Reinhardt, Molly seized the opportunity came out with a blistering attack on Player for not standing up for Papwa.

'I have the greatest admiration for Papwa's impeccable behaviour throughout his golfing career. No golfer in the world has suffered the insults that have been handed out to this first-class sportsman,' she wrote.

Chapter 7: Reaction

Player tried painfully hard to make plain his belief that the Vorster government was doing the best it could in a difficult situation. He called Reinhardt a 'sweet old lady'.

Molly pounced on that one, too. She now had the most popular SA name in the world on the tip of her épée, and her *Sunday Times* readership soared. She said she did not mind being called old, or a lady, but sweet she never was.

Letters to the editor, pro and con Player, glutted the mail and were run every Sunday under a streamer 'MOLLY-GARY LETTERS'.

'Not good enough', according to some newspapers who thought that Player should have taken a stronger stand and not condoned the treatment that was being handed out to Papwa.

Despite the bannings, threats and intimidation, or perhaps because of it, Peter Louw , the secretary-general of the South African Non-European Golf Association (which along with the South African Golf Union and the PGA, who had been campaigning on Papwa's behalf), received a letter from Howard R Taylor, the director of the Carling World of Golf Championship, extending an invitation for Papwa to participate in that year's tournament which was scheduled to be played at Royal Birkdale, Southport, England, 31 August – 3 September 1966.

Taylor stated in the letter, that: on the basis that "our action recognises the fact that Mr Sewgolum was unable to complete his qualifying tournaments through no fault of his own and that in the four qualifying tournaments in which he participated, he had made a very good showing," Taylor however, specified that Papwa's acceptance was for that year only.

The aim was to stage a true world championship for golf and make another contribution: 'to international understanding by bringing together golfers of all races, creeds and colours in friendly competition.'

In 1966 the brewery tournament board had expanded the qualifying field to include the champions from eight zones. Zone 1 USA, Zone 2 Canada, Zone 3 Mexico, Central America, South America, and the Caribbean, Zone 4 Great Britain and Northern Ireland, Zone 5 Europe, North Africa, The Middle East, Zone 6 Africa, Zone 7 Asia, and Zone 8 Australasia.

Each qualifying player earned a minimum of $500 for expenses and could also stand to win lucrative prize money – always useful for a man like Papaw, who was forever struggling to make ends meet.

Those participating included, inter alia, Bruce Devlin, Billy Casper, Al Greenberger, Jacky Cupid, Roberto De Vicenza, Bernard Hunt, Julius Boors, Christy O'Connor, Harold Henning, Gary Player, Doug Sanders, Mike Slouched, Johnny Pot, Peter Allis, Neil Coles, David Snell, Ramon Seta, Lionel Plats, Gene Littler, Keel Nagle, Bob Charles, and Peter Thompson.

The competitors program also included a death notice for the previous year winner Tony Lemma who was tragically killed in Illinois, USA on July 24th. Lemma had won the 1965 Carling World Event at the Pleasant Valley CC in Massachusetts and was to play at Royal Bridal as the defending champion.

After two rounds the only South Africans making the cut were Trevor Wilkes (151), Bob Verwey (151), Barry Franklin (150), Papwa Sewgolum (146), who was a shot behind Harold Henning (145).

For the third round Papwa was paired with George Archer (USA). They were in 17th position trailing the leaders Bert Yancy, followed by Kel Nagle, then Australian Bruce Devlin and Peter Butler.

Those trailing Papwa included iconic golfers Bruce Crampton, Jim Ferree, Charlie Sifford, Doug Sanders, Gay Brewer, Dave Stockton, Christy O'Connor, legendary Moe Norman, Billy Casper, and Roberto de Vicenzo amongst others.

Finally, Bruce Devlin, 28, won his third PGA tournament. Great Britain with a four-round total of 286 nipping US golfer Billy Casper, who had a great last two rounds, by one stroke.

Papwa finished 6th against the world's best on 293 – a terrific performance, and by so doing, qualified for the event again the following year, returning to SA some R2,500 richer.

Banned from playing in SA tournaments, and with only small purses available in Rhodesia and on the TPA Non-European Tour, he had no alternative but to look further afield to try and support his family.

In the convoluted thinking at that time, the Nationalist Party in power by banning him from playing in SA, seemed more concerned

Chapter 7: Reaction

with keeping Papwa away from the local media limelight, especially where people of colour were concerned, even though with his passport in tact, he attracted substantial world media attention whenever he played abroad.

Papwa

Papwa playing at Royal Birkdale GC during the Carling World Golf Championship. Photographer unknown

There were more forays overseas. He first went to Toronto, Canada to compete in the Carling event at the Board of Trade GC, which was won by Billy Casper, but with a score of 152 for the first two rounds he failed to make the cut. Still the appearance money of $500 was not to be sniffed at.

Chapter 7: Reaction

Then it was on to his long-awaited debut on the 1967 US tour where he signed up to compete in tournaments in Dallas, Houston, New Orleans, Oklahoma City, Dublin, and Toronto.

Among his spectators at the Houston event during the opening round was the previous year's US tour money leader, Billy Casper, who wanted to see for himself this upside-down grip that he'd heard about.

William 'Billy' Earl Casper Jr. was one of the most prolific tournament winners on the PGA Tour. Like Papwa, Casper started as a caddie to rank seventh all-time in career PGA Tour wins with 51, across a 20-year period between 1956 and 1975.

Casper with a total of 69 Professional wins, won three major championships and a Senior Major, represented the United States on a then-record eight Ryder Cup teams, and twice PGA Player of the Year (1966 and 1970), twice leading money winner, and won five Vardon Trophy awards for the lowest seasonal scoring average on the Tour. He was also inducted into the World Golf Hall of Fame in 1978 (the year after Bobby Locke's induction).

Respected for his extraordinary putting and short-game skills, Casper was a superior strategist who overcame his distance disadvantages against longer-hitting competitors such as Arnold Palmer and Jack Nicklaus with moxie, creative shot-making and clever golf-course management abilities. Never a flashy gallery favourite, Casper developed his own self-contained style, relying on solid technique, determination, concentration, and perseverance.

Casper couldn't believe how Papwa could hit the ball so far with his reverse grip. 'It was amazing,' Casper told the press that day.

Despite looking forward to his long-awaited US debut (with Casper looking forward to playing against him) Papwa, never a good traveller, was homesick in the US. He struggled to find vegetarian meals and came down with food poisoning at the Houston Open. He returned home, miserable.

'He was always homesick,' recalls Verwey. 'He was just never very happy whenever he was away from Durban.'

Through the summer of 1966/67, Papwa had continuing success on the non-white circuit in SA. Despite reclaiming the 1966 Natal

Non-European title from Rajdaw, and beating David 'Bobby Locke' Motati by 5 shots in 1967, the *POST* summed up his performance as follows: "There were streaks of brilliance by the maestro Papwa. But on the whole, from this showing, he will have to put in some eight hours of practice per day if he is to be in the hunt against top golfers on the White circuit."

The SA non-european golfers played for their richest prize in the 1967 SA Non-European Championship hosted at the King David Country Club. Cigarette manufacturers, Cavalla Ltd, presented a purse of R1000 for the meeting and provided extra funds to help with the tournament's organisation.

The tournament met with success, as the club willingly offered its course, and provided all the accommodation possible for the comfort of the black officials and competitors, and attracted a vast gallery. At the time, Ismail Chowglay was still regarded as the best non-european golfer in the Western Province.

Golfers travelled great distances to attend and take part in the tournament, although the sponsorship was insufficient to cover the prize-money, consequently the entry fee was allocated to further make up the purse: 'It is these people we can really class as sportsmen,' stated Louis Nelson.

The King David CC closed the clubhouse for the duration of the tournament, and no European members or spectators were allowed on the course, much as they might have wished to see the play.

It was expected that Papwa would again be the victor. And he faithfully realised expectations by leading from the start, and holding it to the end, winning by seven strokes with scores of 70 69 72 71 (282) from Chowglay 74 74 70 71 (289), then came Mogoerane and Hlapo.

Despite Papwa being banned by the Vorster government from entering in 'white' tournaments, Fred Paul continued writing applications for permits, and the press kept reporting that they had been turned down, embarrassing the government such that they were now deemed a threat to national security and possible treason.

Papwa was, however, able to campaign that summer on the Rhodesian pro circuit, were he made a strong showing in the second event, as the defending champion, the Bata Bush Babes (R2000)

Tournament, finishing in a tie for 4th place on 286. This was won by Graham Henning on 282. In the third and final event, the Dunlop Tournament, Papwa again finished in a tie for 4th with scores of 72 72 71 72 (285), but a long way behind back-to-back winner Graham Henning on 276.

The banning didn't apply to competing abroad, and after receiving medical treatment, he returned to the UK in July for the 1967 Open Championship.

The venue was Royal Liverpool (Hoylake), and he got through the qualifying stages quite comfortably on a score of 143, but failed to make any headway in the championship proper and came 57th, with Roberto de Vicenzo winning on 278. While overseas, he played in a number of other events in both the UK and on the Continent.

India: Offer you can't refuse

Papwa then accepted an invitation to compete in the 1967 Indian Open tournament in Calcutta. He had become a household name in India where there were few or no international sporting heroes, and there was a great deal of interest in the treatment he had endured as an Indian in a country with a 'white' government.

Fred Paul and Papwa were garlanded at the hotel in accordance with the custom. The Indian people were anxious to meet a son of their soil who had shown the rest of the world that golf was not beyond them. No expense was spared in ensuring that Papwa was looked after.

Contrast this with his coming from a shack with holes in the roof and newspaper stuffed into the windows, and an unbearably hot corrugated iron roof in summer. Now they were provided with an air-conditioned bungalow and a servant.

The saga of Papwa's poor treatment in SA at the hands of the golfing authorities and government had received great prominence in the Indian press over the years, and the Indian people took Papwa to be a national icon, such that he had assumed a god-like status, and his company was highly prized. Mobbed by fans and reporters, he could not even buy the simplest item, like toothpaste, without causing crowds of people to gather.

The status of Papwa as an international sporting celebrity,

something India had failed to produce, ensured that the two attended a social whirl of parties, receptions and dinners where they were wined and dined at the best restaurants.

The Royal Calcutta Golf Clubhouse

The Royal Calcutta Golf Club situated at Tollygunge is affectionately known as the 'Royal' and is synonymous with the game of golf in India. Founded in 1829, the Royal is the oldest golf club outside the British Isles. The oldest is the Royal & Ancient, St. Andrews in Scotland, the home of golf. The golfing heritage and history of the 'Royal' have created a truly hallowed place for the game of golf.

Ladies were very reluctantly admitted to the club meant exclusively for the use of gentlemen in 1886 when the committee voted 43 against 13 on the condition that female members were only allowed to use the course in the mornings.

The area over which The Royal Calcutta course is laid was originally paddy fields, and the course is consequently very undulating. Successive committees built mounds and planted thousands of trees and shrubs to enhance the beauty of the property. However, The Royal's conspicuous features are its strategically located water tanks and natural water hazards. Greens at The Royal are quite large by modern standards, and their undulations make them tricky. The par 4s are long and challenging to score on, where approach shots require

Chapter 7: Reaction

long and medium irons to be hit which test the skills of all the golfers.

Membership of the Club stood at over 2,500. A milestone in the Club's history was the election of the first Indian Club Captain, Kamal Kumar Mitra in 1963.

Being the first golf club in India and where the game of golf was introduced and started in the country, it had a policy of encouraging the local lads working as caddies to become some of the best professionals in the country.

Over the years, The Royal had become very popular venue for many prestigious amateur and professional events including the Indian Open. Later many renowned International golfers would walk these fairways – the most significant ones being – major winners Walter Hagen, Peter Thompson, Payne Stewart, Charl Schwartzel, Louis Oosthuizen among others. Indian greats such as I.S. Malik, H.S. Malik, Billoo Sethi, Ashok Malik, 'Bunny' Lakshman Singh, Jeev Milkha Singh, Arjun Atwal, Jyoti Randhawa, S.S.P. Chawrasia, and Anirban Lahiri, and of course Papwa Sewgolum, have all been a part of the Royal golfing heritage and history!

India had her star system in the 1960s, but Bollywood was in its pre-history. Raj Kapoor was famous, and playback singer Lata Mangeshkar, who sung prerecorded songs for the Indian film industry, was a darling in a million homes. As far as sportsmen and sportswomen were concerned, the biggest stars were Ramanathan Krishnan the first great tennis player, Leslie Claudius, the field hockey player, and cricketer Farokh Engineer, but Sewgolum wasn't far off the pace.

Indian fans had watched carefully since Papwa won the Dutch Open in 1959. His exploits were carefully followed. He was perhaps the first truly pan-Indian sporting star.

Huge crowds came to see Papwa play, and he obliged by signing autographs and shaking hands. However, the organisers at the Royal Calcutta Golf Club were perplexed, given the treatment Papwa had endured, when he patriotically insisted that the SA flag be flown alongside the Indian and flags of the other competing nations. This flag had been deliberately removed as the Indian government had forbidden the presence of the SA flag as there was no diplomatic recognition. Ordinary Indians could not understand his loyalty given all the injustices perpetrated against him and other social minorities in the country.

Several big names were in the field – Peter Thompson from Australia (five time British Open champion), Guy Wolstenholme and Malcolm Gregson from England. However it was a little known Japanese player, Kenji Hosoishi, who took the title on 287, beating Gregson in a play-off.

The press commented on his skill around the greens, and large crowds of spectators followed him around enraptured by his reverse grip, and marvelling at his game, especially the proficiency of his chipping.

But, in the strange conditions, he struggled with the fierce unrelenting heat and exhaustion, and only managed a 6th place tied with Randall Vines and Barry Coxon on 295 – twelve strokes behind the winner in this top-field tournament, not such a bad result in these conditions given the fact that this was his first tournament on the Indian subcontinent.

Meanwhile, despite the fact that Graham Wulff had little contact with Papwa since Nelson, and subsequently Paul had taken over Papwa's management, he was pleased to receive an invitation from the Indian Government to visit India, and to spend two days as Prime Minister Indira Gandhi's guest, and receive an honour from Indira Gandhi[16], not long after she had taken office in acknowledgement of the help he had given his former employee, Papwa.

Unexpectedly, Papwa received a letter dated 20th September 1967 from Brigadier Rodriques offering him the position of The Royal Calcutta Golf Club Professional, with a monthly salary of £250 plus a house, the first Indian offered this position since the club was founded in 1829. Now 38, with probably only another five years of competing at the top level. This was much more than he could earn in SA.

The letter came at a crucial time for Papwa because his career had reached a crossroads. Should he stay in Durban where he was banned from playing in white tournaments, even merely becoming a member

---

16 Indira Gandhi was the daughter of Jawaharlal Nehru, the first and only female Prime Minister of India. Her own bodyguards and Sikh nationalists assassinated her on 31 October 1984

Chapter 7: Reaction

of or just playing on a white-golf course; where he was treated as a second-class citizen with no rights, and where the policy of apartheid was rife with security police following and frightening him and his family?

Or should he accept the offer of becoming the first non-Indian club golf professional at the famous Royal Calcutta Golf course following the election of their first Indian club captain in 1963, and the oldest club in the world outside the UK?

Here he would be paid a respectable regular salary, receive a comfortable home, mix with the cream of Indian society, be respected and admired for what he had achieved, and given time off to play in certain events.

The decision seemed obvious, yet like those Jews who remained in Germany when the Nazis came to power, so Papwa believed the nationalist government would relent and allow him to once again play in the white SA tournaments. After discussing this offer with Suminthra, who didn't want to leave their family and friends, he declined the offer.

He always felt his illiteracy as an embarrassing burden and to some extent, he was an outsider, Suminthra was unhappy about making the move. It seemed safer to stay in South Africa.

Although this decision may have turned out to be a devastatingly poor one for the Sewgolum family, in hindsight, it was a wonderful decision for black-SA sport, as Papwa's trials and tribulations continued to dominate in the spotlight of world opinion as the chisel continued to break another brick in the apartheid wall.

Equally, this was a pivotal moment for the nationalist government. Papwa, through his exploits, exposed SA's golf and golf courses to potentially thousands of tourist golfers every time he played abroad. They could have engage with him by reaching out and using this non-political hero to help break down world opinion, and as a buffer between the races for dialogue and harmonious interaction, but they only saw him as a challenger to the white-man's dominance. The moment was lost. They decided to turn the screw further!

In July 1967, Papwa returned overseas and played in a number of other events in the UK including the British Open at Royal Liverpool

Golf Club, Hoylake. He progressed through the qualifying stages, but did not make the cut for the final two rounds, and on the Continent, including the July 1967 Dutch Open at The Hague where he opened with rounds of 72, 69 to be trailing Guy Wolstenholme by one-shot together with Peter Townsend and Barry Coxon.

Eventually he lost the Dutch Open by a single shot after finishing with an eagle 3 at the 18th, shooting 72 69 73 69 (283) to Peter Townsend's 72 69 69 72 (282), with Graham Henning third (284) after returning the best score of the tournament of 67 in round 3, and in the French Open he came 5th on a score of 281, finally returning home with a windfall of 1,500 pounds.

| 1967 | Peter Townsend | England | Haagsche | 282 | 1 stroke | Sewsunker Sewgolum |

Peter Townsend (wins (14))
- 1966 English Men's Open Amateur Strokeplay – Brabazon Trophy
- Represented Great Britain twice in the Ryder Cup
- ☐ European circuit (5)
- ☐ Other (8)
- ☐ Senior European Tour (1)

In the background in 1967 was South African-born 'coloured' cricketer Basil D'Oliveira from Cape Town who was as talented at cricket as Papwa was at golf, and who had left to play professionally in England. When he was selected for England to play in SA, the Vorster government stopped the tour – 'teams comprising whites and non-whites' could not be allowed to compete in SA.

Chapter 7: Reaction

Papwa, the champion overseas, a second-class citizen in his own country. Source: Natal Newspapers.

There was an outcry in the British House of Commons. The tour was called off, and SA cricket with Graeme Pollock, Barry Richards, Mike Procter, and a host of other star performers, and which was enjoying a golden era at the time found itself isolated.

The resultant worldwide outcry, with slogans such as 'No normal sport in an abnormal society!' pushed a reluctant cricket establishment to find a way to include playing opportunities for local players of colour.

Two years later, Dawie de Villiers led his Springbok rugby team to the UK, where they faced the full wrath of the anti-apartheid movement.

Attempts by the authorities to soften race laws for soccer had mixed results, and later in 1974 tensions peaked during the final of the 'mixed-race' Chevrolet Cup between Kaizer Chiefs and Hellenic when a riot broke out leading to a pitch invasion. Two years later, Soweto erupted in flames, and the revolution began in earnest.

By clamping down on all interracial sports in 1967, the government made it impossible for Papwa to play in any 'white' tournament golf in SA ever again, nor was he allowed to enter any golf course, not even as a spectator.

Meanwhile, Papwa's erstwhile manager, Louis Nelson's ambition knew no bounds. Not content with his positions as Chairman of the Durban Golf Club, and President of the Natal Non-European Golf Union, he ascended to the presidency of the SA Non-European Golf Association.

Some good news. At this time as Papwa was offered a position at the Chainama Hills Golf Club in Lusaka, Zambia, a country just north of South Africa, but he clearly was not experienced at green-keeping and was not really qualified for the job. However this came to nought in August 1968 when he was informed that no work permit would be granted for him in Zambia.

On 2 December 1968, the General Assembly of the United Nations called upon all its member states to suspend cultural, sporting, educational and other ties with the apartheid government and with South African organisations that practiced Apartheid.

These political changes did not impact upon Papwa's life as he continued to play in the lesser non-European events in South Africa and certain neighbouring countries.

Restricted to playing in non-white tournaments in SA and neighbouring countries, Papwa turned his attention to the 1968 SA Non-European Championship at the Circle Country Club with R1,000 prize money sponsored by Grosvenor Motors BP on offer which he duly won with a record 285 (70 70 71 74) from Tshabalala (293) and Hlapo. By now he was going on 40 and had already peaked as a golfer. The standard of his game had slowly ebbed over the years and was now in decline.

Chapter 7: Reaction

Edward Johnson-Sedibe teeing-off.

Source: Christopher Meister

Politically the apartheid laws of the land were no longer confined to matters of black and white. They embraced all races. Thus it was that the Circle Country Club, being in Natal and situated in nominally a 'black' area, a permit was needed, and obtained from the Department of Planning, 'to allow Coloured, Chinese and Indians to take part in and to watch the event'. At the same time, non-europeans were not allowed to use the clubhouse or any other facilities that were reserved for whites only.

A surprise entry for this 1968 SA Non-European Open championship was 'Eddia' Johnson-Sedibe, winner of the title in 1951 and 1952, and now living in Germany where he was the resident professional at the Verband Golf Club.

By now, since going to compete in the 1959 British Open, Eddia had become the most popular teaching professional in Germany, regularly competing in Europe and finishing within the top 30.

In 1969 there were also reports in the black press of his having built his own golf course and driving range at Gat Waldhof near Hamburg, but this was a gross exaggeration as he had merely conceived the idea after his car stopped on the cobblestones of Gat Waldhof and informed the owner Bernhard Kroger, that he wanted to build a golf course there and that he had already planned the course in his head. Kroger then engaged him to consult insofar as the construction thereof.

However, by the mid-1970s he had reached a stage where he also wanted to participate in the 'struggle', the reason he had left SA, such that he returned to SA, and was subsequently killed in Angola[17].

Unfortunately, he did not witness liberation from the apartheid regime. Today he is still a role model for many young black golf enthusiasts.

Papwa followed that with a win in the Spa Open in Mbabane, Swaziland where he set a new course record with a 69. In Rhodesia, he finished 9th in the Dunlop, shooting 74 72 75 73 (294), followed by a tie for 3rd place with 281 in the Flame Lily. He then won a sponsored tournament in Mbabane, Swaziland, carding a 218 against Cox Hlapo's 223 to win by five shots.

Because of this blatant intervention and repression by the government, the United Nations General Assembly decided in 1968 to call upon all States and organisations to suspend sporting exchanges with South African bodies which practice apartheid. The UN Special Committee against Apartheid began actively to promote the sports boycott all over the world.

Action by anti-apartheid groups, Afro-Asian countries and the United Nations dealt severe defeats to apartheid sport. Apartheid became a major public issue in countries with which South Africa sought exchange in sport.

A rugby tour of Britain in 1969 proved a disaster because of public demonstrations; the British Government was obliged to prevent a cricket tour in 1970 when Afro-Asian countries threatened to boycott the Commonwealth Games.

Massive demonstrations greeted the South African rugby tour of Australia in 1971. The South African team had to be transported in Australian Air Force planes because of trade union action. More than 700 demonstrators were arrested and many were injured because of police brutality. The State of Queensland declared a state of emergency during the tour, provoking a general strike by the trade unions.

---

17 His nephew, is Lieutenant-General Aubrey Sedibe, SA's Surgeon-General. A medical doctor who served in Umkhonto weSizwe (MK), the military wing of the ANC, during the liberation struggle and transferred to the SA Defence Force when MK was incorporated into it in 1994.)

Chapter 7: Reaction

The Conservative Government hoped to arouse racist passions and win the next elections, but it was roundly defeated, and the new Labour Party Government of Gough Whitlam announced a boycott of apartheid sport.

A proposed rugby tour of New Zealand was also aborted because of public opposition and a threat by India and African countries to boycott the Commonwealth Games in Christchurch in 1974.

These campaigns strengthened the anti-apartheid movements and provided tremendous publicity to the struggle for freedom in South Africa. But the successes led to new challenges.

South Africa remained a member of many international sports federations with the help of its Western friends who enjoyed weighted voting in several codes of sport like tennis. The struggle had to be carried on with each of these bodies.

While South African tours of other countries could be disrupted by public action, it was much more difficult to prevent sports administrators in Britain, New Zealand and other countries from organising tours to South Africa.

To overcome the boycotts, South Africa began to send teams abroad with no advance publicity and to spend millions of rand to entice sportsmen and teams from abroad to play in South Africa. It announced "concessions" from time to time, none of which satisfied the Olympic principle of non-discrimination, but were meant to deceive the gullible. The new situation required SAN-ROC to intensify action with constant vigilance and a multi-pronged strategy.

Globally the campaign to isolate SA from participating from international events intensified, and was led by Sam Ramsamy and Peter Hain from the office of SAN-ROC based in London.

There was undoubtedly an awareness that something needed to be done about black golf, and in December 1968 Gary Player played a large part in organising the R1200 Gary Player Invitational golf event, the most lavish ever held in SA for black golfers. Papwa was an easy winner with Tshabalala 2nd (293). His first prize was R500.

What did it matter that he continued to dominate in the black tournaments? A golfer is only as good as his opponents. And while there were a few outstanding black players, they, too, were curtailed in that they were forced to compete against the same pool of players over and over.

Papwa also won the R.L. Bambata Boodhun trophy over 36 holes at the Springfield course, named after the grand-daddy of non-european golf run by Durban Golf Club in his honour since 1948.

The black golfers had a small circuit from the end of December 1968, all played on white courses. First, there was the Natal Non-European Championship at Kloof CC, December 25–26. Next, the South Western District Non-European Championship at Oudtshoorn on December 28–29, and then the SA Non-European Championship January 1-2.

Once again Papwa was the winner of the 1969 SA Non-European Championship, this time at the only black 18-hole club in the country, the new Athlone Golf Club in Cape Town open to all races with scores of 71 76 73 75 (295) from A. Hartzenburg (298). Clearly, the fairways were still rough and ready, the greens challenging, and the southeaster was blowing.

Meanwhile, the Government Bantu Affairs Department had Robert Grimsdell design a championship golf course overlooking the Indian Ocean including a club house at Umlazi, near Durban, for Bantu golfers, which held its first sponsored tournament in June.

Papwa finished yet another year playing for small change. Banned from playing on the rich all-White circuit in SA, and being too poor to travel overseas, Papwa faced a bleak future.

His total earnings for 1969 were a meagre R840. At least 20 per cent had to be deducted for travelling costs, caddie fees and other expenses. That left him with just R672, making his monthly income R56. The three tournaments staged by the Natal(N-E)GU carried a total cash prize of R1,700.

Papwa won all three tournaments. His purses were R100, R100, and R140. Unmistakably, Papwa got a raw deal in so-called parallel but unequal Non-European TPA tournaments. But he had no choice.

His manager, Fred Paul, made attempts to get him a job but had little success. The highest paid job Papwa could get was for R40 per month, with no time off for golf. This meant that Papwa was better off playing golf. The extra R16 kept Papwa in golf – the sport in which

Chapter 7: Reaction

white South African, Gary Player, was making a million.

Papwa now criticised the standard of the organisation of the non-european tournaments and the small purses in the press.

When articles appeared criticising the association, including Papwa's own comments concerning the poor first prize purse disbursement, Louis Nelson, now president of the SA(N-E)GU went on the attack:

Papwa is not the only non-white golfer struggling in South Africa and should stop relying on public sympathy to raise money. Wealthy Indians have dug deeply in their pockets on three occasions to send Papwa overseas and have not got a thing back for it. It is about time he stopped complaining and did a day's work himself. The media should stop paying all this attention to one player – you – when there are other younger players emerging.

Not only did Nelson criticize him in the press, but now the chairman of the non-european Durban Golf Club, Nelson had the club send Papwa a letter, criticising him for not carrying out his coaching duties, alleging that he had no interest in coaching beginners. Despite denying this allegation and offering to add extra time to coaching his position as the club's professional, the 'club' was not satisfied with his response, reviewed his position as club professional and terminated his position.

At this time, an unofficial world golf ranking of the best players during the 1960s was released by Ainsworth Sports.

Rankings for SA golfers[18]:

- 3 – Gary Player
- 50 – Harold Henning
- 165 – Cobie le Grange[19]
- **177 – Papwa Sewgolum**
- 198 – Denis Hutchinson

---

18 Retief Waltman's name is missing despite his victories in 2 SA Opens and the Dutch Open, as well as his invitations to play at the 1959 & '64 Masters.

19 Cobie le Grange achieved a world ranking of 15 in 1964/65

- 208 – Bobby Verwey
- 222 – Brian Wilkes
- 273 – Barry Franklin
- 309 – Allan Henning

Obviously Papwa's victories on the so-called parallel but unequal TPA Tour was not taken into account, nor the difficulties apartheid presented insofar as his limited permission to play in SA tournaments, his banning, and that his passport was withdrawn.

Soon afterwards, the UN General Assembly called on all its member states to suspend sporting ties with SA. In the UK, the Halt All Racist Tours (HART), which was headed by SA-born activist Peter Hain (later 'Lord', and a British cabinet minister), began baring its teeth and, in 1969, severely disrupted a rugby tour of the UK by an all-white SA team.

After the 1967 the All Black tour to SA was withdrawn by the New Zealand government because of the apartheid regime's refusal to grant visas to Maori players. The 1970 tour went ahead with four Maori players included.

However, the propaganda was unsuccessful. SA having been excluded from the 1964 Tokyo Olympics, was formally expelled from the International Olympic Committee in 1970. There would be many more sporting boycotts to come. According to the famous dictum of the anti-apartheid SA Council on Sport, there could be 'no normal sport in an abnormal society.'

The 1970 SA Non-European Championship was held at Benoni and the Ohenimuri Country Clubs where the winner, Papwa, won R250 for his efforts with scores of 77 67 69 74 (287) – the 67 equaling the course record – from Tshabalala 75 70 74 76 (295), Mogoerane and J. Ranjith 4th on 302.

Meanwhile, there was a problem insofar as the obscure distinction among blacks between amateurs and professionals. Relatively little control was exercised to separate the two codes and a major problem was that, unlike their white equivalents, the blacks did not have separate bodies for the paid and amateur ranks.

Chapter 7: Reaction

Pushback

With the ban on black golfers continuing, the SA Non-European GA, under the presidency of Louis Nelson, sent six black golfers (excluding Papwa) to compete on the 1970 British and Continental circuits. These included Vincent Tshabalala, Ismail Chowglay, Martin du Preez (player/manager), and Richard Mogoerane. The intention was to make the presence of black golfers recognised in international golf. 'We want to ensure a continuity of participation of non-white golfers in international golf following the breakthrough made by Papwa Sewgolum,' stated Nelson.

Chowglay, now 37, shot 71 74 72 77 (294) in the German Open at Krefelder GC and came a credible 6th, winning £250, although he missed the cut at the French Open by one shot shooting 72 71 (143).

The night before The Open qualifying tournament each player sat working out his round for the next day. Unfortunately, it did not proceed as planned, as the morning dawned cold, windy, and drizzling. Chowglay opened with a 74, Tshabalala a 75, but Martin du Preez and Richard Mogoerane were well off the pace. They all missed the cut.

Once again it demonstrated that had Chowglay been given the opportunity in his prime locally and been able to travel overseas, who knows what he may have accomplished. He certainly could win. Meanwhile, reporters and others were keen to interview the South Africans concerning political issues but were given short shrift.

In July, Nelson was suspended as chairman by his own Durban Golf Club. Why? The accusations ranged from poor financial record keeping to failing to honour the committees' requirements.

Nelson reacted by taking the golf club to court after making it a personal issue between himself and the members of the committee. He finally settled the matter on the Supreme Court steps, and the committee was not found liable for any losses in their personal capacity. He had involved the club in legal costs in the amount of R2,000, and certain members then generously paid these expenses on behalf of the club.

The general feeling among the 162 registered members of the club was that Nelson had involved the club in unnecessary litigation and legal costs and that the committee had the competency and right to suspend him.

In July 1970, the general membership of the Durban Golf Club decided to elect new officials at the annual general meeting. Fred Paul, Papwa's manager, was elected as secretary, with Ken Singh as the new chairman.

Nelson, after ten years at the helm, was bundled out of office. The meeting was the first of its kind in the history of black sport in SA, following his contemptuous disregard for the club's constitution and failure to produce the information required in connection with the records of the club, and the scant respect in his treatment of the committee.

Nevertheless, Nelson was still the President of the SA(N-E)GA where earlier in the year he had attacked Papwa for trying to raise funds for a trip abroad. By now he was very much the golf guru, so much so that when he died in 1973, tournaments disintegrated.

Paul meanwhile, retained his faith in Papwa and continued in his efforts to raise funds through begging, borrowing, scrimping, and saving. Eventually his labours were rewarded.

In view of the ban on Papwa, several prominent Durban Indian businessmen were approached by C K Naidoo to put up money to sponsor him in early 1970. Not only provide him with money to play overseas but would also support his family in his absence. Naidoo stressed that this move was not politically motivated rather it was "to give Papwa a chance".

Following his annual trip up north to compete on the three-tournament 1970 Rhodesian circuit, Papwa was back in the UK for his last Open Championship played at St. Andrews. There were several SA black players in the field including Durban caddy Lawrence Buthelezi and the long-hitting Vincent Tshabalala.

Papwa shot a record-breaking 64 in the qualifying tournament. However, he shot 72 and 78 in The Open proper to miss the cut by one shot. One-shot ahead of him was Player who was playing day-in-day-out, while Papwa had little tournament and competition play worth the name, going from 'bush' golf to the atmosphere of St. Andrews.

Buthelezi, however, made history in that he was the first Zulu to play in the Open Championship. There were several South African non-white players in the field, but only Buthelezi and Papwa got

Chapter 7: Reaction

through the 36-hole qualifying stages (a wonderful achievement by Buthelezi).

Lawrence Buthelezi possessed all the required skills to compete with the world's best golfers

Jack Nicklaus won the event, which included Gary Player and Papwa playing in his in his last Open Championship, as participants.

He rose from caddy duties as a schoolboy to help feed his family, to competing with the world's best golfers in the 1970 British Open on golf's hallowed ground, the St Andrews golf course in Scotland.

Described as a maestro of the "pigeon-egg sized ball and stick game", Lawrence Buthelezi made his mark on the green.

Having slugged it out with a premier crop of golfers at the Open, a lingering question for many was what Buthelezi would have achieved had he not entered the game via the back door, received proper mentorship and equal opportunities.

Attending high school was not a luxury that Buthelezi's family could afford because of their dire financial circumstances, so some of them worked on local farms.

Their meagre earnings had to be supplemented and Buthelezi made his contribution by working part-time as a caddy at the local Howick Golf Club.

Although he had to eventually drop out of school, his fulltime caddying job not only gave him the opportunity to hone his golfing skills, it also paved the way for his employment with the winery group. The trajectory of Buthelezi's life hit the up and up from the time he met "Mr Henning", a salesman for the winery group (previously known as Gilbeys).

According to his daughter Brenda: *"My father developed a close bond with Mr Henning, which was beneficial for him. He became his caddie and Mr Henning then hired him as his personal driver. He helped my father with his golf skills and when he relocated to Pinetown, he recommended my father replace him."*

Buthelezi was with the company from 1961 until his retirement in 1993. Brenda said he was very passionate about golf but was unfortunate not to get the opportunities to advance his game.

"He was not allowed free access to local facilities, like all people of colour back then. They could only use the facilities on certain days and times."

To play in a tournament in Durban, Brenda said Buthelezi once made the long trek from Howick on foot.

"That meant spending the night sleeping in the bushes as he walked towards Durban. That was a good example of my dad's persistence and determination. I'm pretty sure the golf clubs he had early on would have been donated to him.

"My dad played with people like Papwa Sewgolum, Gary Player and Vincent Tshabalala in the latter stages of his career, he was also invited to a round of golf with a former US ambassador in Durban."

She said when he spoke about qualifying for the British Open he did so with fondness.

"He also got to visit Buckingham palace and toured the UK. That trip opened doors for him."

Brenda said he went on overseas trips and visited various parts of the African continent thereafter to play golf. Playing golf exposed him to how well-off people lived and that sparked his aspiration to provide his family with a better quality of life than what he had been accustomed to while growing up.

According to Mervyn Naidoo in the Sunday Tribune, an article in the "SaveMor Guild" published in September 1971 described him as "Natal's top African golfer". In the same article Buthelezi was quoted saying Sewgolum was the "greatest black golfer".

He played in many tournaments with a lot of success, and trophies from events, even triumphing over Papwa, and donated some of his trophies to people staging development events.

Petrus Mbewu, Buthelezi's former colleague, said he was a fantastic man who made others aware of their rights and was passionate about whatever he did.

"He was in a car accident (1980s) near Nottingham Road (Midlands) that left him unable to play golf as he did before and told me how disappointed he was because of the opportunities playing golf brought him."

Having derived much joy and respect as a seasoned golfer, Buthelezi offered his golfing expertise to anyone who asked for assistance and he was very involved with developing the game in initiatives that involved schools, especially in Umlazi and Chatsworth.

"Apartheid has robbed many people of many things. Had Lawrence been playing with the current generation of players, he would be playing on the world stage."

Despite Naidoo's generosity, Papwa was running short of money and he would have to fly home if he could not find further backing. An appeal was made to the Western Province Coloured Golf Union but it was turned down with regrets. Lionel Theys, secretary of the Union, explained that the Athlone golf course was a terrific drain on their resources and that this made it impossible to help Papwa.

Later in the year Papwa played for the Rest of the World against Britain, losing his match to Brian Barnes by one hole. Clearly he was still good enough to represent the 'Rest of the World' but not SA.

But for Papwa, there was no one speaking out for him, no protests, and no boycotts when he was explicitly banned from playing in the Natal Open.

Then out of sheer malice the apartheid government 'revoked his passport', trying to limit the amount of exposure he could receive overseas and the resulting reflection on their policies, thus closing off any possibility of competing internationally, meaning that he could not make a living playing golf in the international arena either. Checkmate!

In March 1970, Gary Player's contradictory political statements continued as he deplored the banning of Papwa and the refusal of a visa for Arthur Ashe. Of course by now, Player was under huge pressure at numerous United States tournaments by anti-apartheid groups objecting to his participation.

Player said that Papwa should be allowed to play in South African golf tournaments – 'South Africa would show the rest of the world that it doesn't hate people of colour by letting a guy like Papwa play' – although he added a caveat that the door should not be thrown open to all non-europeans, and that each player should have to qualify.

Australian Peter Thompson (five-time British Open champion) also spoke out against Papwa's banning, pointing out that Papwa was Player's competitor, but now restricted from playing in the world arena despite being a loyal South African mentioning his raising of the flag incident at the Indian Open.

In the ensuing years, denied the right to play the game he loved, Papwa was said to be a broken man, who struggled to survive and stared forlornly at his golf trophies.

Earlier that year, there had been a number of professionals from Britain and Ireland on the SA circuit, and most of these golfers had decided to skip the Rhodesian tournaments in favour of the more lucrative Zambian circuit. Seven of them were promptly thrown in jail when they arrived in Lusaka because they had been to SA.

These were the years of sanctions and boycotts, and sporting contact with SA was *verboten*. The matter was eventually cleared up, but the seven had to spend a night in jail.

Two other players were based in Zambia and one of them, Simon Hobday was served with deportation orders because he had taken part in tournaments south of the Zambezi.

In 1971, the government smarting from the hostile reaction from

Chapter 7: Reaction

governments and organisations around the world, and in the face of mounting pressure to allow non-racial golf, introduced the concept of 'Open International Tournaments'. These competitions allowed top black golfers to play in a few leading tournaments including the SA Open, provided they were players of adequate standard, which led in August 1971 to the formation of the Non-White Professional Golfers' Association.

There were three Open International Tournaments, the PGA Championship, the SA Open, and the General Motors Classic.

Gary Player convinced Vorster, to allow Lee Elder[20] to play in the December 1971 South African PGA Championship."

In this context, the season beginning with the PGA championship at Huddle Park on November 24, provided 'another crack in the wall' and made history in the professional game. Among the black qualifiers who played all four rounds were Solly Sepeng, L. Letsoala, Daddy Naidoo, Richard Mogoerane, and with the best score, Ismail Chowglay. Papwa, however, was not included in the list – he was 43 by now and his best golf was behind him.

Now changes for which Papwa had been one of the catalysts, but were too slow to benefit him, opened the way for younger sportsmen to inch their way into open participation.

As was reported in the press: 'For the first time in a tournament field there will be players of mixed race – several non-white players from SA, including Indians and Africans; an American Negro, Lee Elder and a Chinaman from Formosa, Lu Liang Huan ('Mr Lu')'.

For four days, blacks and whites mingled on a 'Whites Only' golf course as though it were the established South African way of life.

For four days they sat together in the stands; for four days they played together on the course; for four days they ate and drank together in the clubhouse – "Lee Elder and Papwa were allowed to use the clubhouse, but not the 'white toilet,'" Dale Hayes said, disgust in his voice – and for four days nobody gave it a second thought.

Sadly, Papwa, the shuttlecock of sports apartheid for so many years and the man who had done all the front-running for mixed golf,

---

20 In 1974, Elder became the first Black golfer to compete in the Masters

was now too old to savour the honours out there on the fairway.

Interviewed in the comfort of the clubhouse lounge, Papwa said; 'Look at all the golfers, Black and White mixing freely. It's marvellous to be treated as a golfer for a change and not some sort of freak. I'm very happy for the young non-Whites who have their golf careers ahead of them. But it's come too late for me. I'm now 43. There's nowhere for me to go, but down in this tough game of nerves. I'm just about all washed up.'

A large group of his own people told him that he must not play in multinational tournaments, but golf was his only livelihood. Then there were some who said he should play because as long as you play, you embarrass them. As long as you humiliate them, it will tell the world that this multinational thing doesn't work. But neither of the two forces would meet.

The 71/72 season had not been particularly good for Papwa. His long reign as the SA Non-White golf champion ended on the 72nd green at the Benoni Country Club in the 1971/'72 season. Papwa had been held to a tie by Vincent Tshabalala in 1965, and finally, it was to Tshabalala, that he eventually relinquished his stranglehold on the SA Non-European Championship when Tshabalala on 292 beat him by a single shot.

"Vincent Tshabalala is the new champion," heralded the news report. He beat Papwa by one shot – yet he came so close to losing the title. Tshabalala had a four-shot lead on Papwa going into the third round after a par-71, but Papwa whittled down the lead to a nail-biting finish.

Both had good drives at the last hole. Tshabalala had a tough third onto the green while Papwa was on the edge of the green for his second, and was left with a reasonable putt for a three. He missed, and Tshabalala holed to win by one shot, followed by Daddy Naidoo 294, Ronald Anooplal 296, Johnson Chetty 302, and D. Mukwevu 303.

His best showing had been at Mbabane in the Swaziland Holiday Inns tournament, March 1971, where after a final round 67 he finished 3rd behind Denis Hutchinson and Cobie le Grange. Precluded by the laws of the land from competing in the 'white' circuit in the Republic he, as Hutch put it at the prize-giving, 'came in well from the cold.'

Chapter 7: Reaction

After 63 holes it was clear that the top spots would go to Hutch and le Grange, so the fight was on for the third position. At least five players were in real contention, but in the end, it was Papwa who stood up best under strain. His final round of 67 not only secured third place for him but was the best return for the entire day.

After his passport was finally returned in 1971 a decision was taken that Papwa would not return to the UK and Europe, but that the possibility of his playing in New Zealand and Australia was being considered. This did happen towards the end of the year, in fact, he travelled with Gary Player, who finally, discretely sponsored him and helped fund the trip. That trip took him to play in the Dunlop International event at the Manly Golf Club, Sydney, to which they travelled from their hotel in the heart of the city by hovercraft across the waterways, boats and yachts to beachside Manly, and where both he and Gary refused to discuss politics, and as usual Gary claimed they were there to play golf.

Papwa was not immune from political debates. While in Sydney he claimed he had been pressured into signing an anti-apartheid statement at his hotel, and which he later claimed to have inadvertently signed given that he was not able to read. 'I am interested only in golf, and not politics. I want nothing to do with the anti-apartheid movement in Sydney or elsewhere'. Accordingly he came in for criticism for not taking up the fight on behalf of those in distress in his own country.

On 17 November 1971, he entered the Christchurch Garden Classic in New Zealand without notable success.

Player also arranged a number of invites to tournaments in the US, but unfortunately Papwa once again became homesick and returned home after only competing once. He simply did not have the stomach and the support team.

It is, however, interesting to speculate why at long last Player stepped in to sponsor Papwa. Clearly Player was under immense pressure not only in America, but also around the world whenever he played. He was an easy recognisable target who had publicly embraced the apartheid policy and who regularly played golf with Prime Minister Vorster.

The Mark McCormack management agency managed Player's

business affairs for many years promoting him as one of the big three – together with Jack Nicklaus and Arnold Palmer (actually it should also have included Billy Casper). Now not only was Player's negative brand under pressure from his sponsors, but it was clearly also affecting Nicklaus and Palmers' brands by association.

Is it not inconceivable that Player was encouraged to take Papwa with him in order to blunt and deflect the protests, and protect the brand of the big-three?

During the latter part of 1973 Player also took Martin du Preez and Hamilton Mbatha, the president and secretary of the South African Black Golfers Association, to Australia for the purpose of telling people in that country that things were fine and well in South Africa, this, despite the fact that no black golfer had been considered for selection at provincial or national level. At this juncture Player still supported the apartheid policies of the government, although his views were softening.

Meanwhile, Player was becoming aware of his social responsibility and established the Gary Player Foundation which looked after the educational and physical wellbeing of some 400 school children. This, however, did not deflect the demonstrators when he next appeared at the 1975 Australian Open where demonstrators chanted 'Racist! Racist!' and a firecracker and a bag of peanuts were thrown at him as he putted whilst the greens were torn up.

Following a few dismal years, re-energised by his 1970 European tour and his sixth placing in the German Open, Ismail Chowglay[21] was once again the SA Non-European Open champion at Kroonstad where he shot 74 74 75 74 (297) winning from Tshabalala 79 73 74 72 (298) and Mogoerane (298) who tied for 2nd.

Mogoerane, the overnight leader, missed a half a metre putt at the 18th and final hole to give Chowglay outright victory. Chowglay was four strokes better than Mogoerane on the final round. Tshabalala had a par 72 for the best final round, but this was not enough for him to

---

21 Chowglay the Clovelly CC caddy-master although denied the permission to give lessons (although he would quietly coach the juniors for free) or work in the pro shop, was allowed to pound ball-after-ball from alongside the 10th tee when the course was quiet, using his three-wood (without a tee) and cutting the corner with drive after drive.

recover from his first round fiasco of 79, which he followed up with a 73 and 74 in the second and third rounds.

But Papwa was still a force in 1972 on the non-European circuit winning the Transvaal Non-European Open and the sponsored Luyt Lager Open for blacks to the tune of R1,000 played at the Ohenimuri Country Club. This 72-hole event was won by 'Cox' Hlapo (now 48) in a sudden-death play-off from Papwa. Hlapo ended the tournament with a tremendous 25m putt for a birdie on the first extra hole.

The leading scores were:

290	–	S Hlapo **S Sewgolum**
293	–	I Chowglay
294	–	R Mogoerane
295	–	R Letsoalo
296	–	V Tshabalala

Overall control of golf in SA at this time was in the hands of an organisation called the SA Golf Council. Its intention was presumably to establish some sort of working relationship between black and white golfers and to coordinate the activities of the various controlling bodies.

Amateur golf was under the control of the SAGU (white) and the SA(N-E)GA (black), while professional tournament golf was under the control of the SA Professional Golf Association (white) and the SA Professional Players Association (black). Another body called the SA Bantu Golf Union registered by Vincent Tshabalala was considered not to represent Bantu interests throughout the whole country and was denied membership of the SA Golf Council.

From the start it was evident that the two professional bodies did not always see eye to eye, each one jealously guarded its own domain and demanded absolute loyalty from its members. Notwithstanding these differences, it is of interest that it appears that Papwa was able to play in events under the control of both of these professional bodies and also those under the control of both of the amateur bodies.

The Vavasseur Natal Open was under the SAPGA, the Masonite Tournament was under the SAPPA, the SA Open was under the SAGU and the SA (N-E) Open was under the SA(N-E)GA.

Meanwhile Papwa, who was unhappy with the direction in which the organisation of black golf was heading, boycotted the Oris Stroke-Play Championship at Houghton. 'I refuse to be a political football,' said Papwa. 'I'm getting tired of non-white golf officials who put themselves above the game.'

In Natal, Daddy Naidoo and 16 other golfers refused to take part in an event carrying a R300 first prize.

What was this all about?

The reason was that Louis Nelson, as chairman of the SA(N-E) GA, had now become instrumental in the formation of the Non-White South African Professional Players' Association that insisted that all black golfers should be exclusive members of that Association or barred from tournaments under its control.

Papwa and the others refused to join an organisation whose officials were making personality issues and were not affiliated to the white SAPGA. Participation under these conditions might get them barred from the multiracial tournaments.

Another issue worrying the non-european golfers was the compulsory use of the bigger American ball in all SAPGA tournaments. Robert Ntshingila, well know in golfing circles and well travelled, felt it would be unfair and would put non-Europeans at a disadvantage. So too did Simon 'Cox' Hlapo, the seasoned veteran amongst black golfers, who said he was shocked. Brian Henning heading the SAPGA refused to back down.

As a consequence in October 1973 the SA Professional Players Association fought back, suspending eight professional golfers for two years for taking part in multinational events, and Papwa was fined R50.

Meanwhile, two important developments took place.

The South African Council on Sport (SACOS) was established in 1973 as a non-racial sports federation. Uncompromising on apartheid, it played a crucial role as a partner of SAN-ROC in advocating equal opportunity for all races in sport and merit selections, thereby reinforcing the international boycott. Its declaration that there could be "no normal sport in an abnormal society" was a powerful antidote to the propaganda of the apartheid regime and the maneuvres of white sports bodies which made false claims of non-discrimination.

Sam Ramsamy managed to leave for Germany to represent the non-racial sports bodies during the Munich Olympics. A founding member of SACOS, he joined SAN-ROC, linking internal and external resistance, became chairman of SAN-ROC in 1976 and executive chairman in 1978. He proved to be ideally suited to lead the campaign in the new stage.

He established excellent relations with African, Indian, Caribbean and other sports federations, and secured recognition for SACOS from the Supreme Council for Sport in Africa. He maintained close contact with anti-apartheid groups around the world. He also developed personal contacts with many sports editors and South African correspondents in London so that the boycott received great attention. Above all, he was in constant consultation with colleagues in South Africa and secured close cooperation between SAN-ROC and the ANC leadership in exile.

Cracks in the wall

Shortly after John Vorster took office in 1966 he announced that South Africa would no longer dictate to the international community what their teams should look like. Although this reopened the gate for international sporting meets, it did not signal the end of South Africa's racist sporting policies.

At this time, SA's racial profile abroad had been severely tarnished. A sequence of demonstrations in Australia and New Zealand had ensued, and the issue around cricketer Basil D'Oliveira formerly denied the opportunity to play without restriction in the county of his birth, gained great publicity.

Suddenly Papwa was not the only sporting hero increasing pressure on the apartheid government – 'a country at war with itself.'

☐ Cricket: The Basil D'Oliveira Affair

In 1968 Basil D'Oliveira, a Coloured South African-born cricketer who had represented England in Test cricket since 1966, was selected for the proposed tour to SA. Having moved there six years earlier, D'Oliveira was considered part of the team, but the SA government had different ideas about the 'coloured' cricketer – prompting a crisis that shook apartheid.

Vorster went against his policy by refusing to permit D'Oliveira to join the English cricket team on its tour to South Africa. Vorster said that the side had been chosen only to prove a point, and not on merit.

D'Oliveira left SA primarily because the era's apartheid legislation seriously restricted his career prospects on racial grounds and barred him from the all-white Test team. Manoeuvring by cricketing and political figures in both countries did little to bring the matter to a head. The Marylebone Cricket Club's (MCC) priority was to maintain traditional links with SA and have the series go ahead without incident.

Vorster sought to appease international opinion by publicly indicating that D'Oliveira's inclusion would be acceptable, but secretly did all he could to prevent it.

D'Oliveira was then omitted from the England team to tour SA; they insisted that this was based entirely on cricketing merit, but many in Britain voiced apprehension and there was a public outcry. After Tom Cartwright's withdrawal because of injury on 16 September, the MCC chose D'Oliveira as a replacement, prompting accusations from Vorster and other SA politicians that the selection was politically motivated. Attempts to find a compromise followed, but these led nowhere.

"Dolly" was eventually included in the team as the first substitute, but the tour was cancelled after negotiations broke down, and the MCC announced the tour's cancellation on 24 September.

The D'Oliveira affair had exposed SA to the world as a racist state. More than two decades of sporting isolation would follow coming to an end only in 1991 after the release of Nelson Mandela.

Protests against certain tours brought about the cancellation of a number of other visits, including that of an England rugby team touring South Africa in 1969/70.

Sporting boycotts of SA were already underway by 1968, but the D'Oliveira controversy was the first to have a severe effect on SA cricket. The SA Cricket Board of Control announced its intention to remove racial barriers in SA cricket in 1969 and formally integrated the sport in 1976. Meanwhile, the boycott movement escalated sharply, leading to SA's near-complete isolation from international cricket from 1971.

Dr Ali Bacher, the former head of SA cricket, was forthright in his views about D'Oliveira when he was interviewed by the BBC. 'He showed conclusively that black people in SA, given the same opportunity as whites, had that ability, talent, and potential to become international stars.'

Gerald Majola, the chief executive of Cricket SA, said: 'The circumstances surrounding 'Dolly' being prevented from touring the country of his birth with England in 1968 led directly to the intensification of opposition to apartheid around the world and contributed materially to the sports boycott that turned out to be an Achilles heel of the apartheid government.'

The significance of the Vorster's decision was that D'Oliveira, irrespective of the fact that he was now holding a British passport, was born in Cape Town of mixed race, and, therefore, unacceptable lest other black South Africans living abroad think they too could compete against white SA.

Vorster approved the inclusion of Maori players in the New Zealand All Blacks as they had been included the previous year. Further, the difference was that Vorster made a distinction between those born in SA and those born abroad – satisfying his own views of foreign and domestic players.

Just as Papwa had put a human face to the realities of petty apartheid when he was forced to accept his prize in the rain, the D'Oliveira affair exposed the lengths to which the SA government would go to achieve the acceptance of apartheid to watch their nations favourite sport, and by extension their nation's approval, thereby perpetuating the system that now so many South Africans took for granted.

The public relations disaster around D'Oliveira was followed by the "White Bans" which occurred in 1971 when the Chairman of the Australian Cricket Association – Sir Don Bradman – flew to South Africa to meet Vorster. Vorster had expected Bradman to allow the tour of the Australian cricket team to go ahead, but things became heated after Bradman asked why Black sportsmen were not allowed to play cricket. Vorster stated that Blacks were intellectually inferior and had no finesse for the game. Bradman – thinking this ignorant and repugnant – asked Vorster if he had heard of a man named Garry Sobers. On his return to Australia, Bradman released a short statement: "We will not play them until they choose a team on a non-racist basis."

In South Africa, Vorster vented his anger publicly against Bradman, while the African National Congress rejoiced. This was the first time a predominantly white nation had taken the side of multiracial sport,

Chapter 7: Reaction

suggesting that more 'white' boycotts were around the corner. Almost twenty years later, on his release from prison, Nelson Mandela asked a visiting Australian statesman if Donald Bradman, his childhood hero, was still alive (Bradman lived until 2001).

☐ **Rugby: The All Blacks**

In 1960, nearly 160,000 people signed a petition opposing that year's tour to South Africa by an 'all white All Blacks' team. Groups like the Citizens' All Black Tour Association campaigned with the slogan 'No Maoris – No Tour'. Others argued that politics had no place in the sport.

In the end, Wilson Whineray's team left as planned, their aircraft narrowly missing demonstrators who were sprinting across the runway at Whenuapai airport. Despite protests, the controversial rugby tour went ahead. The issue of sporting ties with SA would eventually split the country in 1981.

For the 1970 tour of SA, a solution in the form of a compromise was devised for Maori and Pacific Island players. They would be considered 'honourary whites'. It was a term applied by South Africans to certain ethnicities, giving them most of the rights of white citizens.

While this placated some, many were still angered. Protest organisation HART was formed in 1969 with significant Maori input. The tour went ahead with Sid Going (who was Maori) and Bryan Williams (Samoan) participating as honorary whites. While the New Zealand Maori Council saw this compromise as acceptable; the Maori Women's Welfare League opposed the tour.

In 1973, the government, under Prime Minister Norman Kirk effectively forestalled planned protest actions when it intervened to cancel a planned Springbok tour of New Zealand as the team was to be selected on the grounds of race rather than merit.

In 1976, the All Blacks toured SA, with the blessing of the then-newly elected New Zealand Prime Minister, Robert 'Piggy' Muldoon (who subsequently acted as the narrator in the Rocky Horror show after his term as Prime Minister ended).

Twenty-five African nations protested against this by boycotting the 1976 Summer Olympics in Montreal. In their view the All Black tour tacitly supported the apartheid regime in SA. The five Maori players on the tour, Billy Bush, Sid Going, Kent Lambert, Bill Osborne and Tane Norton, as well as ethnic-Samoan Bryan Williams, were again granted honorary white status in SA.

Concerned about possible disruption of Commonwealth Games, the white Commonwealth countries agreed to the "Gleneagles Agreement" of 1977 to discourage competition with South African teams; a similar declaration was adopted by sports ministers of the Council of Europe the next year. This was thus the beginning of action at a governmental level in Western countries and of "third party boycott" (of teams and countries collaborating with apartheid sport).

Boycotts and bannings were now starting to take their effect on white SA golfers. Gary Player was the all-too-visible target of anti-apartheid demonstrators around the world. Wherever he played, he was regarded as a spokesman for apartheid – or at least the one tangible target its opponents could easily attack.

There were even death threats. 'Every week,' he says, 'Every week. In America, Australia, Europe, for about two years. It was not easy. At the PGA Championship in 1969, in Dayton, Ohio, they threw ice in my eyes. They threw telephone books at my back. They charged me on the green. They threw balls between my legs as I was about to putt. You know, it's hard to comprehend. And I lost the PGA by one shot. This was my best tournament I ever played (he told the author).

And I had it everywhere I went, Everywhere!'

Player talks of the injustice of it, and of the black players he supported and sponsored during the 1970s, including Papwa and Vincent Tshabalala, and he mentions his iconic one-white-leg/one-black-leg pants that he wore at the 1960 Open at St. Andrews. They were, he says, 'a quiet protest, of bringing white and black together.'

'We were brainwashed,' concedes Player.

Meanwhile, the Black Panther movement denied it had made threats on Player's life, and Arthur Ashe, barred by the apartheid government from playing in the SA Tennis championship, added fuel to the fire saying that he feared for Player's safety.

Chapter 7: Reaction

1960 The Open: Youthful Gary Player's black and white pants.

In 1971, entries of SA Golfers were turned down in Scandinavia, Greece, and elsewhere. Sally Little was persuaded not to enter the British Amateur championship because the organisers feared demonstrations.

"As a young South African girl playing professional golf in the apartheid years, I faced a number of obstacles. I was boycotted and humiliated all over the world. In many instances, I was kept out of tournaments, not being allowed to pursue my passion."

At the same time, a professional golfer for the first time was refused permission to play in a tournament because he was a South African as Bobby Cole's entry in the Volvo tournament in Sweden was turned down. 'Since Cole is from South Africa we are unable to have him enter our tournament. Sorry.'

'I'm still often asked why I stopped playing tournament golf at such a young age,' said Dale Hayes. 'It was politics. Hugh Baiocchi and I arrived in Athens to represent South Africa in the World Cup of Golf, played a practice round and took part in the pro-am before being told that we would not be allowed to tee up in the tournament. In fact, we were given 48 hours to leave Greece – I got fed up with the uncertainty of playing under such conditions.'

Although no golfers were affected as severely by the politics of SA as were Ramnath Boodhun, Papwa Sewgolum, Vincent Tshabalala, Richard Mogoerane, Ismail Chowglay, Edward Johnson-Sedibe, and Simon Hlapo, white golfers were inconvenienced and singled out for special attention from anti-apartheid protesters overseas.

In 1976 the British PGA tried to withhold payment of prize money to Simon Hobday because of his Rhodesian/SA connections, and Gary Player missed out on huge money by not being allowed to play in Jordan.

In the late 1970s Sweden stopped South Africans from competing, and when they arrived at the borders of France, Spain and the Netherlands, they were never sure if they would be allowed in.

Light peeping through

With mounting international pressure, the government announced that five events in the 1973/74 season would be designated as 'open internationals' and the top four black golfers on the Order of Merit would not be required to qualify for multinational tournaments on the SAPGA circuit. These open international events attracted the usual entry from the leading black players.

In the PGA championship, Papwa and Chowglay were the best, tied on 299 but a long way back. The SA Open was played at the Durban CC, a course very much to Papwa's liking. It was won by Bob Charles on 282 from Bobby Cole, Vinny Baker, and Graham Marsh, with Papwa finishing in a tie for 11th place. He was let down by a 77 in the last round.

Those making the cut in the General Motors Classic at Wedgwood CC were Richard Mogoerane, Ismail Chowglay, Solly Sepeng, and Z Manunda.

Chapter 7: Reaction

But Papwa was not yet finished, and in 1974 he once again showed his dominance and won the SA Non-European title played at Glendower Golf Club for a record tenth and final victory when he made up 10 shots on Tshabalala in the final round to win by 1-shot.

He also won the Tournament of Champions, Natal Non-European Open, and Griqua Gold Cup, Meanwhile, Gary Player was winning The Masters (USA) and The Open (UK).

October 1973, the Masonite Africa Ltd with R1500 prize money was won by Papwa after a tense fight-back by Theo Manyama. Plans were afoot that this would be one of ten tournaments for black golfers in the following season.

In May, Papwa won the 54-hole LTA Masters R3000 Non-European Tournament at Observatory GC. He scored 218 and was followed by R Mogoerane (219), V Tshabalala (220) and I Chowglay (221).

Also in 1974, to assist the Athlone Golf Club, Cape Town, with the financing of their new clubhouse, Gary Player played an exhibition match featuring Sewgolum, Tshabalala and Chowglay.

'Athlone will be one of Player's sternest tests in his golfing career,' stated *The Cape Times*.

Prior to the challenge match, Player held a golf clinic for the spectators who had come to watch this epic encounter.

By then Papwa (with A. Hartzenburg, runner-up in the 1969 SA Non-European Open on his bag) had a thick-set build, compared to the lithe, slim 'boyish' ladies man Chowglay (with Abe van Rooyen, the 1970 WP N-E champion carrying his bag).

Long-hitting left-handed Chowglay scuffing up the turf instead of a tee, using only a 3-wood, out-hit Papwa who was a little shorter than Player. But that did not matter, and despite the sandy lies off the fairway and poorly conditioned fairways, once Papwa got near the green, he put on his short-game display.

The challenge caught the public's imagination, and was watch by a mixed-race gallery of more than 2,000, and together Tshabalala, Chowglay, and Sewgolum more than held their own against Player, with Player going round in approximately 67, Papwa was also round in 3-under par-69, Chowglay 71, and Tshabalala 72, with Player/

Chowglay beating Sewgolum/Tshabalala 4/2.

Funds raised enabled the Athlone GC to be a home for local golfers, particularly the coloured community golfers, including some outstanding talent, and continue to operate for a few more years.

Papwa receiving the Masonite Trophy for winning the 1973 Tournament of Champions in Durban

CHAPTER 8: VIVE LA FRANCE

Handing over the crown

At this time, Chowglay (now 41), together with Tshabalala, was perhaps still the leading player after Papwa, and he was part of a group of professionals sponsored by Becks Lager, touring the country giving golf lessons. A newspaper report stated that he qualified for the 'White' PGA circuit and would be eligible to compete in eight tournaments.

Within the concept of open international events and the fact of black golfers being restricted to these, it was for the most part business as usual for the next few seasons.

The names of the leading black golfers competing in the designated tournaments tended to repeat from year to year, tournament to tournament – Chowglay, Tshabalala, Mogoerane, Naidoo, Manyama, Sepeng, Motati, Mamashela, Mavundla, Chetty, Molefe, and Papwa Sewgolum, although Papwa was playing less and less.

Ismail Chowglay, Vincent Tshabalala, Papwa Sewgolum

The 1975 Vavasseur Natal Open in January was one of the open international events. Papwa finished on 77 73 70 72 (292) for a share of 13th place. Also doing well was Chowglay (294) and Daddy Naidoo (295).

Finally, though, a major breakthrough, when in September 1975, Piet Koornhof, the Minister of Sport, announced that the South African professional golfing tour would in future be open to all races.

Golf was the first sport chosen for this complete reversal of government policy, a decision which many commentators ascribed to the fact that both Koornhof and Vorster were themselves keen golfers.

Trumpeting the decision, Ted Partridge, the editor of *SA Golf*, wrote: "By removing all barriers of race and making merit the strict yardstick by which a man's qualification is measured, golf has become the first major sport to win the battle of politics."

The decision was a lucrative one – the changes saw South Africa allowed to play in the World Cup of Golf which Bobby Cole and Dale Hayes win in Caracas Venezuela from Isao Aoki and Masashi 'Jumbo' Ozaki, whilst the South African PGA boasted new sponsorship highs.

By this stage, Papwa was already 46 and Chowglay 42, with their best years behind them. Outside of such events the usual personal, legal and sporting limits, oppression and segregation continued.

It was now time for Vincent Tshabalala aged 32, to take up Papwa Sewgolum's mantle.

Six foot one, Vincent started working out as a caddie after school at Rietvlei Golf Club, including caddying for Gary Player, who also spent time coaching him. He saved up for a mixed bag of golf clubs, one at a time costing R5 each, to pursue his passion for golf, a sport that was historically a white sport. Later he worked as a very gifted mechanic before he devoted his life to his greatest passion.

During the 1965-70s on the non-European TPA Tour he had six wins, four second-place and one-third place finish. He was, however, barred from the Southern African Tour in his prime during this period as a result of apartheid.

Like Papwa and Chowglay, Tshabalala used a cross-handed grip to good effect with his long irons, and was ranked the number one long-iron player on the 1976 Sunshine Tour. He also had an excellent

Chapter 8: Vive La France

short game.

He tied the 1965 SA Non-European Open with Sewgolum and won the title in 1971, '77, and again in '83.

The problem remained that black golfers including Vincent had great difficulty in raising finances for competition. Many of them worked outside the game during the off-season to fund their competitive play. Vincent worked as a mechanic when not touring.

Then in 1974 Gary Player sponsored Vincent and took him overseas to Australia where Player won his seventh Australian Open in spite of enduring anti-apartheid demonstrations who ventured on to one of the putting greens in the middle of the night and wrote 'Go Home, You Racist Pig' in white lime powder.

1974 Australian Open Royal Melbourne GC

It was the beginning of further troubled times for SA golfers abroad where they faced a hostile reception when interviewed and on the golf course, with some of the greens vandalised by the demonstrators. 'After all, I was there,' said Vincent. 'And I was also targeted by Australian racists who referred to me as 'smoke.'

'I remember standing on the tee at a par-3 – 160 metres from the pin – and they were saying things like, 'The smoke won't get it over the water.' I stepped back to regather myself, and then I hit a 5-iron at the flag, two feet from the hole. Vincent never lost for words, 'I turned around and said; this smoke can play!'

Later they went to America, and Player arranged for Vincent to play two PGA Tour events – the Kemper Open and the IVY-Philadelphia Golf Classic. In those two tournaments Tshabalala only broke 80 once.

Tshabalala then competed in the US Open – the first SA black golfer to do so. No mean achievement!

During 1975, Papwa competed in as many of the former white-only tournaments as possible but though he often made the cut, he routinely finished outside of the top ten, and out of the money. Washed up and wounded, he did not play as much golf as before, preferring to spend the day fishing at the nearby Umlazi River where he had good memories of fishing with his father as a boy, and nights at the shebeen regaling stories of his golf triumphs to admirers who would buy him drinks.

He again travelled to the UK in 1976 and, among other events, appeared in the Kerrygold Tournament at Waterville in Ireland. This was the last overseas trip.

With his killer instinct fading, weight ballooning, and his health deteriorating, Papwa became a shadow of his former self, but he took a central interest in the establishment of a strong association for black golfers, and the encouragement of young talent.

Still, the Papwa era hadn't quite ended, as the old maestro confirmed once again that he was still the best black golfer in the country when he took first prize of R300 in the R1500 Natal N-E Open, nine shots ahead of his nearest rivals Ismail Chowglay and Ram

Chapter 8: Vive La France

Rajdaw on 303, followed by A Collins (306) and J. Ranjith (307).

Richard 'Boikie' Mogoerane, the winner of the SA Non-European Open in 1973, won again in 1976 played at Durban, while Papwa won the Western Province Non-European Open.

Meanwhile, Raymond Ackerman, playing with his youthful friend Rita Leveten (2010 Southern Africa Golf Hall of Fame inductee) at Clovelly Country Club, thought he was a hotshot golfer with a possible career, that was until he played Denis Hutchinson in the SA Amateur and lost 10/8, so instead he turned his attention to building his Pick 'n Pay empire.

So it was in January 1976 that Ackerman approached Prime Minister B.J. Vorster with Minister Connie Mulder in attendance, and informed him that he was opening Clovelly to all races.

Mulder's immediate reaction was 'over my dead body', but Vorster sent him packing, telling him to 'get out of the office'. He then confirmed that Ackerman could proceed if 87 per cent (an arbitrary figure which he plucked out of the air) of the members agreed. Most of the members agreed, and the club became the first golf club in apartheid SA to be opened to all races.

Another chink in the armour!

Three months later, the new Minister of Sport, F.W. de Klerk, (the future Prime Minister who would release Mandela) used this loophole to allow all sports clubs to choose their membership, thereby opening sports clubs to all races.

Vincent Tshabalala had learnt the game, not on the emerald, tree-lined courses that proliferated throughout 'white' SA, but on a scrubby, eight-hole course laid out on waste ground. The greens were not green but dusty brown, and the concept of a hazard was unknown because the whole course was a hazard.

He did well in the 1976 Dunlop Masters at Kensington, finishing 5th on a score of 273 (Papwa finished on 289) and also in the Rhodesian Dunlop Masters on 285 for a share of 8th place.

Vincent was unable to play in the majority of tournaments on the Southern African Tour in his prime, but once again with the assistance of Gary Player, who financed his trip, he gained entry to tournaments on the European Tour in 1976.

And so it was that he made his European Tour debut at the Madrid Open at Puerto de Hierro finishing tied for the 45th place. Then onto The Open, won by Johnny Miller, where Vincent came 56th.

The following week, Vincent on an extremely tight budget, set out for France, and the famous Le Touquet Golf Club.

Not having money for a caddy, Tshabalala had to pull his own golf cart and judge his own distances. But as a former caddy, he never needed to consult with a caddy for the line as he had developed a flair for 'reading' the green.

At that time, touring professionals during practice rounds would often attach a wheel to their cart with an odometer measuring distances as they made their way around the course, judging these and writing them down in a little notebook for reference during the tournament.

Set within superb natural surroundings – between the forest and the sand dunes – Le Touquet Golf Club is one of the most beautiful of European courses, surrounded by a vast forest and an opaline sea, a mere two hours from Paris. The 18-hole La Mer Course, a typical British links course, was built in 1931 by the renowned architect Harry Colt together with Charles Alison, and ranked in 1976 as one of the top 20 courses in Europe.

Measuring 5,648m (now 6,343m), this par-72 golf course started in the flat land soon threading its way into the ever larger dunes as the round progressed, undulating fairways, prolific pot bunkers, not to mention the awaiting gorse and heather rough, which demanded concentration and precision. All this and the blustery wind that funnelled down the Channel whipping across the exposed links, seldom benign and could seriously damage any score card, and with wonderful sea views of the Channel from elevated tees.

Opening with a 434m par-5, followed by a long 187m par-3, then a short 324m par-4, and a short 410m par-5, allowed the golfer to get away with a fast start and then claw back the round with par-5s at the 15th and 17th holes.

On May 4, 1976, at the French Open, Vincent knew he was in 'the zone', the clubhead moved all the way back to the top of his swing as rhythmically he swung the club back, feeling every little motion, and

Chapter 8: Vive La France

then the momentary pause. It felt like he had all the time in the world, amazingly smooth and mechanical, as he aimed for the top of the flag, trying to drop the ball from the fairway directly into the hole as the clubhead made solid contact with the ball spraying up the turf. And his confidence grew as his short game, his real strength, came to life.

He opened with a solid 70 despite pulling his own golf cart, leaving him two shots behind the leader, Salvador Balbuena (winner of the Portuguese Open three weeks earlier), in a group of players in fifth position with Neil Coles, Sam Torrence, and Simon Hobday.

It was still all smiles after the second round with another comfortable 70, which kept him in the hunt although Balbuena had pulled clear, now with a 6-shot lead over Vincent, but only three ahead of Hobday.

The third round was played on a morning, crisp as Vincent's golf, as he swung round in a remarkable 66 now only three shots behind of Balbuena, tied with Simon Hobday who shot a 69. Roaring back through the field after a poor second round was Sam Torrence with a course record 63, now a shot back of Vincent and Hobday, together with English Ryder Cup star Neil Coles.

Vincent started out the final round three behind Balbuena, and after ten holes, he was 5-strokes adrift. But the Spaniard lost a ball for a six at the 11th, a turning point, and then ran up a three-over par-8 on the 14th after hooking into the rough three times.

Like an Americas Cup yacht sweeping past all opposition, Vincent took the lead and held onto it shooting a 67 for 272 (16 below par), as Balbuena played conservative golf and a 72 as the South African blazed to the trophy by two strokes over the Spaniard.

To put this into perspective, previous winners of the French Open have included Jose María Olazabal, Colin Montgomerie, Retief Goosen, Sam Torrance, Robert Allenby, Nick Faldo, Seve Ballesteros, Bernhard Langer, Sandy Lyle, Greg Norman, Dale Hayes, Brian Barnes, Peter Oosterhuis, David Graham, Roberto de Vicenzo, and in 1951 Hassan Hassanien, Egypt's greatest golfer.

And so it was that Vincent Tshabalala, a 35-year old black South African who had been working as a motor mechanic two years previously, while pulling his own golf cart, snatched a shock victory by winning the French Open, on May 9, 1976, just two months before the Soweto uprising, with scores of 69 70 66 67 (272), beating a top international field. He finished two strokes ahead of Salvador Balbuena, with Simon Hobday, Neil Coles, and Sam Torrance sharing 3rd place, and with Seve Ballesteros 6 shots adrift, winning €3,570 (Severiano Ballesteros won it the following year, whilst Dale Hayes had won it in 1974).

Salvador Balbuena Bruna (1950 – 9 May 1979) was a Spanish professional golfer who won the 1976 Portuguese Open on the European Tour and the 1976 Morocco Grand Prix. Also in 1976, Balbuena was selected for three international teams: He represented Team Spain in the Philip Morris International (a 16-country knockout tournament); Team Continental in the Double Diamond International (played 1971-77); and Team Continental in the Hennessy Cognac Cup (vs. Team Great Britain & Ireland). It was quite a debut season, and Balbuena appeared poised for great success.

On May 10, 1979, on the eve of the 1979 French Open in which he was due to play, Balbuena joined several fellow Spanish tour players at a restaurant for dinner. With him that night were Antonio Garrido, Manuel Pinero and Jose Maria Canizares. During dinner, Balbuena collapsed. An ambulance was called and rushed him to a hospital, but it was too late. Balbuena died on the way. He had suffered a massive heart attack. Balbuena was only 29 years old.

According to Peter Alliss' 1983 The Who's Who of Golf, almost all of the other Spanish golfers in the field for the French Open withdrew in tribute to Balbuena. Seve Ballesteros, however, carried on, and gave his tournament winnings to Balbuena's wife.

- ☐ TSHABALALA Vincent SA 69 70 66 67 = 272 (-16) € 4,907
- ☐ BALBUENA Salvador SPN 67 66 69 72 = 274 (-14) € 2,944
- ☐ COLES Neil ENG 69 69 68 70 = 276 (-12)
- ☐ HOBDAY Simon RSA 69 67 69 71 = 276 (-12)
- ☐ TORRANCE Sam SCO 69 74 63 70 = 276 (-12)

Chapter 8: Vive La France

French Open 1976 winner Vincent Tshabalala

I owe everything to Gary Player, who helped me with my game and programme of physical training, and helped my family. He will be over the moon about my win, which means I will not have to pre-qualify for the British Open. I played that in 1970 but I didn't make the last two rounds.' He was the first African black man to win on the European Tour.

In 2010 Vincent was delighted to meet Sally Little for the first time at his induction into the Southern Africa Golf Hall of Fame at Oubaai, George, and taking her aside, he drew out a torn well-worn old article from his wallet. 'I always wanted to tell you that when I won the French Open, I drew inspiration from this newspaper clipping which I carried in my pocket throughout the tournament. It told the story of Sally Little who earlier that month had become the first South African female to win a Major in the United States when you triumphed at the Women's International in South Carolina.'

The following months their careers were to be overshadowed by the tragic Soweto uprising.

Returning home to Soweto in July with €4907, and despite the 'necklacing', a common horrifying death for black collaborators (burning tyre containing petrol placed over the head), and with the '(Winnie) Mandela football club' in their yellow tracksuits terrorising the residents with kidnapping, torture and murder, Tshabalala was immediately selected by the SAPGA, headed Brian 'Bruno' Henning (later one of the founders of the US Champion Tour), to partner Gary Player in the World Cup – the **FIRST BLACK SPORTSMAN to be selected to REPRESENT AND PLAY FOR (WHITE) SOUTH AFRICA** – which invitation he immediately turned down! [22]

This was despite Gary Player being his friend and mentor, and irrespective of the money and status he would earn. He declined for good reason as Soweto went up in flames during the 1976 July student riots following an attempt to enforce Afrikaans language requirements on black African students, and the mood of the black population was sullen and threatening.

Vincent lived in Soweto, the centre of the unrest, and an acceptance of an invitation to represent 'white' South Africa abroad was potentially dangerous to himself and his family.

At the same time, he felt he was being used by the Apartheid government and the PGA to placate the protests directed against white golfers abroad as he was only ranked 14th on the SA Order of Merit, such that he did not deserve his place, and accordingly his selection was merely for political expediency.

Furthermore, the invitation was to represent the SAPGA in this world event, even though they would not let him be a member, nor did he have the same rights as the other 'white' professionals to vote.

This was simply glossed over as it did not occur to them – they had allowed him to play under the new dispensation, and surely this was enough?

The upshot was trouble with the SAPGA, and its president Brian Henning. They had obviously wanted to put on a 'black' face in the world arena to deflect the criticism and banning now levelled at those white golfers playing internationally, and especially Gary Player.

---

22   Hugh Biaocchi took Papwa's place and partnered Player to 4th place. Player won the individual title.

Chapter 8: Vive La France

1976 Soweto uprising

For no valid reason, the winner of the French Open, Vincent Tshabalala's entry for the SA Open was turned down, leaving the black golfer furious.

Further, he was suspended not only by SAPGA but now also by the black controlling TPA body for having taken part in a 'white' tournament.

In order to enable him to play in multiracial tournaments, and thus get around this ban by both the SAPGA and the Black TPA Tour, he formed the 'South African Bantu Golf Union' on the advice of Minister Piet Koornhof.

But it seems he was soon forgiven as that season he played nine events and would finish joint 7th in the Sumrie-Bournemouth Better-Ball (with John O'Leary), 17th at the Italian Open, and joint 21st in the Piccadilly Medal.

In January 1977, Vincent won the SA Non-European Open in Durban with scores of 73 75 73 70 (291) and for a fourth time in 1983 shooting 74 74 75 74 (297). However, he was then banned from playing in the Zambian Open because he was South African.

Vincent was inducted into the Southern Africa Golf Hall of Fame in 2010, the year after Papwa's induction, but as a final irony, this author was contacted by Grant Wilson, CEO of the Sunshine Tour, and informed that both the Sunshine Tour and Johann Rupert did not approve of Tshabalala's selection for induction. The basis for this was a letter he had written to the Minister of Sport Steve Tshwete complaining that the Sunshine Tour, under the guidance of Rupert, were not providing sufficient opportunities for more black players to compete in local tour events, favouring white overseas players instead.

The Hall of Fame induction committee was split insofar as proceeding, but Harry Brews, Sally Little, Peter Sauerman, and Barry Cohen had their way, although we had to compromise with the rest of the committee by simultaneously agreeing to induct Richard Mogoerane and Theo Manyama.

Finally, Vincent was inducted into the 2010 Southern Africa Golf Hall of Fame ironically together with Brian 'Bruno' Henning, who previously had him banned.

CHAPTER 9: END OF THE ROAD

Papwa's death

Going forward to the summer of 1976/77 the earnings of professionals after the first six events on the South African circuit make interesting, if somewhat sad, reading. Under the headings Position on Order of Merit, Name, Winnings, Tournaments Played and Stroke Average, the list reads as follows:

1	Player G	R19 362	(5)	68,40
2	Baiocchi H	18 937	(6)	68,66
53	**Sewgolum S**	R258	(2)	73,62
56	Mpharu E	230	(2)	73,75
62	Manyama T	163	(2)	74,12
63	Nkabinde S	153	(2)	74,37
67	Chowglay I	116	(1)	76,25

It is clear that the black players only played 1-3 tournaments compared to their white counterparts playing 5-6 events. Cost of traveling and playing in the event together with having their entry accepted showed there was still a long way to go to even the playing field.

Papwa's final tournament was the 1977 Natal Non-European Open which he won for at least the seventeenth time in a minimum of 21 starts.

He was ready to concede that his career was effectively over. Interviewed by sportswriter Norman Canale in 1978, Sewgolum noted that while it was heartwarming that golfers of all races were beginning to mix freely, 'it's come too late for me.'

Papwa battled with his health, and on more than one occasion he was forced to withdraw from tournaments or return home prematurely from overseas trips because of health problems. That he should have decided to remain at home comes as no real surprise.

Canale observed: 'Sadly, Papwa, the shuttlecock of sports apartheid for so many years and the man who did all the front-running in the movement for mixed golf, was now too old to savour the honours out there on the fairway.'

That same year Gary Player won his ninth – and final – Major championship, the US Masters at Augusta. While it marked the end of an incredible chapter in Player's life, a new one was opening as he would win a further nine Majors – on the lucrative seniors' Championship Tour.

Whether Papwa still experienced the shame of the Natal Open saga, the discouragement he felt at not being able to compete, or years of prejudice held against him, his career was over. He faltered in the tournaments where he could compete and never properly recovered, both on and off the golf course.

This slowly broke his spirit, leaving him with nothing but a dream. He started to become overwhelmed by loneliness and took to drink. He seemed apologetic for having let down the community. He was a victim of the apartheid system.

On the 4th of July 1978, Rajen Sewshanker said his father, Papwa, began complaining of chest pains at his Riverside home. He spent the evening in bed, but didn't sleep well. The following morning he died following a massive heart attack.

He dared to dream and succeeded in the face of overwhelming adversity, He was relatively young, only 49 years old, not always in the best of health, and, perhaps most significant of all, he had had enough.

The community came together to provide a decent burial. The body was bathed, anointed with a mixture of water and sandalwood, and daubed with turmeric powder and water. It was garbed in new cloth, and flowers, incense and rose water decorated the coffin. An enormous cavalcade snaked its way from the family home to the Clare East Crematorium (which is next to the renamed Papwa Sewgolum

Chapter 9: End of the Road

Golf Course, formerly the Springfield Golf Club) such that there's a fairway in-between the crematorium and the Umgeni River.

When the open coffin was removed from the hearse, it was carried through a tunnel of friends and family who held up golf clubs in the air to form a symbolic arch. While his son Deepraj chanted a Hindu prayer commanding his father's spirit to be reincarnated[23].

The funeral pyre was lit and the flames consumed the body of this Durban giant. The ashes were then collected and Sewgolum's sons released them into the Umgeni River where they washed into the Indian Ocean.

The golf club salute to Papwa's funeral in 1978 (photographer unknown)

'The struggle for him had ended.' He was a champion. Our Champion!

'What counts in life is not the mere fact that we have lived, it is the difference we have made to the lives of others that will determine the significance of the life we lead' – Nelson Mandela

---

23   Hindus believe that within 10 days the soul of the deceased is believed to acquire a new body, and the consequences of the last life, its rewards and punishments are unfolded.

Papwa

The difference between Player and Sewgolum was that the doors that opened for Player to enter the golfing world and carve out his remarkable story were bolted shut for Papwa.

'I lost my mother when I was eight, my father worked in the mines, and I had a three-hour round trip to school every day before coming back to make my own supper,' Player said. 'But even though I went through all that, it was nothing compared with what Papwa had to endure.'

Papwa was, in the best sense of the word, a simple man who saw himself neither as a symbol nor as a political flag-waver. He asked only for the chance to play and express his talents.

As the first black man to play in a white tournament he competed at the 1961 SA Open at East London trailing not clouds of glory, but red tape in the form of a group areas permit which excluded practice time, drinks at the bar, and the opportunity to change his shoes in the locker room. Such was Papwa's introduction to first-class tournament golf in SA, and it says much for his character that he rose above these indignities and got on with the job of earning a living in the only way he knew.

He was a golfer who spent too long on the sidelines to achieve his full potential, and his early death emphasises this sad fact. He has, however, a place in the game's history not only for what he did, but how he did it, and colleagues will doff their caps in memory of a gentle, unassuming man – who achieved far more than ever he realised.

On his untimely death, the National Party Minister of Sport, Dr Piet Koornhof in an ironic twist, sent a telegram to his family paying tribute to this 'grand master of golf' in these words 'I am very sorry to hear of your great irreparable loss. He was a fine golfer, a great man, and will be sorely missed.'

'He really knew what he was doing on the golf course. Soft spoken, he was no fantastic striker of the ball, but he could move it left and right. He knew how to get around a golf course, and he really knew what he was doing. A really nice guy, a credit to golf, and a credit to the game,' said Denis Hutchinson.

'A genius around the greens, it was a privilege to know Papwa as a Champion and as a Gentleman,' said Dale Hayes.

Chapter 9: End of the Road

'South Africa has produced many Champion Golfers but few the equal of Papwa, by then a folk hero with no money, a drinker with a bad heart. Papwa fought hatred with love. From a hundred yards in, Papwa was dynamite. His short game was undoubtedly his greatest strength. The fact that he is relatively unknown to South African golfers today is a great shame,' said Gary Player.

'I always had the impression that he could have gone down as one of the best golfers in the world had he been blessed with the right opportunities from a much younger age,' said Bobby Verwey.

It's one of golf's great traits that, irrespective of class, colour or upbringing, the only conflict is between a man and the ball. Sure, there are challenges, like the weather, and opponents, and internal fears, but they have only as much influence as you allow them to. When you stand over a stroke, it is just you and the ball. When he played a shot he switched off, there was nobody around him, nobody in front of him. He had a very relaxed way of playing and accepted the bad times.

Player and Papwa might have shared a course on only a few occasions, but their common adversity meant they had more in common than most, even as they were reminded of their differences all too often. It was an ironic role-reversal, in that Player's trouble started when he left SA, and Papwa's occurred whenever he came back.

That's the beauty of sport. Even after the greats pass on, their legend grows with time and their legacy is there for all to see, forever.

This unassuming son of a fruit seller dared to dream and succeed in the face of overwhelming adversity, which included a racist golfing establishment and – in a classic irony of apartheid logic – a government which actively undermined his accomplishments and outrageously humiliated and scorned him.

Beating Player in the Natal Open and matching the golfing cream in the SA Open attested to the quality of Papwa's ability. Who knows what heights he would have reached as a golfer, were it not for apartheid? Yet, because of apartheid, the lives of Player and Papwa panned out so differently.

While Player went on to become one of the greatest players the game has known and a multi-millionaire, Papwa died penniless, a pauper, and broken man because he was denied the opportunity to do what he loved most in life – play golf at the highest levels.

'And he was very, very talented,' said Player. 'He was relatively short off the tee but had a very good short game, and was, in my opinion one of the best and most accurate players I have ever seen within 40 yards (36m) of the green, and he had a very good temperament. He's

Chapter 9: End of the Road

been an extremely controversial subject in South Africa. It was tough for him. He came along at the wrong time, unfortunately. But in the meantime, he's given a lot of people, particularly young Indian golfers a lot of encouragement. Any young Indian golfer coming along can have Papwa as a hero.

And he faced enormous restrictions to his freedom throughout a short career that was sabotaged by the racist regime. How do you ever say what a man's future would have been?" asks Player, finally.

But then he proceeds to do just that: 'If you want to make a comparison, he was just under a Harold Henning. Harold Henning was just a little better than him. He would have had a very nice future.'

"He never learnt to better himself and he spent the money he made on keeping his family going. If he had stayed under our guidance, we would have arranged for him to have royalties on clothing, shoes, and sporting equipment bearing his name. With his publicity and fame and the fact that he was a hero in the eyes of the Indian community they would have sold well. He could have been a world champion were it not for apartheid", reflected Graham Wulff.

Unfortunately, we will never know just how far Papwa could have gone had he been given more opportunities in the 1950s-60s. In his prime during the 1960s he lost that period from 1966–1972 when he was banned. While his victory over Player in the 1965 Natal Open could have been a stepping stone to greater things had he lived in any other time or circumstance, it was seen as a symbolically threatening event by the apartheid leaders of the time.

Discussing his father, Rajen Sewshanker notes that Papwa 'thrust South Africa in the glare of the international spotlight and marked a significant turning point in South Africa's relationship with the civilised world when he won the 1963 Natal Open'.

Papwa was regarded as a man looking for trouble instead of an athlete passionate about his game. An illiterate Indian man beating a white man at an elitist sport was merely unacceptable – what if this defeat eradicated the misguided notion of white supremacy? In the government's eyes, Papwa had to be stopped.

Rajen continued: "This happened when he was in his prime and it hit him hard. Golf was his trade and he didn't have anything to fall back on. He was emotionally and physically crippled. Alcohol was an escape".

To complicate matters, although non-political, Papwa suddenly found himself thrust into the political limelight as the 'symbol of the anti-apartheid sport movement'. The sport's boycott that followed led the fight to end apartheid and helped bring about the day when Nelson Mandela would honour Papwa Sewgolum who still remains one of the greatest golfers to come out of SA.'

In March 1983 the Durban Golf Club printed a new scorecard embossed with an image of Papwa against the background of sugar-cane fields, whilst in December 1985 the Durban Golf Club hosted a tournament in memory of Papwa.

On 23 January 1993, Papwa was the first sporting personality to be honoured with a figurine at the Durban History Museum "because he was an exciting and different character. Although he was a sportsman, he played an interesting political role" stated Gillian Berning, and joined other famous personalities, such as Shaka, Dingaan, Alan Paton, King Edward Masinga, Mahatma Gandhi, Albert Luthuli and John Dube.

September 1993, the city of Durban honoured the memory of Papwa when the Papwa Sewgolum Golf Course – formerly the Linear Park Golf Course – was opened in Springfield by Margaret Winter, a former mayor.

In 2004 the changing tides of democracy ensured Papwa was further honoured for his excellent achievements in the field of golf and his perseverance and courage in the face of debilitating apartheid laws. He was awarded the 'Order of Ikhamanga in Silver' from President Thabo Mbeki, South Africa's highest honour for achievement in the performing arts and sport.

For a long time, Durban Country Club officials attempted to portray the outdoor ceremony as a magnanimous gesture – "it would not be fair for Papwa to go inside to get his trophy, out of sight of his enormous following," according to the club history. "It certainly was not a slight to Papwa – rather one of consideration to enable his fans to see him in his moment of glory."

Chapter 9: End of the Road

The model of Papwa, caddy and golf bag

However, in 2005, the Durban Country Club, where the infamous prize-giving ceremony took place, unveiled a memorial plaque on the outside wall of the clubhouse, facing the 18th green, honouring Papwa.

In Honour: Sewsunker 'Papwa' Sewgolum

This plaque was commissioned by the members of the Durban Country Club to commemorate local golfer Sewsunker 'Papwa' Sewgolum's historic victories in the 1963 and 1965 Natal Open Championships, making him the first person of colour to win a professional golf tournament in South Africa. We salute the talent of this self-taught legend of the game

The plaque concludes: *"The club apologises for what had happened four decades earlier".*

Durban Country Club chairman Ray Lalouette described the 1965 Natal Open awards ceremony as 'an ignominious debacle that must have been the source of much embarrassment and humiliation for a fellow human being at a time when he should have been experiencing joy and jubilation.'

'No matter what the background, or the rules of the land, it must have been an experience that caused hurt and shame for him and his family.'

'It is therefore fitting and appropriate that I, as the current chairman, take this opportunity on behalf of the members of the Durban Country Club, to apologise to Mrs Suminthra Sewgolum and to Mr Sewgolum's son, Rajen, and his family for the suffering you have endured as a result of that most unfortunate incident.'

'We have commissioned this plaque to serve as a permanent reminder to all those (and especially golfers) who walk this way, that Papwa Sewgolum was a remarkable man.'

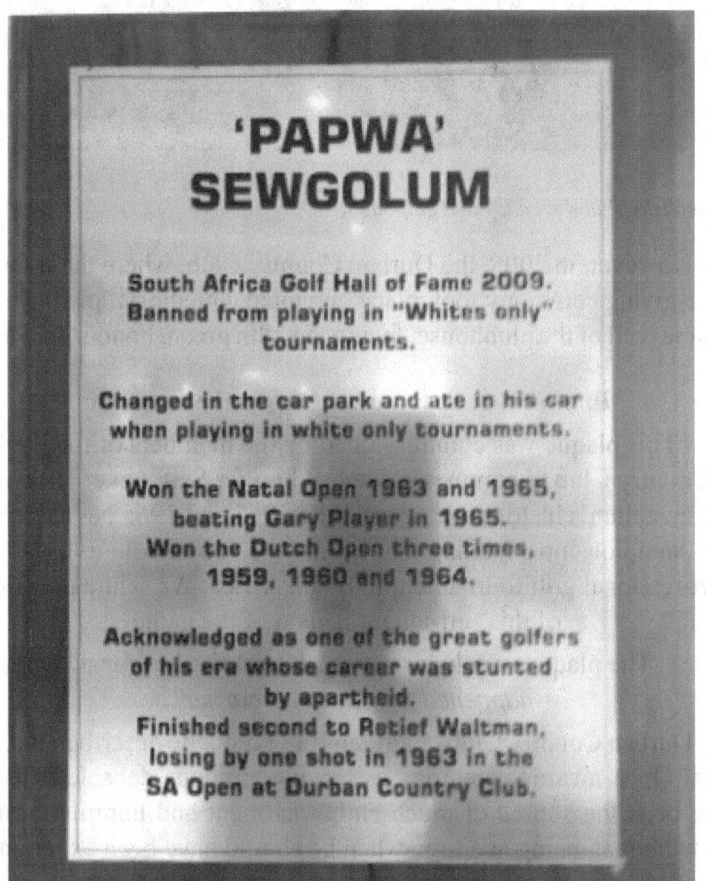

Chapter 9: End of the Road

However, the plaque does not take into account all Papwa's victories on the supposed parallel non-European tour as classified 'professional tournaments in South Africa', nor does the Durban Country Club 'where people matter and values count', make any mention on its website of the most famous golfers who won tournaments there (together with Sid Brews, Bobby Locke, Gary Player, and Ernie Els), its former home-grown champion and local hero. Papwa simply gets an unsympathetic page in the 1982 club history, blaming the victim for the misfortunes that befell him by concluding: 'Sadly, brilliant golfer that he was, Papwa seemed to lack the determination and discipline to remain at the top.'

Also in 2005, Christopher Nicholson's biography of Papwa Sewgolum: *'From Pariah to Legend'* was published, followed by Maxine Case's book *'Papwa Golf's lost Legend'*, while a documentary film about his life, *'Papwa: The Lost Dream of a South African Golfing Legend'*, had its première in August 2005, a life that was lived 'in triumph and in loss', Craig Urquhart also dedicated one chapter to Papwa as one of the ten best South African golfers in his book *'The King of Swing'*.

In 2009, Sewsunker 'Papwa' Sewgolum was inducted into the Southern Africa Golf Hall of Fame by Vincent Tshabalala, alongside Gary Player, Bobby Locke, Nick Price, Sally Little, Ernie Els, and Retief Goosen, all multiple major winners, and in 2010, the Durban Golf Course was renamed after him, "The Papwa Sewgolum Municipal Golf Course", an 18-hole flat woodland course situated in the suburb of Reservoir Hills, one of the few municipally-owned tracks in SA.

Finally, in 2017 Rajen Sewshanker received the South African Sports Trust award on behalf of his father from President Motlanthe.

As Craig Urquhart, in his book 'The Kings of Swing' comments, 'A good man, a great golfer and a beacon for all of South Africa, Papwa Sewgolum may not have won a Major, but the role he played in leveling the courses in this deeply fractured land can never be under-estimated.'

Whatever the truth of the conflicting details of the prize-giving, the incident was just one of countless apartheid assaults that Papwa endured. But as a potent symbol of exclusion, it turned into a firestorm, starting with press commentary at home and abroad.

Papwa

Chapter 9: End of the Road

In 1966 Gary Player went on to pen his infamous lines: 'I am a man of Verwoerd and apartheid' in his book, *Grand Slam Golf*. Player – the 'white champion' – although he changed his public position as circumstances changed in SA, was at that time deeply involved in the apartheid-support system established by the state, and as such, at that time, he never challenged the fact that one of the few golfers in the world capable of beating him was banned by racism from even making a living out of golf, instead Player went on to become a multi-millionaire.

Papwa – the 'black champion' – on the other hand, even embarrassed his hosts in India by insisting when he played there that the SA flag was flown alongside those that represented the countries of the other players in the tournament.

However, the memory of Papwa remains strong and continues to inspire future generations of golfers. He was a symbol of the sports-boycott movement. He went on to become an international symbol against Apartheid in sport, and his reach in this field stretched beyond just South Africa. Even Australia was made an example of when Papwa was denied by the authorities to play there in 1958.

He was an ethnic Indian golfer and highlighted the struggle of non-Europeans to compete in sports in an era of apartheid. But thanks to this country's laws at the time, which were subsequently declared a crime against humanity by the UN, his golfing achievements were limited.

Under difficult circumstances he managed to make it with determination, guts, class, skill and most of all determination..

Papwa Sewgolum died penniless, and yes, he drank, says Rajen; it was his way of overcoming the disappointment. He became a very sad person. But he was never bitter, and his influence transcended way beyond the mere sport of golf, and as a result of his achievements he was able to make a huge impact on the dismantling of an entire political system, and the termination of apartheid.

He was much mourned as the following tribute attests. *'Many racial barriers in sport have been removed and the general atmosphere these days is far more relaxed than it used to be. Agreeable though this may be (as far as it goes), it is salutary to remember that only a few years ago the attitude to multiracial sport was a curious mixture of patronage, bad manners and grudging enlightenment. The golfer who started it all, Sewsunker "Papwa" Sewgolum, died this week. Good player though he undoubtedly was, any consideration of his career must really concentrate on the man himself-on his tolerance, good humour and instinctively gentlemanly behaviour. Papwa was, in the best sense of the word, a simple man who saw himself neither as a symbol nor as a political flag-waver. He asked only for the chance to express his talents (upside down grip and all) on golf courses here and overseas'.*

He was not an emotional man, at least outwardly, but it is not difficult to imagine his bitter-sweet feelings when he won the Natal Open, only to receive the trophy outside in the rain because of permit limitations. His successes overseas included three victories in the Dutch Open and the consistency that was the hallmark of his game kept him regularly in the prize lists at home.

With the passing of the years Papwa became part of the scene, which was all he ever wanted, and the cruder humiliations were no longer the lot of his professional life unassuming man-who achieved far more than ever he realised.

'I have always admired people who achieved in spite of adversity. He did a lot in spite of what he had, and had to deal with,' said Sally Little (two-time LPGA major champion).

"In my day, everybody who followed golf in Southern Africa knew about Papwa," Nick Price (former World Number 1).

Ben Crenshaw, with his childlike wonder of golfiana in all its forms, will sometimes encounter a player of a certain age, with a certain accent, and make this plea: *Tell me all about him – tell me about the man they call Papwa!*

And Gentle Ben will lean back and hear the remarkable tale of Sewsunker "Papwa" Sewgolum, with his dark skin and cross-handed grip and magical short game, South African golfer of Indian descent and a world-class talent who, at times in his prime, could not compete in the national championship of his homeland.

The prohibition that black sportsmen faced continued until the abolishment of apartheid in the 1990s, when the sporting walls that Papwa had first and most spectacularly pounded on, would, at last be

Chapter 9: End of the Road

reduced to the rubble of history.

In the years since liberation, the golf establishment and government have worked to bring golf to black youngsters[24]. Academies and bursaries have been set up and talent identified and given opportunities. The majority of black golfers, however, still face the obstacles of poverty, a lack of facilities and limited opportunity. It is a measure both of how far the sport needs to move forward, and of the stature of Papwa's achievements that no other SA golfer of colour, other than Vincent Tshabalala and Lewis Chitengwa[25], have so far won a major national open tournament either in SA or overseas.

He was a champion!

---

24 Like the (Sally) Little Golf Trust focusing on black junior school girls.

25 In 1993 Zimbabwean, Lewis Chitengwa won the World Junior Championship beating the defending champion Tiger Woods. The following year, 1994, he beat Rory Sabbatini and Tim Clark on his way to winning the South African Amateur Match-Play championship. He featured prominently on the American university circuit and was playing on the Canadian Tour, preparing himself for a tilt at the PGA Tour when he died of a rare form of meningitis. Nick Price, the former world number 1, stated his protégé would surely have won a major. His father and coach, Lewis Muridzo, the first Zimbabwean of colour to play in white tournaments locally and abroad, also coached Vijay Singh when he first played the tour in Southern Africa.

SEWSUNKER 'PAPWA' SEWGOLUM
(December 1928 – July 1978)

- Mother was blind, lived in a shack, didn't go to school – illiterate
- Went to work at 11 following the death of his father
- Taught himself to play golf with a wooden stick
- Played with the 'wrong' reverse grip
- At 16 won the Natal Indian Open
- Late 1957 shot 59 in a caddy tournament at Beachwood
- First black golfer to win a European National championship tournament – the Dutch Open
- Won the Dutch Open (3) runner-up (1) – first player to win it three times (in 4 attempts)
- Won the Natal Open (2) – his first two attempts
- Banned from playing in SA tournaments, and passport withdrawn

Citations

☐ 1960 Member British PGA
☐ 1970 Rest of the World vs. Britain
☐ All Tournaments won – 77 (at least)
☐ Open tournament wins – 10 (excludes non-European titles)
☐ Lesser SA Tournaments (18)
☐ TPA Tour: SA Non-European Open (10) 2nd (1) – Provincial titles (38) 2nd (9)
☐ SA Non-European Sportsman of the Year 1959, '63/4
☐ SA Order of Merit 1964/65 3rd – despite being prevented from playing in two events
☐ 2004 Awarded the Order of Ikhamanga in Silver
☐ 2009 Inducted into the Southern Africa Golf Hall of Fame
☐ 2010 Papwa Sewgolum Municipal Golf Course named after him

Chapter 9: End of the Road

- 2017 South African Sports Trust award

*Disadvantaged by apartheid – prevented from playing the SAPGA 'white' tour – and overseas

Record

Amateur
- Natal Indian Open 1945

Professional – Open tournaments
- Dutch Open 1959, 60, 64, 66 4th, 67 2nd, 70 6th
- The British Open 1963 13th, 67 57th
- SA Open 1963 2nd, 64 3rd, 65 12th, 70 11th
- Natal Open 1963, 65
- Grand Prix Series First Leg 1963
- Grand Prix Series Second Leg 1963 2nd
- Kensington Open 5000 1964 8th
- Cock 'o North (Zambia) 1964
- SA Dunlop Masters 1965 3rd, 66 11th
- LiquidAir 5000 1965 15th
- SA PGA 1965 5th, 66 11th
- Flame Lily (Rhodesia) 1965 5th, 66 8th
- Carling World Golf Championship 1966 6th
- Bata Bush Babes (Rhodesia) 1966
- Rhodesian Dunlop Open 1966 5th
- French Open 1967 5th
- India Open 1967 6th
- Swaziland Spa Open 1968
- Mbabane Holiday Inn 1971 3rd

Professional – Non-European TPA tour
- SA Non-European Open 1960, 61, 63, 64, 65, 67, 68, 69, 70, 74

- ☐ SA Non-European Open 1971 2nd
- ☐ Natal Non-European Open 1954, 55, 57, 58, 59, 60, 61, 62, 63, 65, 66, 67, 68, 69, 70, 74, 75, 77
- ☐ Natal Non-European Open 2nd 1956, 64, 71, 76
- ☐ Griqualand West Non-European Open 1960, 61, 63, 64, 65, 67, 69
- ☐ Western Province Non-European Open 1960, 64, 69, 76
- ☐ Western Province Non-European Open 1968 2nd
- ☐ Transvaal Non-European Open 1964, 65, 66, 67, 69, 70
- ☐ Transvaal Non-European Open 1972 2nd
- ☐ Eastern Province Non-European Open 1964
- ☐ Eastern Province Non-European Open 2nd 1963, 68
- ☐ OFS Non-European Open 1966, 69
- ☐ OFS Non-European Open 1968 2nd
- ☐ Natal Midlands Non-European Open 1959, 60
- ☐ R200 Sponsored Invitation 1964
- ☐ R.L. Bambata Boodhun Trophy 1965, 66 2nd
- ☐ Natal Thunderbird Classic 1965
- ☐ Transvaal Invitational 1966
- ☐ Gary Player Trophy 1967
- ☐ Gary Player Invitational 1968, 69, 70
- ☐ Kimberley Non-European Open 1968, 69
- ☐ St Michael's Non-European Open 1968, 71
- ☐ Luyt Lager 1972 2nd
- ☐ Tournament of Champions 1973
- ☐ Coca-Cola Open 1974 2nd
- ☐ LTA Masters 1974, 75 2nd
- ☐ Griqua Gold Cup 1974

*Records incomplete

Chapter 9: End of the Road

Gary Player: Questions

John Vorster, a keen golfer and enthusiastic supporter of the Nazis during World War II. Gary Player was a regular golfing companion – something else that attracted a great deal of criticism.

One day Player went into Vorster's office. 'And I said to him, please, I'd like to break down the apartheid barrier in sport,' Player recalled. 'You know, to go to a man like that was tough. And I said I'd like to invite Lee Elder, the black American golfer, to South Africa. I thought he was going to tell me to get out. Instead, with those thick bushy eyebrows and head still bowed, he said, go ahead. And that was a start.

I'm very pleased I did play golf with Vorster, because had I not, I could not have gone into his office and achieved that. I was able to contribute a very significant thing to our country. I had set a trend, but once we could get an international player of colour here, there is no doubt that was the start of breaking down apartheid for all sports.'

For many, this kind of "reform" was nothing but tokenism: government propaganda intended to counter the rising international outcry against apartheid.

It was 1971 and Elder said he would play in SA, but only under certain conditions: Other black professionals must be allowed to compete, in front of mixed crowds, and have full access to all the amenities, such as the clubhouse. Player – and Vorster – agreed.

In other quarters, the National Party government branded Player a traitor for inviting African-American tennis star, Arthur Ashe and his compatriot, golfer Lee Elder, to SA.

Lee Elder recalls that distant summer of 1971. 'Gary asked me to come,' he says gently. 'We were good friends, and we still are today. I wanted to try to help in any way I could.' Elder, a year older than Player, is something of a pioneer. At a club with a complex history in matters relating to skin colour, in 1975 he became the first black person to enter the grounds at the Masters as a competitor, opposed to a caddy or waiter.

In SA, he played in tournaments and exhibition matches with Player, including one in Durban where the proceeds went to a school for black girls.

Elder's lasting memory of the trip is a big dinner one evening at the famous Wanderers Club in Johannesburg.

Vorster was part of the receiving line, shaking hands with all the guests as they arrived. Right before it was Elder's turn to meet the prime minister, Vorster abruptly left the receiving line, walked over to the main table, and sat down.

'It was in the newspapers there the next day – Vorster snubs American golfer,' says Elder. 'The reason he gave was that the proceedings were taking too long, and he wanted the festivities to start on time.' Elder shakes his head; 'The thing about Gary, he was always proud to be South African. He's a good friend. He didn't deserve to be targeted. These things are a lot different now.'

Is there still racism in golf? 'Oh, yeah,' replied Elder to the rhetorical question. 'You have a generation that's been taught a certain way by their parents. A lot of improvements, but it's going to take time, generations until we get to the day when we don't see the colour, we see the person.'

Three tournaments that year would be classified as 'international' events that were open to golfers of colour, with more to follow in subsequent years. Similar initiatives took place in other sports. Selected hotels and restaurants were also accorded 'international' status. Papwa played in these golf events, but his best years were gone.

There were still restrictions, however. Dale Hayes recalls that black players weren't allowed to use the same toilets as whites. And for many, this kind of 'reform' was nothing but tokenism: government propaganda intended to counter the rising international outcry against apartheid.

'Those tournaments were really just a window dressing on the situation in South Africa,' says Dennis Bruyns, executive director of the SA tour from 1981–1991. 'The black players in South Africa couldn't go to any of our main venues for 51 weeks of the year, but in the fifty-second week, when the tournament was on, then they could go and play and have a drink in the bar. Basically, the Group Areas Act didn't apply for that one week. It was all part of a grand plan at the time. There was a huge effort to try to sell this to the world.'

Bruyns, a former tour professional, choose his words carefully

Chapter 9: End of the Road

concerning Player's role in creating the 'international' events: 'I think to an extent he was used,' he says. 'He was doing it from his heart. They were more political than he was. They saw an opportunity.'

Gary Player, the super-fit, small, neat man dressed in dark outfits was known as the Black Knight. His working rules were strict and uncompromising – health, diet, practice, and physical strength, something he advocated long before it became popular.

He was denied a place in the Commonwealth Ryder Cup team because he would have represented a pariah state, and he did much to narrow the race gap as the true reality of apartheid finally struck home.

However, Player found himself embroiled in the race issue following the release of his 1966 book 'Grand Slam Golf', where he had written: 'I must say now, and clearly, that I am of the South Africa of Verwoerd and apartheid ... a nation which ... is the product of its instinct and ability to maintain civilised values and standards among the alien barbarians ... The African may well believe in witchcraft and primitive magic, practice ritual murder and polygamy; his wealth is in cattle.'

These words, phrases, and inferences were deemed patronising at best, racist at worst, and his image suffered in some quarters.

Christopher Nicholson in his book *'Pariah to Legend'*, says the events were 'a charade. This kind of thing was nothing but an attempt to put a positive face on apartheid. Gary Player was part of that.'

Nicholson further criticises Player's role in the '70s in the so-called 'Committee for Fairness in Sport', and the conservative newspaper, *The Citizen,* both of which, he says, were government-funded operations.

At that stage, according to SA writer Christopher Merrett: 'It is a matter of undisputed historical fact that Player was a notorious apologist and propagandist for apartheid,' as seen in his book in 1966, the year after he was beaten in the Natal Open by Papwa, although there is no mention of Sewgolum.

Player goes onto say he won an amazing comeback victory against Tony Lema in the Piccadilly match-play tournament in 1965 because he got to thinking about his country, 'maligned, misunderstood, pilloried by people who can tell us how to order our affairs from a range of 6,000 miles without ever coming down to South Africa and seeing for themselves and trying to understand.'

Certainly, his political colours were still firmly nailed to the National Party flagpole more than a decade later when it emerged Player had been a member of the secret clique assembled by Eschel Rhoodie and his 'Infogate' pals to back the launching of the English Nationalist voice piece, The Citizen, during the BJ Vorster regime.

Insofar as Player's golf slacks featuring one black and one white leg were concerned, Nicholson is quite clear: 'It seems to me that one black leg and one white leg was rather an endorsement of the separateness apartheid espoused.'

Both Player and Sewgolum professed only to be golfers, uninterested in politics, but as Nicholson shows, Player – the 'white champion' – although he changed his public position as circumstances changed in SA, and as more pressure was brought to bear when abroad, was deeply involved in the apartheid-support system established by the state.

However, in hindsight, one should reflect upon the 'white society' South Africans were brought up in AT THAT TIME. A white person growing up in SA, separated from Africans due to apartheid policies, unless they were interacting on a personal level, were brainwashed through the apartheid controlled media, and for Player, who was never exposed to university politics, to be asked to play golf with the Prime Minister was viewed as an honour.

Chapter 9: End of the Road

Liberal universities in and around the early 1970s saw UCT student Geoff Budlender, the SRC President, reject Vorster's insinuations 'with the contempt it deserved', as for the first time police beat up white students demonstrating for free black education at St. Georges Cathedral, and then violently carried protesting students off UCT's Jameson stairs. Neville Curtis, NUSAS President, having been tipped off, escaped through the mountains to New Zealand via Lesotho, while Steve Biko at Fort Hare was telling touring UCT law students that they wanted a clear polarisation between blacks and whites, and white liberals merely muddied the water. Meanwhile, the law student moot room was a breeding ground for Anton Lubowski and others. Outside of the university no one was the wiser except for some newspaper headlines.

Growing up with a father working on the mines, and no mother, Gary Player was not part of this world, although travelling and competing outside of SA he should have becoming aware that all men are born free and equal.

In Player's case, it should also be remembered that from 1961, Helen Suzman was the sole voice of South Africa's oppressed until 1974 when six colleagues joined Helen in Parliament. Suzman became known for her strong public criticism of the governing National Party's policies of apartheid at a time when this was unusual among white people. She found herself even more of an outsider, as she was an English-speaking Jewish woman in a parliament dominated by male Calvinist *Gereformeerde Kerk* Afrikaners.

At that time, the Progressive Party was the lone voice speaking out in parliament against apartheid, with the 'white party' only supported, in the main, by affluent liberal English-speaking whites, especially the Jewish community, and for the rest, the vast majority supported the apartheid policy.

It is likely that Player had a double purpose for initiating the invitation for Lee Elder to play in SA, both in an attempt to deflect political contempt aimed at him while playing in international events abroad, as well as to help create the impression of trying to break down barriers within SA by enabling leading black golfers to participate in white-only tournaments. Similarly, in the 1970s, he started to assist Sewgolum insofar as a trip to Australia and New Zealand, and especially his sponsorship of Tshabalala financially and through tournament invitations to break into the international golf circuit.

In 1974 he appeared to modify his political views in his autobiography *'Gary Player World of Golf'*, where he goes on to say: 'As in every country, there are things that are obviously wrong, and a great many of us are working hard to rectify them. I must say, however, that in all my travels across the world I've never seen a country where white and black get along as well together as in my country.'

Player was also asked by government officials to entertain a few very important overseas businessmen by playing golf with them when they came to SA. He says it seemed harmless enough and nothing more than a good public relations exercise. At first, he declined as he had an arrangement to appear in Australia for a sizeable fee, but then they also offered albeit a lesser fee, so being a patriot, he agreed. He goes on to say that if they had told him it was to advance the cause of apartheid he would not have done it.

The question, however, must be asked why is it that only Player is targeted for not assisting black golfers, especially Papwa Sewgolum? Other great SA golfers were playing competitively such as world champions like Bobby Locke (four-time major champion – top 20 all-time ranking) and Harold Henning (over 50 worldwide victories).

Later in the 1980s as the reality of apartheid was appreciated by Player, it dawned on him that as a sportsman of his eminence in SA, that it was not possible to separate politics from sport. There is no doubt that he both changed his views, and subsequently spoke out forcefully against apartheid and inequality, while at the same time raising millions of dollars for the disadvantaged, as well as funding his own school for disadvantaged children: 'then suddenly I realised that it wasn't equal, apartheid was a dreadful policy.' But this was too late for Sewgolum and Chowglay.

In 1987, in an interview with the *LA Times*, Player disavowed the system of apartheid, stating: 'We have a terrible system in apartheid… it's almost a cancerous disease. I'm happy to say it's being eliminated… we've got to get rid of this apartheid,' and 'the wind of change has at last reached South Africa, and our country will be the better for it.'

Chapter 9: End of the Road

While in an interview with Graham Bensinger, Player discussed his early support for apartheid stating that the SA government had 'pulled the wool over our eyes' and that the people were 'brainwashed' into supporting these policies.

Clearly as an international figure he played a significant role in breaking down apartheid by finally speaking out as his understanding and appreciation of the ills of apartheid changed. Why it took so long is a mystery.

However, Player's more recent recollections are interesting: 'Protestors of South Africa's apartheid policy gave me grief for a couple of years. I didn't believe in apartheid, and I surely wasn't responsible for it, but I was a ripe target. They burned awful statements into the greens where we were playing. I got death threats at my hotel every day. At the 1969 PGA Championship, a guy screamed just as I stroked a 10-inch putt, and I missed and lost by one. At Merion, during the 1971 US Open, we kept guns in the house where I was staying. I struggled through it, and you know something? It's easier to fight than to run away. It was a tough two years. But Nelson Mandela, who spent over 20 years in prison, had it a whole lot worse.'

Player was awarded the 'Order of Ikhamanga in Gold' for exceptional achievement in 2003 by President Mbeki for excellence in golf and contribution to non-racial sport in SA.

He could have done more to assist Sewgolum! At least he could have spoken out in support of Papwa. Of course Papwa was seven years his senior, so it was probably easier to assist Tshabalala who was seven years younger than Player, and who Player could mentor.

'Mandela taught us to look forward,' said Player. 'He said you cannot live in the past. You cannot have bitterness in your heart. It's like when you play golf – if you make a bogey, you better forget it and get a birdie on the next hole. There's a great spirit in South Africa. We've made bogeys. We're making birdies now.'

How could it be that Papwa Sewgolum and Ismail Chowglay, who regularly had pages and pages of copy written about them in the Indian, Coloured, and Black-read newspapers and magazines in both SA and India, heroes and icons to millions of Blacks, Coloureds, and Indians, would be abandoned by both black and white, as well as the golf bodies, and be allowed to pass away in abject poverty primarily due to apartheid?

Final word

This then is the story of 'Papwa' Sewsunker Sewgolum, the man apartheid tried to forget, Papwa dominated the sports pages newspapers and magazines, read by millions, and how this forgotten icon assisted the anti-apartheid sports movement which ultimately led to the dismantling of apartheid.

Golf is a worldwide sport with an international audience, and as such it reaches many more countries and people than any other game played in SA. The fact that Papwa Sewgolum came onto the scene at just the time that Nelson Mandela and others were being locked away was hugely significant, not only for the citizens of SA but also the international community.

Against all the odds, those golfers of colour, competing abroad in The Open and other tournaments shone the spotlight on apartheid, especially when Papwa Sewgolum won the Dutch Opens, and then the Natal Opens, and opened the eyes of the world to the inequality of the apartheid system locally, while abroad the anti-apartheid sports movement had their figurehead when photographs of him receiving his trophy in the rain in 1963 went viral.

This led to sports boycotts, thereby stopping white golfers from competing internationally, which not only impacted negatively on the government, but also on the psyche of the population used to our golfers carrying the flag and winning abroad, and how the rest of the world viewed apartheid. It had a major impact in helping to break down the golf sporting barrier, and apartheid in its totality, even if Papwa was not necessarily politically active.

Sewgolum was also a hero to India's population looking for sporting heroes outside of cricket, tennis and hockey, and this further drew India's attention to the iniquities of apartheid. India's campaign against South Africa led directly to the country being barred from the Olympics.

By beating Gary Player in 1965, Papwa defeated the national government's sporting icon, and the white population's favourite son.

Chapter 9: End of the Road

It was the most 'apolitical' of political sporting victories.

While he did not live long enough to experience some of the benefits that would accrue to for non-racial golfers later on, he and his successes can be credited with helping to pave the path for those that followed.

In moving forward from this painful reminder of our divided past, perhaps the greatest tribute we can all pay to the 'deferred dream' of Papwa Sewgolum is to find and nurture a Tiger Woods from SA, a new class of golfers who would make us all proud and smile when recalling the names of Sewsunker 'Papwa' Sewgolum, Ramnath 'Bambata' Boodhun, Edward Johnson-Sedibe, Vincent Tshabalala, Ismail 'Boy' Chowglay, Joe Dlamini and Simon 'Cox' Hlapo while they now walk on greener fairways.

SOUTHERN AFRICA PLAYER RANKINGS

South Africa has truly been one of the strongest producers of golfers throughout the world. They have not only dominated the local Sunshine tour, but has also been forced to reckon with in the international competitions.

From the Black Knight, who entered onto each golf course like a valiant knight going into battle, to the Big Easy with his elegant swing, we have produced some of the best golfers in history! From making their own dents on the PGA tour to their amazing wins in our very own Sunshine and TPA tours.

However, before we talk about the best and even the greatest player from Southern Africa, we need to address the issue of the Colonial policies and Apartheid where people of colour are concerned. Afterall, there was the TPA Tour, a professional golf tour for people of colour from the 1960s-1980s.

This tour was purported to be the equal to the South African circuit according to the government. Of course this was not the case for many reasons. Let me list a few:

- The money was hugely inferior
- Tournaments were only played on proper golf courses (not bush courses) from 1960.
- Tournaments were usually hosted only at the end of the year when players could get time off from work.
- But how can you then compare these professionals with those playing the white tour?
- When they were allowed onto 'white' golf courses, they were breaking 'white' course records in tournament play. Players such as Papwa Sewgolum, Ramnath Boodhun, Simon Hlapo, Lawrence Buthelezi, Ismail Chowglay, and Vincent Tshabalala.

SA Player Rankings

- Some may say, "look at their record overseas",, but these folk were usually caddies who had to work fulltime, unlike some of the white professionals, were not sponsored abroad, and didn't have funds to travel and play abroad.
- Yet those very few who managed to travel abroad, like Chowglay, Tshabalala, Johnson-Sedibe, William Manie, and Papwa had amazing successes. Even world number 1 at the time, Billy Casper came to watch him play and was astounded. What could they have achieved?
- It was difficult for golfers of colour to play on normal golf courses when they wished to both due to the expense as well as inability to become members.
- Practicing before the event was forbidden and tournaments were 36 holes a day
- Participants were not allowed in the clubhouse.
- The cost of traveling to events was difficult given the pittance prize money on offer.
- Most were caddies and had to work for a living, rather than practice fulltime like many white participants.
- Only a limited number of participants were of the highest level. This limited competition.
- No white spectators were allowed

Yet with the balmy sunshine umbrella, South Africa golf flourished were it on manicured fairways or bush-golf. Competition was strong, and we emerged as the most successful major winning nation outside of America. An incredible achievement.

In fact, such an incredible achievement that the American PGA sought to conspire to ban Bobby Locke form playing against the Americans after he quite literally dominated them winning tournament-after-tournament and setting the largest winning totals whilst breaking the scoring records.

There were simply some professionals who objected to this upstart by winning what they regarded as their bread-and-butter earnings. But when finally the PGA had a change of heart motivated by the spectators it was too late and Locke was lost to them.

Gary Player's best tournament, as told to the author, wasn't any of his 9 majors but rather when he came second to Raymond Floyd, with spectators rolling balls between his legs as he putted, throwing ice in his face, belittling him, and having to play with armed security following death threats.

Sally Little had to change allegiance to the USA to continue competing. Whilst Dale Hayes retired from touring at 28 after being thrown out of Caracos at the World Cup, and the list goes on.

Let's immediately start with the best golfers (not greatest), that is those who at stages in their lives played the best golf.

Pound-for-pound if there were different weight levels, Bobby Cole and Ramnath Boodhun were possibly the best.

Were we to consider the 'BEST' rather than the 'GREATEST' we may have Bobby Locke topping the list. Afterall besides being 'banned' from the US Tour for being too good, he won the SA Open nine times, that is every time he entered, and virtually lost the sight of his eye after winning The 1957 Open. Famous golfer, Denis Hutchinson, 'the voice of golf' would certainly agree.

Denis Watson would have been the PGA Tour 1984 money winner and US Open winner were he not penalised 2-shots despite getting a ruling he could wait longer for the ball to drop into the hole as it 'was moving'.

Retief Waltman retired at 25 having already been invited to play in The Masters and already the winner of 2 SA Opens to take up a calling in the ministry.

Wayne Westner may have also been in this list having won two SA Opens and the World Cup before severely injuring his wrist, and Tim Clark, born with an arm deformity had to retire early when the long putter ruling changed, and Sally Little was off the LPGA Circuit for two years in her prime with major health issues.

Then there's the curious case of Maud (Titterton) Gibb 1908 Womens Amateur Championship 1908 winner playing for Scotland although she did play for England. Relocating to South Africa she won the South African ladies champion in 1913 and 1914 when she also became the first President of the SA Ladies Golf Union.

The list may look like this:

All-Time Southern Africa BEST Golfers
1. Bobby Locke
2. Gary Player
3. Ernie Els
4. Nick Price Zimbabwe
5. Retief Goosen
6. Sally Little
7. Denis Watson[26] *Zimbabwe*
8. Louis Oosthuizen
9. **Sewsunker 'Papwa' Sewgolum**
10. Retief Waltman
11. Sid Brews
12. Harold Henning
13. Mark McNulty *Zimbabwe*
14. David Frost
15. Maud (Titterton) Gibb

*Best golfer ranking is based on ability and not necessarily how many majors or tournament victories

---

26 1984 Watson lost the US Open by one shot, BUT he received permission from his official referee to wait longer than 10 seconds for the ball to fall into the hole, which it did. He was subsequently penalised two shots (reduced to one shot penalty the following year).

All-Time Greatest BLACK Golfers (pre-1994)
1. Sewsunker *'Papwa'* Sewgolum (1954–77)
2. Lewis *'Clever Boy'* Chitengwa (1991–01) Zimbabwe
3. Vincent Tshabalala (1965–83)
4. Ismail *'Baby-face Boy'* Chowglay (1955–83)
5. Simon *'Cox'* Hlapo (1953–68)
6. Joe Dlamini (1983–1990s) Swaziland
7. Ramnath *'Bambata'* Boodhun (1920s–34)
8. Edward *'Eddia'* Johnson-Sidebe (1951–68)
9. Richard *'Boikie'* Mogoerane (1966–83)
10. Lawrence Buthelezi (1958–67)

Looking in – David *'Bobby Locke'* Motati, William Manie, RT Singh, Mokgeteng John Mashego, Daddy Naidoo, Ronnie Ditsebe, *'Star'* Naidoo, S Swartz, *'Polly'* November, Sammy *'Slamming'* Daniels, David Phala, Bob Nkuna, Raydmuth Rajdaw, Jacob Gumbi, Ramphal Tiney.

All-Time Greatest Golfers
1. Gary Player (ranked 1 unofficial – 9 majors)
2. Bobby Locke (ranked 1 unofficial – 4 majors)
3. Ernie Els (ranked 1 – 4 majors)
4. Nick Price Zimbabwe (ranked 1 – 3 majors)
5. Retief Goosen (ranked 3 – 2 major)
6. Sally Little (ranked 2 – 2 majors)
7. Louis Oosthuizen (ranked 3 – 1 major)
8. Sid Brews (ranked 5 unofficial – 8 SA Opens)
9. Mark McNulty Zimbabwe (ranked 3 – 1 senior major)
10. David Frost (ranked 3 – 1 senior major)
11. Harold Henning (50 victories – Canada Cup)
12. **Sewsunker 'Papwa' Sewgolum** (77 victories - 10 SA N-E Opens)
13. Dale Hayes (ranked top 10 – World Cup – retired 29)
14. Charl Schwartzel (ranked 5 – 1 major)

15. Tim Clark (ranked 15)
16. Trevor Immelman (ranked 12 – 1 major)
17. Rory Sabbatini (ranked 8)
18. Denis Watson Zimbabwe (1 senior major)
19. Retief Waltman (2 SA Opens – retired 25)
20. John Bland (35 victories)
21. Cobie le Grange (ranked 15 – wins 18)
22. Lewis Chitengwa Zimbabwe (World Jnr Champion / SA Amateur – died 26)
23. Fulton Allem (15 victories)
24. Bobby Cole (13 victories – World Cup)
25. Reg Taylor (all-time best amateur)

39	**Vincent Tshabalala**
66-75	**Ismail Chowglay**
75-90	**Joe Dlamini** *Swaziland*
100s	**Ramnath Boodhun;**
100s	**Simon Hlapo**
100s	**Lawrence Buthelezi**

CHAPTER 10: RECORDING HISTORY

Southern Africa Golf Hall of Fame

2010 Vincent Tshabalala's induction into the Southern Africa Golf Hall of Fame: Barry Cohen, Hugh Baiocchi, Vincent Tshabalala, Sally Little, Dale Hayes, Cobie le Grange, John Bland

Source: Barry Cohen

In 2009 December, the SA Golf Heritage Trust hosted their first annual Southern Africa Golf Hall of Fame Induction awards at the Hyatt Regency Oubaai, George, where Papwa was inducted.

The following year the SA Golf Museum was opened by Gideon Sam (SASCOC) at Oubaai, built and funded by Harry Brews and Barry Cohen.

'There are displays of memorabilia at the SA Museum of Golf that can only be bettered at the R&A museum at St. Andrews and at Royal Blackheath. It should be compulsory for all young golfers to pay the museum a visit so that they can stroll through the history of the

game in South Africa.' – Dale Hayes

This heritage centre specifically featured a subset on black golf, including special sections on the TPA Tour, Papwa Sewgolum, the iconic black golfers, and the lost history of black golf.

Gary Player reading his citation in the Hall of Fame. Right Papwa Sewgolum's citation

Southern Africa 'Black' Hall of Fame Inductees
Induction
Class 2009
Sewsunker 'Papwa' Sewgolum
Class 2010
Vincent Tshabalala Richard Mogoerane Theo Manyama
Class 2012
Peter Louw
Class 2014
Simon 'Cox' Hlapo

Class 2015
Joe Dlamini
Class 2017
Lewis Chitengwa
Class 2018
Ismail 'Boy' Chowglay

Harry Brews Award
Class 2013
Honourable 'Ntate' Andrew Mlangeni

Golf Hall of Fame 2010 Induction: Hugh Baiocchi, Duggie Donnely (famous European Tour commentator), Vincent Tshabalala, Dale Hayes, Louis Oosthuizen

Source: Barry Cohen

Chapter 10: Recording History

2010 General Bantu Holomisa, Richard Mogoerane, Vincent Tshabalala at the Southern Africa Golf Hall of Fame Induction invitational golf tournament, Oubaai.

Source: Barry Cohen

Honorable Ntate Andrew Mlangeni receiving the 2013 Harry Brews award with inductees Debbie Symon (Dave's daughter).Wendy Warrington, Bobby Cole.

Source: Barry Cohen

Raymond Ackerman congratulating Andrew Mlangeni on the receipt of the Southern Africa Golf Hall of Fame 'Harry Brews' award 'for his selfless contribution.' (The Hon. Malangeni went to jail with Nelson Mandela for 27 years).

Source: Barry Cohen

2016 Induction: Dan Retief, Joe Dlamini, Senator Mike Temple.

Source: Barry Cohen

CHAPTER 11: STATISTICS

SEWSUNKER 'PAPWA' SEWGOLUM
Professional wins 77

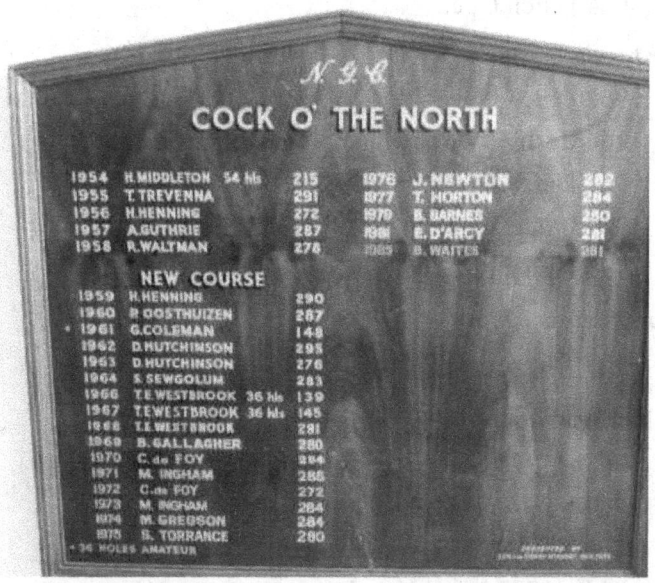

Southern Africa circuit wins (5)
- 1963 Natal Open
- 1964 Cock of the North (*Zambia*)
- 1964 Grand Prix Series First Leg (Gary Player 2nd)
- 1965 Natal Open (Gary Player 2nd)
- 1966 Bata Bush Babes (**Rhodesia**)

Other results
- 1963 South African Open 2nd (won by Retief Waltman)
- 1964 South African Open 3rd (tied Gary Player & Bob Charles)
- 1964 Grand Prix Series Second Leg 2nd (won by Gary Player)

- 1965 South African PGA 5th
- 1965 Flame Lily *(Rhodesia)* 5th
- 1966 Rhodesia Dunlop Open 5th
- 1971 Mbabane Holiday Inn *(Swaziland)* 3rd

European circuit wins (3)
- 1959 Dutch Open
- 1960 Dutch Open
- 1964 Dutch Open

Other results
- 1966 Dutch Open 4th
- 1966 Carling World Championship 6th
- 1967 Dutch Open 2nd
- 1967 India Open 6th
- 1967 French Open 5th

Major championships
- 1963 The British Open 13th

TPA Non-European Tour wins (66)
- 1960 – 1974 South African Non-European Open (10)
- 1964 – 1970 Transvaal Non-European Open (5)
- 1966 – 1969 OFS Non-European Open (2)
- 1954 – 1977 Natal Non-European Open (18)
- 1960 – 1976 Western Province Non-European Open (4)
- 1964 – Eastern Province Non-European Open (1)
- 1960 – 1969 Griqualand West Non-European Open (7)
- 1959 – 1974 Other Non-European Tournaments (18)

Papwa: Tournament Records

*Note: The more important tournaments were often played at the end or the beginning of the year such that they may have been designated as the tournament for either year. I have only surmised the actual year based on my research and newspaper articles.

Chapter 11: Statistics

SOUTH AFRICAN NON-EUROPEAN OPEN

YEAR	FIRST	SECOND	THIRD	FOURTH	FIFTH	COURSE
1960	S Sewgolum (308) 80 80 74 74 (308)	RL Brown (310)				Milnerton *first white course*
1961	S Sewgolum 75 73 76 73 (297)	S Hlapo (305)	I Chowglay/PL Paul (307)		J.Semenya (311) / RT Singh(314)	Kloof & Royal Durban
1962	I Chowglay 72 74 74 77 (297)	Percy/P Mazibuko 73 74 76 78 (301)	J Semenya 79 72 72 79 (302)	PL Paul/ S Hlapo/ R Ditsebe	*8th S Sewgolum (308)	Kimberley
1963	S Sewgolum 75 77 75 74 (301)	I Chowglay 74 77 80 83 (314)	S Chakane 75 84 75 82 (316)	R Ditsebe/D Motati/R Tiney (318)		Walmer *par 75*
1964	S Sewgolum 71 72 70 75 (288)	E. Lee & J Semenya (309)		I Chowglay (310)	S. Hlapo (315)	Glendower
1965	S.Sewgolum/V Tshabalala 77 74 69 71 (291) 74 74 73 70 (291)		I Chowglay (292)			Alexander
1966	D Motati (292)	V Tshabalala				Bloemfontein

Year	Winner	Runner-up	Third	Venue
1967	**S Sewgolum** 70 69 72 71 (282)	I Chowglay (289)	S Mogoerane	S Hlapo	King David
1968	**S Sewgolum** 70 70 71 74 (285)	V Tshabalala (293)	S Hlapo		Circle CC
1969	**S Sewgolum** 71 76 73 75 (295)	A Hartzenberg			Athlone
1970	**S Sewgolum** 77 67 69 74 (287)	V Tshabalala (295)	R Mogoerane (302)	J Ranjith	Benoni & Ohenimuri
1971	V Tshabalala (292)	**S Sewgolum** (293)	D Naidoo	R Anooplal	Benoni
1972	I Chowglay 74 74 75 74 (297) *62 qualifying record	V Tshabalala & R Mogoerane (301)			Kroonstad
1973	R Mogoerane	I Chowglay	R Anooplal		Wedgewood
1974	**S Sewgolum** 77 69 75 70 (291)	V Tshabalala 70 70 72 80 (292)			Glendower
1975	UNKNOWN				
1976	R Mogoerane				
1977	V Tshabalala 73 75 73 70 (291)				Durban

Chapter 11: Statistics

PROVINCIAL RESULTS

TRANSVAAL NON-EUROPEAN OPEN

1964	**S Sewgolum** 76 70 65 73 (284)	E Borman 76 71 75 82 (304)	J Netshitopeni (307)	Vincent Tshabalala (308)	Percy Mazibuko (309)	Benoni
1965	**S Sewgolum** 70 70 71 71 (282)					Glendower
1966	**S Sewgolum** 69,70,70,73 (282)	S Hlapo	R Mogoerane	D Motati	J Gumbi	
1967	R Mogoerane (302)	**S Sewgolum**	S Hlapo			
1968	I Chowglay 73 69 73 73 (287)	N N'kosi (307)				
1969	**S Sewgolum**	I Chowglay				Benoni
1970	**S Sewgolum**	V Tshabalala/S Sepeng/R Anooplal				
1971						
1972	V Tshabalala (295)	**S Sewgolum (297)**				Ohenimuri

O.F.S. NON-EUROPEAN OPEN

1966	**S Sewgolum** 69 70 70 73 (282)	S Hlapo 69 76 75 71 (291)	R Mogoerane 73 75 75 76 (299)	D Motati 77 77 73 74 (301)	J Gumbi 75 77 75 75 (302)/ Z Mavundla 74 77 74 77 (302)
1968	R Mogoerane (302)	**S Sewgolum** (304)	S Hlapo (306)		Bloemfontein
1969	**S Sewgolum**	R Anooplal			Bloemfontein

NATAL NON-EUROPEAN OPEN

1954	**S Sewgolum**
1955	**S Sewgolum**
1956	**S Sewgolum** *lost playoff*
1957	**S Sewgolum**
1958	**S Sewgolum**
1959	**S Sewgolum**

Chapter 11: Statistics

Year	1st	2nd	3rd	4th	5th	Venue
1960	S Sewgolum 74 72 75 73 (294)	RT Singh 76 79 79 79 (313)	S Hlapo & P Mazibuko			Royal Durban
1961	S Sewgolum 73 73 71 73 (290)	PL Paul 77 76 79 71 (303)	J Semenya 80 77 73 76 (306)	C Shakane 76 80 74 79 (309)	RT Singh 78 78 78 75 (309)	
1962	S Sewgolum					Kloof
1963	S Sewgolum	J Semenya				Circle
1964	S Sewgolum 72 71 73 75 (291)	D Motati 76 76 74 75 (301)	L Buthelezi 75 74 79 78 (306)		R Rajdaw 79 72 76 80 (307)	Maritzburg
1965	Raydmuth Rajdaw (293)	S Sewgolum (294)	S Hlapo (297)			Kloof
1966	S Sewgolum 70 71 73 74 (288)		V Tshabalala			
1967	S Sewgolum 71 76 69 70 (286)	Ram Rajdaw 69 80 72 75 (296) *69 course record	Reggie Naidoo (am) 78 77 72 76 (303)	L Polagadu 74 80 70 80 (304)	D Motati 79 78 71 78 (306)	Maritzburg
1968	S Sewgolum 71 76 69 70 (286)	J Ranjith 74 72 74 79 (299)	M V Naidoo 76 75 75 76 (302)	V Tshabalala 80 75 69 78 (302)	D Motati 72 75 78 78 (303)	Maritzburg

1969	**S Sewgolum** *by 2 shots*			Stanger
1970	**S Sewgolum**			
1971	V Tshabalala	**S Sewgolum**		Maritzburg
1972	V Tshabalala 73 69 59 71 (282)	Johnson Chetty 81 69 68 70 (288)		Windsor Park
1973	J Dlamini			
1974	**S Sewgolum**			Maritzburg
1975	**S Sewgolum** 73 73 77 71 (294)	I Chowglay / R Rajdaw 78 75 76 74 (303)	A Collins (306)	I Ranjith (307)	Circle
1976	I Chowglay *play-off*			
1977	**S Sewgolum**			

Chapter 11: Statistics

WESTERN PROVINCE NON-EUROPEAN OPEN

1960	**S Sewgolum**	RL Brown	Alex Njokweni	
1961	P van Dieman	I Chowglay		
1962	A November			Westlake
1963	I Chowglay			Royal Cape
1964	**S Sewgolum** 68 65 72 70 (275)	I Chowglay / P van Dieman (302)		
1965	I Chowglay			
1966	I Chowglay			
1967	I Chowglay	Wally Lewis	D Motati	King David
1968	I Chowglay (297)	**S Sewgolum** (305)		Athlone
1969	**S Sewgolum** 74 74 76 72 (296)	V Tshabalala (298)		Athlone
1970	Abe van Rooyen 284	R Mogoerane	Vincent Tshabalala	Daddy Naidoo	Athlone

299

1971	I Chowglay 79 76 72 75 (302)	Abe van Rooyen (306)	Wally Johannesen	Percy Lendis	Athlone
1972	A 'Polly' November				Athlone
1973	I Chowglay				Athlone
1974					
1975					
1976	S Sewgolum 78 70 76 77 (301)	J Chetty (307)	S Dondashe (309)	Noel Maart (310)	

EASTERN PROVINCE NON-EUROPEAN OPEN

1963	I Chowglay (309) *course record	**S Sewgolum** (310)	Walmer
1964	**S Sewgolum**	I Chowglay	Walmer
1965-67			
1968	I Chowglay	**S Sewgolum**	

GRIQUALAND WEST NON-EUROPEAN OPEN

Year	Winner	Runner-up	3rd	4th	Venue
1960	**S Sewgolum** 69 72 72 72 (285)				Kimberley
1961	**S Sewgolum** 75 68 69 73 (285) **68 course record*	Jacob Gumbi (308)			Kimberley
1963	**S Sewgolum** (285)	I Chowglay (293)			Kimberley
1964	**S Sewgolum** 77 72 74 72 (295)	I Chowglay 75 75 73 78 (301)	S Hlapo 80 76 77 77 (310)	P Mbuyisa 83 77 77 76 (313)	D Motati 83 82 76 75 (316)	Kimberley
1965	**S Sewgolum** 71 69 70 71 (281)	S Hlapo 75 69 71 71 (286)	J Semenya 75 77 73 78 (303)	S Sepeng 80 74 78 77 (309)	D Mcumola 79 79 77 77 (312)	Kimberley
1966	S Sepeng	S Hlapo			
1967	**S Sewgolum** (300)	S Sepeng 78 78 75 72 (303)	S Hlapo 78 79 74 76 (307)		
1969	**S Sewgolum** 78 78 75 69 (300)	R Anooplal			

NATAL INDIAN OPEN

1946 **S Sewgolum** Curries Fountain

OTHER NON-EUROPEAN TOURNAMENTS
NATAL MIDLANDS

1959	**S Sewgolum** *play-off*	Laurence Buthelezi		
1960	**S Sewgolum**			

F.O.S.A OPEN

1961	Shan Poonsammy 71 74 (145)	Ceasar Shakane *play-off	**S Sewgolum**		Umgeni
1966	Collin Appalsamy 68 72 (140)	**S Sewgolum** 68 73 (141)	Phillip Mhlongo 70 77 (147)	L Buthelezi 75 72 (147)	R Tiney 76 74 (150)	Springfield

TRANSVAAL INVITATIONAL

| 1966 | S Sewgolum (273) | S Hlapo (275) *65 third round | Israel Khumou | | | Wynberg |

R200 SPONSORED INVITATION

| 1964 | S Sewgolum 72 70 (142) | A Collins 75 70 (145) | PL (Fred) Paul 78 71 (149) | Daddy Nair 76 (151) | 75 C Skakane 75 77(152) | Durban |

BAMBATA MEMORIAL TROPHY

| 1965 | S Sewgolum | | | | | Springfield |
| 1966 | Ramphal Tiney 69 68 (137) | S Sewgolum (138) | Daddy Naidoo 73 74 (147) Philip Nhlongo 77 70 (147) | | DL Solanki (148) | Springfield |

THUNDERBIRD R500 CLASSIC

| 1965 | S Sewgolum 70 72 72 72 (286) | A Collins 76 69 72 74 (291) | PL Paul 75 73 76 76 (300) | | | Springfield |

GARY PLAYER TROPHY

| 1967 | S Sewgolum 69* 71 (140) *course record | R Mogoerane 74 71 (145) | I Chowglay (148) R Tiney 79 69* (148) *course record | 8th (152) L Buthelezi, H Lewis, P Mazibuko | D Motati 77 78 (155) | Paarl |

KIMBERLEY OPEN

| 1968 | S Sewgolum | Kimberley |
| 1969 | S Sewgolum | Kimberley |

SWAZILAND SPA OPEN

| 1968 | S Sewgolum | Swaziland |
| 1970 | V Tshabalala | Swaziland |

GARY PLAYER INVITATIONAL OPEN

1968	S Sewgolum (218)	S Hlapo
1969	S Sewgolum	
1970	S Sewgolum		Benoni

ST MICHAELS OPEN

| 1968 | S Sewgolum | | | St Michaels |
| 1971 | S Sewgolum | S Hlapo | | St Michaels |

LUYT LAGER

| 1972 | S Hlapo | S Sewgolum | I Chowglay | R Mogoerane | Ohenimuri |

LTA MASTERS

| 1974 | S Sewgolum (218) | R Mogoerane (219) | V Tshabalala (220) | I Chowglay (221) |
| 1975 | D Naidoo | S Sewgolum | | |

GRIQUA GOLD CUP

1974   S Sewgolum   Durban

COCA COLA OPEN

1975   D Naidoo   S Sewgolum

TOURNAMENT OF CHAMPIONS

1974   S Sewgolum

Chapter 11: Statistics

Notable Performances

1957	Shoots 59 in caddy tournament	Papwa Sewgolum
1959	Dutch Open – 1st	Papwa Sewgolum
1960	Dutch Open – 1st	Papwa Sewgolum
1963	Natal Open – 1st	Papwa Sewgolum
1964	Cock o' North (Zambia) – 1st	Papwa Sewgolum
1963	The Open – 13th	Papwa Sewgolum
1963	SA Open – 2nd	Papwa Sewgolum
1964	SA Open – 3rd	Papwa Sewgolum
1964	Dutch Open – 1st	Papwa Sewgolum
1964	Grand Prix Series 1st Leg – 1st	Papwa Sewgolum
1964	Grand Prix Series 2nd Leg – 2nd	Papwa Sewgolum
1965	Natal Open – 1st	Papwa Sewgolum
1964	SA Open – 3rd	Papwa Sewgolum
1965	SA Masters – 3rd	Papwa Sewgolum
1966	Bata Bush Babes (Rhodesia) – 1st	Papwa Sewgolum
1966	Dunlop Tournament (Rhodesia) – 5th	Papwa Sewgolum
1966	Natal Open – 4th	Papwa Sewgolum
1967	Bata Bush Babes (Rhodesia) – 4th	Papwa Sewgolum
1967	Dunlop Tournament (Rhodesia) – 4th	Papwa Sewgolum
1967	Carling World Championship – 6th	Papwa Sewgolum
1967	Dutch Open – 2nd	Papwa Sewgolum
1967	Indian Open – 6th	Papwa Sewgolum
1968	Swaziland Spa Open – 1st	Papwa Sewgolum
1970	The Open Qualifying round (St Andrews) – 64	Papwa Sewgolum
1971	Coca Cola – 1st	Papwa Sewgolum
1974	SA Non-European Open – 10th victory	Papwa Sewgolum

AUTHOR'S NOTES

This author (aged 11) watched Retief Waltman win the 1964 Western Province Open at Clovelly from Player, Henning and Locke, and so inspired, especially after the Clovelly hero and honourary member, Bobby Locke following repeated calls of 'Bobby, Bobby, Bobby', threw his golf ball into the crowd to the cheers of the spectators.

This seemed like fun such that I managed to swop some pram wheels I was using to make into a go-cart for a friend's late-father's wooden-shafted set of right-handed clubs and a canvas bag.

Soon I was caddying at Clovelly for pocket money, and playing junior golf with Sally Little. I also became very friendly with the Clovelly caddy master, Ismail Chowglay, who took the juniors under his wing, 'illegally' playing and coaching us. Consequently, I was one of those in the gallery watching the challenge match between Player, Chowglay, Sewgolum, and Tshabalala at Athlone GC in 1974.

At university I was involved with the 1972 student demonstrations for free black education at St George's Cathedral, and carried off UCT's Jameson stairs by police, met Steve Biko at Fort Hare, and studied law with Anton Lubowski (both politically assassinated).

Playing off a scratch handicap, I participated in the Australian and SA Amateur championships, and coached golf at Coolum GC, Australia, whilst I represented SA at the World Corporate Golf Championship Final at La Manga, Spain.

I subsequently heard that Ismail Chowglay had died in poverty and wrote a letter to Compleat Golfer remembering him which became the 'letter of the month'. This drew the attention of Harry Brews, who in 2006 asked me to head up the 'Sid Brews Golf Development Trust' with its stated objective being to build a golf museum and honour those who had made a contribution to the game. This offer of becoming involved with Harry Brews drew on my passion for sport and especially golf.

Authors Note

When the trust ran out of funds in 2008, I took over the funding, organising and hosting our first induction event in December 2009, and after researching, designing, and opening the museum in 2010, I became aware that there was not much recorded concerning black golf and I set out to research the subject. At the same time, the induction committee decided to introduce a new category for induction, namely 'disadvantaged', where different criteria were used for induction. Through this project, I became friends with Vincent Tshabalala and Rajen Sewshanker.

2019 I released 'Blazing the Trail', the history of Black golf in Southern Africa, and in 2020 'Let me Play', Black golfers, including Papwa Sewgolum stories.

In 2021, as a director, together with chairman Jeff van Rooyen, we launched 'Finding the Fair Way Foundation' both with the aim of raising funds and benefits for caddies, and to ensure that they were contracted as permanent employees by their golf clubs with all the ensuing benefits, rather than as the historic private contractor system.

UNISA has since come on board to assist with a caddie skills audit with a view to up skilling them, whilst the Government is looking to close loopholes in the legislation thereby confirming that caddies are permanently employed by their respective golf club. At the same time on 10 March 2022 we hosted a successful fundraising golf event and dinner at Country Club Johannesburg in aid of the caddies nationally.

Interesting how a small pebble and the ensuing ripples after stumbling across the 1964 WP Open at Clovelly and watching Waltman, Player, Henning and Locke would lead me all the way to this book.

I have also taken the liberty of ranking my top Black players, as well as the inclusive all-time Southern Africa players (white and black), something which has never previously been undertaken – I trust this is not too controversial.

Barry Cohen

*I took one liberty of including the musical King Kong in Sewgolum's narrative. In fact, this musical only reached the West End in 1961 (not 1959), as this popular heavyweight boxer's tragic life story 'musical' was being performed to mixed-race audiences in SA at that time.

BIBLIOGRAPHY

Books

- *Papwa Sewgolum – From Pariah to Legend,* News & Views by Christopher Nicholson (Wits University Press, 2005) reviewed by Terry Bell.
- Black Sash Records (1974) Everyone's guide to the pass laws.
- Brews, H. *South African Golf, Volume One: Blazing the Trail, The Story of South Africa's First Internationally Famous Golfer,* Cape Town: Published under the auspices of the Sid Brews Golf Development Trust.
- Canale, N. (2013) *Snakes in the Garden of Eden,* Cape Town: Don Nelson Publishers.
- Case, M. (2015) Papwa: *Golf's Lost Legend.* Kwela Books.
- Corcoran, M. (2010) *Duel in the Sun: Tom Watson and Jack Nicklaus in the Battle of Turnberry,* Simon and Schuster. ISBN 9781439141922.
- Fall, R.G. (ed.). (1960) How far the underprivileged have advanced in the game? *South African Golf.*
- Fall, R.G. Golfing in South Africa.
- Joyce, P. (2014) *The rise of the phoenix,* Zebra Press.
- Kerr, W.M. (1997) *The history of Royal Durban Golf Club.* Durban: Colorgraphic.
- Mallon, B. and Jerris, R. (2011) *Historical Dictionary of Golf.* Scarecrow Press. p. 864. ISBN 9780810874657.
- New York Times (1966) *'Gary Player ties for Second',* AP. 20 February. Retrieved 20 April 2017.
- New York Times 1966. Player shoots a 72 for 286 to take South African Golf. *The New York Times.* AP. 7 February. *Retrieved 20 April 2017.*

Bibliography

- Meister, Christopher: Golf Historian & Writer – Hamburg Area, Germany.
- Clarence Harry Moore & Heather Heath: Autobiographical Anecdotes of the SA War; Growth of Golf in Natal & Transvaal; South Africa's first Golfing Dynasty 1900 – 2000
- The Fifties People of South Africa – Black Life: Politics-Jazz-Sport
- Muir Ferguson, R. *The wonderful golf of Ramnath* B. Bambata.
- Nicholson, C. (2005) *Papwa Sewgolum – From Pariah to Legend*, Johannesburg: Wits University Press.
- Norval, R. (1951) *King of the Links: The story of Bobby Locke*, South Africa: Maskew Miller.
- Norval, R. (1965) *Gone to the Golf,* Citadel Press.
- Norval, R. (1954) *King of the Links*, Bailey & Swinfern.
- O'Donnell, P. (1973) *South Africa's Wonderful World of Golf,* Cape Town. Don Nelson Publishers.
- Partridge, Ted: *The World of Golf.*
- Player, G. *Gary Player World Golfer.*
- Player, G. (1966) *Grand Slam of Golf,* London: Cassell & Company.
- Player, G. and McDonald, M. (1992) *To be the Best.* London: Pan Books.
- 'Presidency Communications Research Document: The National Orders Awards, October 2004' [online] Available at: info.gov.za [Accessed 31 March 2009]
- SA History – Sewsunker 'Papwa' Sewgolum.
- Sauerman, Peter: Premier Golf Historian writing – Various.
- South African Golf Association website: History of Non-European Golf.
- The Compleat Golfer Guide to Golf 2000. Cape Town: Ramsay Son & Parker (Pty) Ltd
- The Mercury (2018) A talent apartheid tragically denied – *Honouring Papwa's memory* 17 April 2018 / Selvan Naidoo.

- Urquhart, C. (2013) *The Kings of Swing*, Zebra Press.
- Vlismas, Michael (2012) *Extraordinary Book of South African Golf,* Johannesburg: Penguin Books.
- Webb, Richard: Narrative Media SA.
- 2005 Documentary film 'Papwa: The Lost Dream of a South African Golfing Legend'.

Newspapers, Magazines, and Interviews
- Boodhun Sujatha (Ramnath 'Bambata's grand-niece)
- Bruyns Denis
- Buirski Tony
- Cape Times: Various
- Compleat Golfer: Various
- Daily Despatch – 1992
- Drum: February 1964; 30 January 1966
- Evening Post – 1963 March 2; 1964 March 15; 1993 March 22
- Fall, R.G. South African Golf Magazines, 1960
- Golf 15 Augustus 1959 & 1960 – *officieel organ van her Nederlandsch Golfcomite*
- Golf Digest: Various
- Hlapo Bernnedett ('Cox' Hlapo's daughter)
- Hutchinson Denis
- Longhurst, H. 'South Africans at Muirfield' in Sports Illustrated (America) 13 July 1959
- Mandblad: First indentured Indians Durban
- Sewshanker Rajen (Papwa's son)
- Selvan Naidoo, CEO, 1860 Heritage Centre
- South Africa Golf magazine: Various 1926 – 1982 – Editor R.G. Fall, later P Sauerman
- Sports Illustrated
- Sunday Tribune 24/01/1993 Yogin Devan
- Sunday Times – various

Bibliography

- The Masters Golf Society 10th Anniversary programme
- The Bantu World October/November 2015
- The Daily News: July–August 1959, '60' 64; February 1963, '65, March 22, 19 93
- German Golf Magazine 'Plock' (Delius Clasing Verlag, Bielefeld) 2006 article
- The Golfer's Annual 1953/4
- The Leader: March 13 1959; July – September 1960; March 02 1963; November 1963; July 1967, '70, '77
- The Mercury: 15 January 1973
- The Natal Mercury 01 February 1952
- The Post: 29 November 1964; Various
- The Star 19/11/38
- The Top Ranked Golfers of the 1960s (ainsworthsports.com)
- van Rooyen, Abe
- Vlismas, Michael (2012). The Extraordinary Book of South African Golf. Penguin UK. ISBN 9780143529729.
- Zonk: July-August 1959, September 1959 pg 27, 29, 1960, January-February 1963, February 1964 pg 29

Websites
- "A.D. Locke Beaten". The Glasgow Herald. 8 March 1957. p. 4.
- Blackenterprise.com/1998-black-enterprisepepsi-golf
- Books.google.co.za/books?id.vol29no2-magazine
- catdir.loc.gov/catdir/samples/simon031/2002025156.html
- Dailypress.com/news/dp_xpm
- "Former SA golfer Vincent Tshabalala dies". SABC. 4 June 2017.
- From Caddying for to Playing With Player October 15, 2014
- "Gary Player Ties for Second". The New York Times. AP. 20 February 1966.
- Horne, Cyril (13 July 1963). "Final Aggregates". The Glasgow Herald.

- https://allafrica.com/stories/201609051428.html
- https://athlonsports.com/golf/golf-course-review-wintergreen.
- https://nationalmuseumpublications.co.za/greens...
- Infoplease.com/people/lewis-chitengwa
- Mallon, Bill; Jerris, Randon (2011). Historical Dictionary of Golf. Scarecrow Press. p. 864. ISBN 9780810874657.
- "Papwa' Sewgolum: little known great". Brand South Africa. 4 September 2005. Retrieved 24 September 2019.
- 'Papwa Sewgolum' dies in Durban". The Glasgow Herald. 6 July 1978. p. 15.
- "Papwa: The Lost Dream of a South African Golfing Legend (2005)". imdb.com.
- Passing on Ambition from Father to Son by Paul Spencer Sochaczewski Bibliography and International Herald Tribune Aug. 25, 1998
- "Player Shoots a 72 for 286 To Take South African Golf". The New York Times. AP. 7 February 1966.
- Reason, Mark (6 May 2006). "Meaning of life lay in Bible, not birdies".
- "Reason: Money is not everything, even in sport". Stuff.
- South African Golfers
- "South African Open, Golf Tournament". where2golf.
- Thefreelibrary.com>Business>Black Enterprise>September1, 1998
- "The Long Road to Non-Racial Golf in South Africa and the Trail Blazed by Papwa Sewgolum". South African Golf Association.
- history.saga.co.za/indexb4cd.html?id=122
- "Torrance finishes joint third". The Glasgow Herald. 10 May 1976. p. 19.
- "Townsend is Dutch Open champion". The Glasgow Herald. 25 July 1967. p. 4.
- yesteryear profile with Daniel Nhakaniso / Munyaradzi

Bibliography

- Madzoker
- ☐ "Vincent Tshabalala – Career Highlights". Sunshine Tour.
- ☐ Wikipedia – various
- ☐ https://en.wikipedia.org/wiki/Indira_Gandhi
- ☐ World Cup
- ☐ www.pgatour.co.za
- ☐ www.theopen.com
- ☐ www.golfdigest.com/story/papwa
- ☐ www.brandsouthafrica.com/tag/gary-player
- ☐ www.athlonenews.co.za/news/golfing-great-reminisces-about-his-career-15226813
- ☐ www.abaphenyi.co.za/news/2018/05/04/department-of-sports-ruled-offside
- ☐ www.thestandard.co.zw/2017/04/23/zims-black-golf-trailblazer
- ☐ www.golftheunitedstates.com/story/235
- ☐ www.nytimes.com/1998/08/25/opinion/meanwhile-passing-on...
- ☐ www.sochaczewski.com/2009/08/30/my-kids-gonna-be-a-star
- ☐ www.imdb.com/title/tt5847770/?ref_=fn_al_tt_1
- ☐ www.golfclubatlas.com/courses-by-country/netherlands/royal-hague
- ☐ www.golfclubatlas.com/courses-by-country/south-africa/durban-country-club
- ☐ www.britannica.com/place/India/Daily-life-and-social-customs
- ☐ www.scribd.com?...?344558583/The-Casbah-40-1977-April-1977
- ☐ Sewsunker 'Papwa' Sewgolum | South African History Online (sahistory.org.za)
- ☐ Papwa Sewgolum: little known great-Proudly Indian-Indian Cooking and Indian Culture
- ☐ 'Papwa' Sewgolum is likely the best golfer you've never heard

- of When Papwa outplayed Player (dailymaverick.co.za)
- ☐ Papa Sewgolum-The Forgotten story of Indian origin legend in South Africa-India Golf Weekly | India's No.1 Source For Golf News and Knowledge (indiagolfdigest.com)
- ☐ From Sibaya maintenance administrator to movie actress (suninternational.com)
- ☐ Papwa: A Challenging Image | sportracepower (wordpress.com)
- ☐ Papwa's championship play-Sports Illustrated Vault | SI.com
- ☐ Papwa's Grip | This is the Loop | Golf Digest
- ☐ Papwa: a glory moment beyond golf (pressreader.com)
- ☐ https://en.wikipedia.org/wiki/Retief_Waltman
- ☐ Australia:– South Africans Gary Player And Papwa Sewgolum In Big Golf Tournament After Refusing To Comment On Politics, Apartheid.-British Pathé (britishpathe.com)
- ☐ TODAY IN KIMBERLEY'S HISTORY 25 SEPTEMBER – Kimberley City Info
- ☐ Black Golf Wire
- ☐ Blast from the past: Papwa breaks down barriers as he purrs to victory (timeslive.co.za)
- ☐ How apartheid denied a Black golf champ-The African Mirror
- ☐ New Books | How apartheid denied a Black golf champ : New Frame
- ☐ Why Gary Player continues to polarise opinion-KEO.co.za
- ☐ Race and Power in South African Sport (wordpress.com)
- ☐ Indian Community | South African History Online (sahistory.org.za)
- ☐ "Presidency Communications Research Document: The National Orders Awards, October 2004" [online] Available at: info.gov.za
- ☐ Obituary: Durbanite invented Oil of Olay | Witness (news24.com)
- ☐ Made in South Africa – Oil of Olay (thisbugslife.com)
- ☐ Bringing 'golf's lost legend' to life (iol.co.za)
- ☐ PressReader.com – Digital Newspaper & Magazine Subscriptions

Bibliography

- https://www.golfcompendium.com/2020/08/pga-tour-carling-open.html
- https://en.wikipedia.org/wiki/Carling_World_Open
- https://www.abebooks.com/signed-first-edition/...
- www.thegolfauction.com/lot-22432.aspx
- en.wikipedia.org/wiki/Vincent_Tshabalala

www.ingramcontent.com/pod-product-compliance
Lightning Source LLC
Chambersburg PA
CBHW011149290426
44109CB00025B/2544